ISBN: 978-1-5323-9862-9 (hardcover edition)
ISBN: 978-1-7923-0489-7 (paperback edition)
ISBN: 978-1-7923-0490-3 (Ebook edition)

FIRST EDITION printed 2019

Published by ToMack Publishing, a subsidiary of ToMack Entertainment
Cover Design by Anthony Price
Edited by Anthony Price
2nd printing; December, 2019
Copyright registration number 1-7213145831

Yours, Very Sincerely and Respectfully

DEDICATION:

This book was written for many reasons, most of which are explained in the book itself. There are some unspoken reasons as well.

Stephan
Maria
Devon and Eyvonne
Luke
Tecla
Keith and Rosemary

Yours, Very Sincerely and Respectfully

Yours

Very Sincerely

and

Respectfully

By Anthony Price

And

Keith Carey

Other works by
Anthony Price
and
Keith Carey

The Rags to Riches Project
(How to Live Happily Ever After)

The Memory Righter
(with Stephan Price)

The Best Defense

Austin! A Love Story

By Anthony Price
I Am Damaged
The Memory Righter (Radio Play)
Indefatigably, Incessantly, Momentarily Erect

Yours, Very Sincerely and Respectfully

This book was created to tell the story of the importance of Gold Star Families and no disrespect is intended in any way. None of the stories in this book are invented, all are true and told the way I remember them. Names have been changed to respect privacy except in those cases where people are publicly known, or in one case, where the name is necessary for the integrity of the story. In many cases where I thought I should include a name, I was overruled by the editors and the names were completely removed. You may wonder if Betty Jo, Bobby Jo, and Billy Jo are real names, but rest assured, they are real people.

The Gold Star Ride Foundation embarked on an ambitious motorcycle ride in 2018. The purpose of that ride, and ultimately this book, is to honor Gold Star Families, and draw attention to the sacrifice made by those families for the rest of us who live in these United States. Any proceeds from the sale of this book are donated to the Gold Star Ride Foundation. No writer's fees are paid. None.

The ride took place from July 2, 2018 to August 22, 2018 and again from September 18, 2018 to September 28, 2018. During those fifty-eight days, more than sixty families were visited all over the country. Not all of those families' stories are included in this book, because some families requested they not have their stories included, and some are not included because of space and time. Neither are all the locations included in this book.

The omission of any particular family's story does not detract or in any way diminish the sacrifice made by any Gold Star Family. Neither does the inclusion augment or aggrandize any story. The stories of specific families are chosen to best promote the need of all the families.

Yours, Very Sincerely and Respectfully

This Note is included to be sure that any family that feels embarrassed or slighted might understand that the inclusion of any story is because the editors believed that these stories could explain the entire sacrifice in the most compelling manor.

We know who you are, and you are always welcome to call us for any reason. You know how to find us, and we appreciate more than words can express the sacrifice you have had to endure.

The stories in this book go far beyond Gold Star Families. Included are the trials and tribulations endured to make the ride happen and to endure the ride itself. Not many among us have the physical and mental ability to perform the act of riding a motorcycle an average of three hundred, seventy five miles a day – every day, for fifty days.

I hope that this story is written in a way you find informative and entertaining.

Yours, Very Sincerely and Respectfully

Table Of Contents

Yours, Very Sincerely and Respectfully

Introduction

Viola was a young mother in 1966 when her son was killed in Vietnam. A week after her ninety-second birthday, Tony stopped to honor her for her sacrifice in the name of freedom.

The visit went on, as the visits do, with small talk about motorcycles and a few comments about the Hero's favorite childhood activities. They talked about traveling and a few other comments about life and events. Then, the fifteen or so other riders gathered close as Tony read the plaque that was presented to Viola. After which, conversations changed to seemingly unimportant anecdotes as before.

After enjoying the company of each other about Ninety minutes, the other riders, family and friends began to depart, one at a time. With only a few left, Tony rose to leave, gathering a few things he had set on the table for the conversation. Without anyone else seeing it, the ninety-two year old Gold Star Mother, who was showing the signs of age and walked with assistance of others and a walker, reached out with a single finger and touched the back of Tony's hand, inviting him to look at her.

She gently held his arm as he looked her in the eyes, and she mouthed the words, "Thank you."

No one else saw this, and no one heard the words. Someone said something about pictures, and Tony held her hand gently and quietly whispered, "It was my honor."

Poses were presented for pictures, and the guests, including Viola, walked him to his bike. There were a few hugs, and some moist eyes as he started the bike and rolled away.

Tony's thoughts wondered as he thought about riding in the rain, dangerous mountain roads, forest fires and smoke, extreme heights, cold, extreme heat, and ten to twelve hours a day, every day for forty-nine days, to get there. "It was totally worth it," he said out loud to no one there.

Chapter One: Before We Start

In The Beginning

You know that feeling you experience when something traumatic occurs, like falling off your bicycle, or a fender bender in your car? Maybe you experienced it when you fell out of a tree when you were a kid, or when some accident or another took the life of someone close to you. It's a strange, slow-motion sort of experience. It's surreal. That's how I've felt for the last two weeks, all day, every day, since I arrived home from riding a motorcycle more than fourteen thousand miles to honor Gold Star Families across the country. Riding fourteen thousand miles only sounds impressive if you've ridden one hundred miles on a motorcycle. Otherwise, it's just numbers. For those of you who don't ride, or for those of you who do who remain unimpressed, let's talk a moment about what that means.

At an average of fifty miles per, which is actually a high average, fourteen thousand miles is two hundred, eighty hours of sitting on and driving a motorcycle. That's sixteen thousand, eight hundred minutes. That's the equivalent of almost twelve days – twenty-four hours a day. That's the distance from Los Angeles, California, to New York City six times! It's ten times farther in distance than the most distant satellite orbiting around the earth. If the distance from your front door to your mailbox is one hundred feet, fourteen thousand miles is roughly seven hundred, thirty-nine thousand, two hundred times farther than that.

Imagine going to your mailbox seven hundred, thirty-nine thousand, two hundred times on a motorcycle.

That's just distance. I haven't mentioned other factors yet. For example, there was a four day period of riding when the outside air temperature was never below one hundred degrees. For those of you who live in Arizona, I don't need to explain this. For those of you who like to insist, "But it's a dry heat," I'm here to tell you, that card doesn't play. In Minnesota, where I've spent most of my life, every winter people talk of "wind chill factor." This is basically what the air temperature feels like in the wind, because the wind will make it feel like it is colder.

The weather announcers on TV will also talk about a "heat index" in summer. In this case, the humidity will lessen our body's ability to disperse perspiration because there is no place for the perspiration to go when the humidity is too high. The hottest day in Minnesota's (often extreme) humidity in summer might produce a "heat index" or a "feels like" temperature in the high nineties. In Arizona, New Mexico and Texas, where it's a "dry heat" it feels like it actually is. During the four days I rode across those states, it was never below one hundred degrees. Never. The coolest nighttime temperature during this part of the ride was ninety-three.

I collapsed from the heat three times.

There was the day in South Carolina where every inch of riding was in the rain. There was elevation sickness in Colorado (but a very awesome view!). There was smoke in Colorado, Utah, Idaho, Wyoming, Montana, Oregon, and Washington. So much smoke in California that it became a state I could not ride into or through. Then there was smoke in the Dakotas from Canada, too. There was road construction, difficult night riding, strange animals on the road, and I'm pretty sure I'll devote an entire chapter to questionable motels later.

Balancing these extremes of riding conditions, there were people I had never met who became my friends almost instantly. If I ever need to call someone late at night to bail me out of jail, every one of these Gold Star Families are on my short list of people to call. They were, in every instance, the salt of the earth. Selfless human beings who make this world a better place to live.

Before I get into that, maybe you'd like to know how I arrived at a place where doing something that profound was in the cards in the first place. I'll share with you who I am and how I came to have this desire to work for Gold Star Families.

It's not an easy story, just as each Gold Star Family's story is not an easy story. No, I'm not a Gold Star Dad or Son or

Brother myself. I got lucky that way. I served four years in the US Navy, and, thanks to a violent car crash just before my discharge, I am a card-carrying member of the disabled vets club. Neither the disabled vets club nor the Gold Star Family club is a club that you want to join. These are clubs that are handed to you. You can't refuse when they are handed to you.

My life was going along, as lives do, with me never mentioning to anyone that I served, let alone boasting about being disabled. To be sure, I don't boast now. It's just a real part of who I am, and I no longer deny it.

I was a stay at home dad, taking care of my children who were very young, when, after three years of this job, I was fired from it. Well, that's the language I use. In fact, my children's mother chose to divorce me, and in the process, did all she could to destroy anything that seemed like a life of mine, and destroy any sort of relationship with my children that I had built. Through the words she chose to use, which were fiction, the court system laid down the law that I could not see my children without a "court approved supervisor" present - a professional who was paid by me.

Let me paint this picture: I tucked my young son (who was seven at the time) and my young, special needs daughter (who was four at the time) into bed every single night of their lives. We spent every day together. We woke up together. I enrolled them in school. I home-schooled my son through second grade. I taught them to tie their shoes; to ride bikes; to play baseball; to swim; and to do all the things that parents teach their children. Their mother had a job which required her to travel and be away from home between two and five days every week. She was gone more than she was home. More often than not, I was a single parent. Maybe not by the strictest definition, but it seemed that way in practice.

One day, after dropping my kids off at their schools, my daughter's principal called and said, "I just thought you'd like to know that your wife just picked up your daughter."

The pain of losing my children was extremely intense. The unjust manner in which the courts treated me and my relationship with my children lasted years; five years, actually.

When I say "five years," that's how long I was required to pay a supervisor to watch me with my kids. In those days the most I could ever pay was about three hours a week.

The incredibly useless fight in the court system for the permission to be with my kids was devastating. Nothing I had ever experienced in my lifetime prepared me for the pain that came from losing my children. I found myself unable to sleep until a total exhaustion took over, and even then, I would wake up crying only two or three hours later. It was more than a year before anything like normal sleep came my way.

The first three months without my children - unable to even call them on the phone without risking being arrested and jailed (which occurred once) - resulted in weight loss, gray hair, and wrinkles. Dark semi circles formed below my eyes and became part of my physical appearance. I lost nearly thirty pounds and wasn't overweight when the ordeal began.

During this unholy period of time, I met the angel that would be my strength since, through, and still. While our relationship is not as perfect as either of us wish it was, when I adopted the mindset that my children were actually dead - which was how I mentally coped with the loss handed to me by the courts - she was there for me to cry on. When the court ruled that I could not see or call my children for a minimum of two years, she was there to help me cope. It was this shoulder to cry on and my adoption of the concept that my children were dead, that got me through the years since then. I know that concept of thinking they were dead seems extreme, but someday, that story will be its own book, and I'll try to explain it better then.

Five years after it began, the courts finally agreed that I could be with my kids on Wednesdays and every other weekend. My son is now well passed his sixteenth birthday and I am teaching him to drive. Things parents do with their kids.

All of that - the story of my kids - is part of the Gold Star Ride story. Maybe because you know a little of what I went through with my own kids, it's a little easier to understand how it is that I feel the way I feel when I meet Gold

Star Families. Granted, after five years, I get to spend time with my kids again, albeit limited, and Gold Star Families have a permanent loss.

No matter what the courts say, the member of a Gold Star Family who gave up their life is not coming back. Ever. We all need to help them with that, because they died for all of us.

The Ride Is Invented

My wonderful mate, I'll call her MSL (My Special Lady) has an unusual job. She is a tobacconist of some renown in the area known as the Twin Cities. In this position, she was, one day about seven years ago, asked to help raise money for disabled veterans. I was still of the mindset that I don't tell people about my disabilities – or my navy service, for that matter – but she knew. She asked me if I'd like to join her at this event because, as she said, "you're a disabled vet, why don't you come with me?"

I did go along on that fund raising effort for disabled vets, holding onto the thought that it seemed somehow like I was helping a group of hypocrites, since I was a disabled vet, and I couldn't get any help from that group. Come to think of it, aside from the Veterans' Administration and the VFW, no vets' group has ever offered to help me at all. So many organizations have said, "No," when I asked that I've stopped asking.

While I was lighting cigars (because that's what you do when you hang out with a tobacconist) for retired professional football players, baseball players, hockey players, and doing my best to enjoy the moment, I heard a distant rumble that sounded like thunder. I looked up and the sky was a perfect blue. Not only that, but the rumble didn't stop, so I knew it wasn't thunder. It came closer, and closer. I knew pretty quickly what I was hearing. I grabbed my phone, because we all have a camera in our phone now, and ran toward the parking lot, which was only twenty feet away. Sure enough, I saw a motorcycle pull into the parking lot of this private golf facility.

If you're like me, you probably think, "Motorcycles don't go to private golf facilities," and generally, you'd be right. This wasn't just a motorcycle. This was a group – and a large group at that. I recorded a movie of an estimated one hundred, twenty-five motorcycles pulling into this private golf club – right up to the front door.

I started riding motorcycles when I was about ten years old. I've been a fan for a long time. Now, after four and a half decades of motorcycle experience, I average about ten thousand miles each riding season. I felt right at home in the middle of all these motorcycles.

A few of the people on bikes wanted cigars (because that's what you get when you see a tobacconist), so while we talked, one suggested that I ride with them the next day. "Sure," I said. "I've got nothing else planned." (Remember? At this time in my life it was still illegal for me to see my kids.)

The next day was Saturday, and I've told this story many times before. We saddled up on the bike and met the group at a gas station near St Paul, Minnesota. After a few words, everyone started up their motorcycles and we were off. I've been on group rides before, so I didn't pay too much attention to anything outside of my responsibilities: my gas tank was full, my oil levels were topped, that sort of thing. There were more than a hundred bikes that day, and I found myself in the pack with about thirty bikes in front of me and about seventy-five bikes behind me. During rides in groups like this, the leader knows where the next stop is, so I don't have to know that. I just have to stay behind the bike in front of me and in front of the bike behind me. We ride, and hear the sound of all those bikes, and the wind in our hair... well, you know the drill.

Then we pulled into a residential neighborhood, which came as something of a shock to me, because I was thinking that we'd go to a biker bar, or greasy restaurant, or something similar. Then we turned onto a cul-de-sac. I was really surprised.

As all those motorcycles squeezed into that tiny street, making sure they could park without scratching each other's bikes, I noticed the houses on that street. Many were drawing their shades closed and peeking around the corner of the window blinds. It was almost a scene from a movie where all the people were terrified of all the bikers that came to run them out of their homes and take over the neighborhood.

By the way, if you worry about such things, stop worrying. I'll protect you.

The group parked and all the people gathered in the front yard of a single house. I followed the people in front of me and tried to get a good spot to stand where I could see and hear everything.

The guy's name is Rockie Lynne. He was fortunate to have a hit song or two in the world of country music, and I hope he has more. He's quite a talent. On this day, however, he was just the guy in the front of the pack. He was the spokesman for the group. He told us all about the plight of the Gold Star Widow that lived in this house.

As tears welled in my eyes and fell down my cheeks, I knew instantly that working for Gold Star Families was something I would do for a very long time.

A few years later, I learned that Minnesota is seventh in the nation for motorcycle ownership per capita. We were shopping for a bike, so I looked at the other end of that list. I found Louisiana and Mississippi were on the bottom, so that's where I started shopping for my new used motorcycle.

The short story is, I found a bike in New Orleans, and rode it back to Minnesota. That trip was completed in thirty hours, and it included a ten-hour stop in a motel. For those of you who like to count the miles, that trip was twelve hundred, sixty-five miles completed in twenty hours of riding. I don't necessarily promote this sort of riding, but I did it.

If you're familiar with the "Iron Butt" patch, no, I didn't earn one because I only rode nine-hundred, sixty-five miles in a twenty-four hour block of time.

Then, I was out with the group in September honoring Gold Star Families in Minnesota. That's when I approached the board members and suggested we take that mission national. They laughed and laughed. They said, "We all have full time jobs, and we're lucky to be able to ride one weekend a year."

"I understand," I replied. "I can go. I don't have a job, and I can't get one with my disabilities."

Some time passed as we discussed it back and forth, and after a few months, they wished me well and told me I could not use their name. I got together with a doctor and a small business owner, told them about the mission, and they agreed to join me as board members.

Together we filed all the papers to be a 501c3 organization, and I started doing all the work necessary to make the ride happen. Today, the board also includes a retired navy SEAL, who spent twenty-eight years in uniform.

Of course, when I approached MSL, her first reaction was, "Why do you want to leave me?"

"I don't want to leave you," I pleaded. "I just feel it is necessary for someone to do this."

"That's not what it feels like," she said sadly. Then she added with a more practical tone, "How will you pay for it? What if the motorcycle breaks down? How long will you be gone? Why do you have to be the one to go?" and a host of other questions, each as difficult to answer as the one before it.

I don't think I ever explained it so that it could be understood. Not only to her, but to most people who have asked. I think it might be one of those things that if you understand, no words are necessary; if you don't, no words are possible. God put it before me to do; so it's up to me to do it. God will show up again in this story.

I spent months planning a route, trying to find places to go that would be welcoming, calling corporations to ask them to lend their support. Every day that I worked, I also heard MSL asking me, "Why?"

"It's hard to explain," I would often start, "but it's something I truly feel like I need to do."

She had come with me on various rides throughout the years, and she had met some Gold Star Family members, but still she kept asking why I thought I needed to go so far and for so long.

"It's a big country," I would say. "I can't go visit

families in all these states over a weekend."

"Why can't you fly in?" she would ask.

"Because it doesn't mean as much if I'm not willing to put myself out there; if I don't suffer to meet them; they won't care if I come or not," I would plead. "It's not like they actually get anything tangible from me," I would say, although the GSRF is designed and set up to give out money for education and anything else they need.

I kept working. I kept calling. I kept talking, promoting, and trying. I looked at other organizations, and I saw what looked to me to be a bit of an error in charitable work. All of the charities that I studied, and there were many, were doing most of their fundraising by asking their constituents for donations (that's the people they helped). While that might keep you going, it just didn't seem right to me. I thought if the cause was right, then it was right for everyone, and everyone should want to keep it going, not just Gold Star Families, who were my constituents.

I called a big company, who said they liked what I was doing. In fact, every single person I spoke to about the mission of the Gold Star Ride Foundation told me it was an incredible mission and they were very happy that I was doing what I was doing. This Minnesota based, world-wide company said they would be helping us. They would be sending us money. Then they didn't. After a month or two, I called them, only to learn that they love the idea, but decided not to help this year. This became a common response, one I heard more than a hundred times.

I volunteer all my time, as do the other board members. I rode fourteen thousand miles with zero pay. In fact, I paid for most of the trip to Gold Star Families myself and with the help of MSL, who didn't understand why I had to do it in the first place. "Why can't you just ride on the weekends?" she would ask.

"Because it's a big country," I would repeat. "Because I need to attract the attention of the news media, and they won't care if I do one family every weekend for two years."

I called companies that build and sell trailers so I would

have one in case the motorcycle broke down. The trailer also offered another method to help pay for the trip: a moving billboard. I offered to put logos on the moving billboard. Seven trailer companies thought what we were trying to do was great, but none of them would help.

I called companies that build cars and trucks. I called them at their national headquarters. I called motorcycle manufacturers as well. All of them thought what we were doing was awesome. I'd like to tell you all about the great success we had because they decided to help. I can't.

Everyone had a good reason. The car manufacturers told me it was taken care of at the local level. The local level told me it was taken care of at the regional level. The regional representatives told me it was taken care of at the national level. Each of these promised to talk to the correct person for me and make something happen. Nothing happened.

One motorcycle company said they couldn't help because they decided that all their philanthropic work was being done by another veterans' organization. I won't say which one, but I will say that veteran's organization managed to "misplace" *one hundred and sixteen million* US dollars in 2016, which was only a few months before the motorcycle company told me they couldn't help me. All I was asking for was about thirty-five thousand (the retail price of a new bike).

I promoted everywhere and anywhere I could. In 2017, I was interviewed by more than sixty broadcast personalities across the country. I published a dozen or more videos. I sent out press releases to every news outlet I could find. I had daily phone conversations with public relations people.

Incidentally, public relations people are quick and happy to promise you how famous you'll be, as soon as your check clears the bank.

Also in 2017, the phone started to ring.

"Thank you for what you are doing for Gold Star Families," I heard the voices say, over and over again, but what followed was different every time:

My daughter was killed on the one year anniversary of her enlistment in the Marines.

My son always wanted to be a Marine. He talked about it from the time he was six years old.

My wife was in the Air Force.

My dad was a Vietnam Vet. He came home for a while after the war, but the war never left him.

I feel like you're the only one who remembers that my husband gave his life for all Americans.

My dad was taken from me when I was a little girl and he was in Korea.

My son's dad was killed when my son was only 14 months old.

My son was killed.

My daughter was killed.

My husband was killed.

My wife was killed.

My dad was killed.

My mom was killed.

"Thank you so much for calling," I would say, "and I'm sure we'll talk again." At which point I would turn to MSL and say, "It's been a long day."

"I don't know what you've been doing," she said to me one day in 2017, "but whatever it is, it needs to stop."

"Why?" I asked.

"Because," she continued, "you've got bags under your

bloodshot eyes, you look like you're losing weight, and you've been sad for weeks. Something's gotta give, because I want my man back."

I think that was the first time I realized that I had been internalizing all those stories. There were so many stories. Even today, the stories still come in. I've learned a few tricks here and there, and I don't get too depressed anymore when I hear those stories, but I feel for each and every one of those people who call or email me with their stories. Even though we have volunteers now who answer the phones, I have taken the responsibility of talking to each one personally. I do it myself.

We received a few donations in 2017, so we tried using that money to raise more money. We knew there was a great need. We purchased a two week radio ad campaign that burned through a hundred dollars a day without generating a single additional donation.

OK, that didn't work. What next?

In 2017 and early in 2018, we set up vendor booths at various events throughout the region. We received ten dollars here and twenty dollars there, but the big companies of the world kept their distance, until the owner of a prominent restaurant in Minneapolis heard about what we were trying to do. He gave me a phone number for a rep at a whiskey company. He said, "Tell him I sent you. I go through more barrels of whiskey than anyone else in the country, so he'll listen."

At that, we were able to start naming the whiskey company as a sponsor. They provided artwork for inclusion on our website and T-shirts for us to give away. Un-fortunately, we're still waiting for them to cut a check to us to be an official sponsor of what we do, and we've pulled their name off of nearly everything we promote, but we'll take their call when they dial our number.

We had a vendor booth at the Saint Croix Valley Riders Chili Feed, which occurs near the St Croix River every September in between Prescott and Ellsworth in Wisconsin, and we're thankful for that group's assistance. We raised a couple hundred dollars there.

If you like biking and camping, they make great chili and it is a fun event. The Saturday night bon-fire is one you'll never forget.

The professional football championship game was played in Minneapolis in February, 2018, and with it came millions of dollars in hype. We did our best to play along. We nearly got into the country's most wealthy charity party, and we did get into a couple parties that were above average, but not quite as glamorous. The result of these parties was three hundred, fifty dollars in donations, and ten thousand dollars in expenses.

The professional football championship game was not so super for us.

We contacted a motorcycle rental company which rents motorcycles nationwide, and I remember the phone call like it was yesterday. "You could ride from one location to the next, changing motorcycles every few days so none would get all those miles put on it."

"That's a great idea," I said, "not to mention the regular maintenance would be much easier."

"We'll put this together. I'm certain we'll want to partner with you and what you're doing," they said.

I never heard from them again, even though I left no fewer than twelve voice mails, and no fewer than ten emails. They changed their mind, but they forgot to tell me.

It was late in 2017 when I got a call from someone in Washington. He identified himself as the president of the American Legion Riders National headquarters. I was impressed. "Do you know why we call them Gold Star Families?" he asked.

"Actually, no," I admitted. I knew the term, not the history.

"It started a hundred years ago," he explained, "during World War I. Whenever a family received a draft notice that their eighteen year old son had to go to Europe; that notice came with a small flag with a blue star on it." He paused just enough for effect before continuing, "Then, if they received the telegram – because in those days, they sent a telegram, not a personal messenger – if they sent a telegram saying the young man was dead, it came with another flag, this time with a Gold Star on it.

"A hundred years ago," he continued, "every person in America knew what a Gold Star Family was. Those families would hang that flag in their windows and the people would lower their heads when they walked passed. They showed respect and dignity to those families. That was lost somewhere along the way. The American Legion decided in the 1950's to resurrect that Gold Star program, and they've been working hard to tell people about it ever since."

A little side note here: I've ridden with American Legion Riders, been a member of the American Legion, and for the most part, I am a huge fan of the American Legion. I encourage other veterans to make sure you look into the American Legion if you need anything. However, the American Legion celebrated its one hundredth anniversary in 2018, and they held their national convention in Minneapolis. When I asked them to help us by providing us a booth at the convention, they became incredibly quiet.

I kept calling people. I kept sending emails to people. I kept going to people's offices to inspire them to help us accomplish our mission and achieve our goals. Our mission quickly became a double pronged fork. On the one side, we needed to take care of Gold Star Families, but on the other, we needed to educate people on *what* a Gold Star Family *is*. On any given day, if I made twenty phone calls to new people, nineteen did not know what a Gold Star Family is.

I stopped to see Rockie whenever I could or whenever he was playing a concert nearby, and while I'd like to say he's a friend of mine, it's more accurate to say we know each other. Even at that, it might be more accurate still to say I know him. I don't know, given the volume of people that he meets every day, how well he remembers me. I do know that when I call his office, it's pretty quiet. Rockie is hard at work promoting his music, performing on stage, and supporting Gold Star Families and our nation's military unlike anyone else I can think of in the entertainment industry, with the possible exception of Gary

Sinise and the Gary Sinise Foundation. I hope someday I can achieve one percent of the workload these two celebrities accomplish for our nation's veterans and fallen heroes.

During one of my short visits with Rockie, I said, "I'm gonna do this ride, and I'd love it if you could ride along when we're in North Carolina. "

"Call me when you know the date you'll be there," he said.

We had met with some of the people at the whisky company and had an informal agreement to promote each other. I was invited to go to events with them, and I did my best to promote them wherever I went. I still have two boxes of their T-shirts shirts in the office that I'd love to give away. The corporation, which is very large, has never made a promise in writing, and the people I was dealing with are all working somewhere else now, so the Gold Star Ride Foundation is basically back at square one with those negotiations.

Back in October, 2017, however, the hype was all about that professional football championship thingy. The whiskey company was trying to have an event in which they would create the world's largest "Old Fashioned" (which is a drink made from whiskey) and the Guinness Book of World Records would stop by and actually say that it was officially the world's largest Old Fashioned. The plan was big and they were going to have a big whiskey drink when they put it all together.

We were talking one day when I was informed that they needed to do something with that Old Fashioned. They had decided to sell the drinks at a bar called Grumpy's in downtown Minneapolis, (a location which has since closed) literally across the street from the stadium featuring the professional football championship game on the day of the game. "Which charity?" I asked.

"Grumpy's gets to make the choice," the reps told me, "and they've already chosen one."

"OK," I said, making sure not to upset any wagons. I didn't think about it again until one day in December when I was driving in downtown Minneapolis for other business. The other business didn't work out and I no longer remember what it was. I found myself rolling passed Grumpy's and there was a parking spot in front of the door.

I pulled in just to say hi to the management and nothing more. "I'm looking for the manager," I said to the bartender.

"He's at the other location," I was told. I thought not much else about it and got back in my car. For reasons I can't really explain, I sort of blanked out until I found my car parked at the other location.

"Hi," I said when I found myself face to face with him, "I'm Tony, and I just wanted to tell you about the Gold Star Ride Foundation."

"Hi Tony, nice to meet you," he said. He shook my hand like he meant it. I told him about what we were planning to do. "I love what you're doing," he said, "I think we'll donate all the sales of that Old Fashioned to you."

"I thought you had a charity already for that?" I asked, sort of.

"I told the company that the money would go to My Kids," he said, smiling. "No, we hadn't chosen one yet, but I know the owners will love your organization."

Bottom line from that story, go to Grumpy's and eat and drink. Grumpy's has been a major player in the sponsorship game from the day they found out about The Gold Star Ride Foundation. The sales of the Old Fashioneds at the bar during the game were just over six hundred dollars the day of the game. Grumpy's rounded the number up to seven hundred, fifty dollars. We posted pictures of the big check on social media, which stirred up some *other stuff*.

The *other stuff* was comments that came from a volunteer who spent some time at an event helping us pass out brochures and business cards. I made the mistake of listening intently as this volunteer shared their personal story of their financial struggles. I made a comment that we didn't have any money, but if we did, I would approve a payment to them for the help they gave us.

This was a very important life lesson for me and all of us at GSRF. Please understand; this volunteer had helped us about a year before the game, the party and the check.

We never did come up with any money to pass on to that volunteer and we regret that. We saw the check from Grumpy's as a promotional tool, and we published the pictures. The (now former) volunteer saw the picture and thought they should receive those proceeds, or at least some of them. Let me say, there was never a promise of payment for being a volunteer; there never has been; nor will there ever be; a promise of money being paid to a volunteer. This was a once only thing and we'll never make a statement like that again, but after hearing the sob story, and after the volunteer had completed the event, I said that if and when we had some money, we'd help them. We had not helped them yet, and we published the pictures.

Please understand that operating a charity with one hundred percent volunteers is still an expensive undertaking. Someone still has to pay for phones, brochures, business cards, websites, and accountants. We have to keep the lights on.

The result was a severe tongue lashing from this former volunteer on social media. The tongue lashing included making false statements that the GSRF was funneling all the donations we receive into the pockets of the board members. There were others on social media who saw this tongue lashing, and commented themselves. I've saved all the messages, but those messages included naming our board members and accusing us all of taking the contributions to the GSRF and lining our own pockets.

I drafted a "note" and published it on Facebook in response to this *other stuff*, and the bad words stopped, however, we had already been blocked from seeing anything they posted, and blocked from the group they administered.

In the essay I wrote and published on social media, I explained how much things cost, and compared other well-known charities financial habits to our own; using all public information. That essay is still available on social media.

The good news is that nothing was ever said again about our organization's finances.

Our work continued. We still needed money, sponsors, equipment, and friends.

We tried to have a formal gala at a private club in Minneapolis back in December of 2017. We had some grand plans. We met with a band manager who represented a Cuban band, and decided to have a Cuban themed evening. We worked with the chef to plan the perfect meal. We worked with the bartenders to plan the perfect drink menu. We studied the calendar to find the day with the least number of conflicting events. We negotiated a limousine service to be sure everyone could come in a nice car. I contacted a handful of retired professional athletes as special guests. All was perfect. Except for one thing:

No one bought a ticket. The event was cancelled before it got off the ground.

I called several printers because, well, we always need stuff printed. I think I called printers in every part of the country. In January, 2018, I finally found one that wanted to work with us. They printed some of our materials for the February football game fiasco. Then: crickets.

It's amazing how the silence of someone can create such a large noise.

In March, we met with the cornerstone of our corporate partners: The Tom Barnard Podcast. Allow a little back story.

MSL was born in and grew up in the Dominican Republic. Her family is all still there. She goes to visit there several times a year, and very often she takes me with her. I've come to learn a lot about this small island nation, and I get around there pretty well.

In the Twin Cities of Minneapolis and St Paul, Minnesota, there are a large number of radio stations. When I last worked in radio in this market (more than twenty years ago) there were more than one hundred-fifty radio stations. For the last three decades, there has been one radio station that is always in the top three for listeners, and usually in the number one spot. This high ranking position is largely because of the guy on the radio in the morning; who has been in that same time slot for more than thirty-three years. At his peak, he pulled a thirty share in the Twin Cities. For those of you who do not follow radio lingo or marketing stuff, this basically means that of the million or so cars on the road during rush hour every morning, almost one out of every three of those cars was listening to the same guy. His name is Tom Barnard, and the radio station is KQRS. You can find it on the FM dial at 92.5.

A few years ago, this powerhouse of morning radio started his very own podcast. While the numbers are much more difficult to track now than they were fifteen years ago, his voice and the things he chooses to talk about are still in demand. His podcast, which is a daily podcast, (another unheard of thing in the podcast industry) has a very large following. I wanted to know more about the podcast, its listeners, and how we could promote our mission on this new medium. I called the general manager to discuss.

We emailed each other trying to get a meeting between Tom and me. While we were trying to arrange this meeting, KQRS was running a promotion. This particular promotion invited people to buy a ticket for a long weekend in Punta Cana, Dominican Republic, with the KQRS Morning Show – featuring Tom Barnard – broadcasting live from a resort there.

After several attempts to get a meeting, I sent an email to the manager saying, "If we can't set this up, I'm just gonna crash your party in Punta Cana."

To which he replied, "If you make it to Punta Cana, I'll move hell and high water to get you a meeting with Tom."

I had ten days to put that together. I know a guy (this is one of my favorite phrases when told of a problem, "I know a guy,") who rents cars in Punta Cana. His name is Melo. I called him and told him I need a car on Thursday. He said he would pick me up at the airport.

I made arrangements with another friend to obtain a "stand by" ticket to Punta Cana's airport. If you've ever flown on a standby ticket, then you know, but if you haven't, well, it's sort of like playing a scratch off ticket in the lottery. Your odds of getting a seat on the plane are reduced a hundred fold from those who have a real ticket.

On the day of the meeting, I waited at the gate of the

Minneapolis airport with my standby ticket as all the passengers – most of which were students on spring break – filled the aircraft. As I sat, I could see the computer monitor hanging from the ceiling, informing me that the plane was full, and it looked like I wouldn't be able to go. If I couldn't go on this flight, there was no plan B. I would not get the meeting.

I was about to give up. I stood and pulled the strap from my laptop bag over my shoulder and looked one more time at the board, when I heard the gate agent call my name. I walked to the counter expecting her to tell me that she had moved my name to the next flight, which was the next day "You got lucky," she said. "Seat twenty-six E didn't show up."

"Thank you very much!" I replied, not sure if I was dreaming. I was assigned the very last seat on the airplane.

Once in Punta Cana, I sent a text message to my guy at the car rental place, Melo. I stepped into a rest room and changed my clothes to be more appropriate for the wonderfully warm tropical climate of Punta Cana. The wonderful temperature of the Dominican Republic is constantly hovering between 80 and 90, and the clothes of the place are always shorts and sandals, unless of course, you're a local who is working a laborious job.

Third world countries do things different than here in the United States, and renting a car is sometimes different from how it's done in the States. I sent another text to Melo and waited. It was 2:15 PM and the meeting time was 4. I enjoyed a Fanta Orange, which is an island favorite, and walked the perimeter of the airport. I texted again. I hadn't received an answer from Melo yet.

I called. He answered. He spoke in broken English. He had forgotten. He'll have one of his drivers here to pick me up shortly.

I waited. And waited. Twenty minutes passed. I called again.

"He is there," Melo said.
"What's he driving?" I asked.
"He's driving a Ford Bronco. Rosso," he said.
"Rosso?" I asked.

"Red," he said.

"It's not here," I said. "No Ford Broncos here at all."

"I'll call him again," he said with a heavy accent.

"Melo?" I said, making sure he didn't hang up, "I have a meeting in 20 minutes. I can't be late."

"No problem," he said. That's the Dominican answer to all questions from U.S. travelers. If my favorite thing to say is, "I know a guy," the Dominican counter to that is, "No problem."

There is no problem to anything that comes along. Looking up and saw a red Bronco.

"Are you Tony?" the driver asked.

"I am," I said, "did Melo send you?"

"Si."

"Good. Let's go," I said, jumping into the front seat next to him.

"Mi nombre es Angel," he said, pronouncing it more like *angle* than *angel.*

"I'm Tony," I said, noticing that he was driving very carefully, slower than other cars on the road. "I've been here before," I said, "I've driven here," I paused. "You don't have to drive careful for me."

"You've been here before?" Angel asked. It was nice that Melo sent a driver who could speak English. "Then don't call me Angel. Call me Veen Diesel!" At that, Angel pushed the accelerator to the floor and began weaving in and out of traffic. I laughed out loud at his reference.

Angel was dropped off at Melo's rental car location, and I proceeded on my own to the resort. I pulled up to the door at 4:01 PM and found Tom waiting patiently for me. Our appointed time was 4:00.

The results of the meeting were far better than I had hoped. There's a lot that goes into this sort of thing, and for the most part, it's not necessary to discuss it here. That was a big day.

I got on an airplane the next day and flew back home. I was back in Minnesota before anyone that went with the radio station to Punta Cana.

Two weeks later, I was a guest on The Tom Barnard Podcast, and I've been a repeat guest ever since. One of the greatest pleasures I've been handed since being assigned executive director by the other board members has been to hang out in the studio with Tom, his family, and his other guests. I don't know if they see it that way, but I think it's a tremendous amount of fun.

A month after sitting with Tom at that beach restaurant in Punta Cana, I heard from the printer again. After three months of silence, we have printing again. T-shirts were ordered, brochures and pamphlets were ordered. Flags were ordered. It was like we were a real organization.

Print Media, MN is the printing company that chose to be one of our sponsors, and we still work with them.

I continued to make contacts throughout the country; continued to hear and read people saying, "What you're doing is fantastic. We can't wait to be a part of it."

That's what I heard from countless hotel chains and oil companies. They couldn't wait to be a part of it. Apparently, "couldn't wait" meant that they *would wait*. They would wait a very long time; most never communicated with us again.

That wasn't universally true, however, because one day I got an email from someone I didn't recognize. We went back and forth with emails until we had confirmed a time to talk on the phone. The result of that phone conversation was a box of equipment from GoPro Cameras. That was another "feel really good about the work you do" day.

Most days were spent reading email, chasing phone numbers, calling people, writing email, radio interviews, oh, and social media. I spent an hour or two every day trying to make social media work.

I did crowd funding campaigns and came to this one conclusion: If you don't need a crowd funding campaign to get people to donate, then a crowd funding campaign will work wonders. If you can't get people to donate without a crowd funding campaign, a crowd funding campaign won't do it either.

I ran ten different crowd funding campaigns on ten

different crowd funding websites. The only money raised was thirty dollars, twenty of which came from me.

We've been lucky since then, with a few donations coming in, but mostly we worked on the sweat of those of us who volunteered time and talent to making the ride work. We received positive responses from Viking Bags, Extreme Fairings, International Cigars and Brandl Motors (Brandl Motors, by the way, sent us a big check. We accomplished a lot with that money, and it was one of the very first checks we ever received. That's why they are still listed on our website, even though they have not sent another check since. They believed in us when no one else did, so we believe in them longer than we should). Still, we needed a shot in the arm to move forward.

Whenever I felt that it was too much, that we didn't have the money; that we didn't have the bike; the trailer; the camera crew; or other bikes that wanted to ride, the phone would ring. "I just wanted to tell you about my son. He was an adopted boy from Korea, and he was in the Delta Forces. He had been in the Army fourteen years when he was shot. One bullet, in the only spot on his body that wasn't covered in Kevlar; his throat."

"I'm so sorry for your loss and I'm so thankful that your son was willing to do that for me," I choked out. Then I knew I would renew my vigor to go on the ride.

At home, MSL was preparing for a high school graduation party for her youngest son, and that was something I lent myself to as much as possible. Once that graduation was completed, and the party had been cleaned up, I dedicated all my time to completing the ride at any cost.

As the ride date came closer, I was becoming a little desperate to raise money and pay for the trip. Donations were (and still are) extremely lacking for our mission. I adopted the mantra that I would complete the ride or die. I slept very little, not because I wasn't tired, but because a few hours after falling asleep, I would wake up with my mind racing. I would get out of bed, open my computer, and go to work.

I wrote radio advertisements that were used in campaigns in Arizona, Florida, Nevada, and of course,

Minnesota. I wrote the ads that Tom Barnard read on his podcast. I produced in my little homemade studio, all the radio ads with my own voice, and all the YouTube Videos that featured my likeness and my voice. I made videos of podcast interviews, and I made videos from nothing, just to tell people what we were trying to do, and about to do.

I wrote press releases and emailed them to news outlets around the country. I spent hours on LinkedIn becoming linked to CEO's, CFO's and CMO's of major companies throughout the country and the world in some cases.

I wrote all the essays and "notes" that were published on social media. I built and maintained the website. I took (and edited) all the pictures, created all the videos, wrote all the copy, scripts and dialogues. I read all the laws, filled out all the applications, applied for all the grants. Every keystroke was made by me.

Then, I took all my notes to the other board members and made sure they agreed with everything I was doing. We still couldn't generate money the way we needed it. It still looked like it would be a massive failure.

Then, our cornerstone sponsor came to the rescue again. Honestly, I don't know how much of this was Tom Barnard personally, and how much was me, and how much was something else. This is what I do know. I called Tom's manager and asked if I could be interviewed on the KQRS morning radio show hosted by Tom. Looking back, I'm extremely glad, thankful, and genuinely happy because I got a "yes."

On June 22, 2018, I rode my motorcycle to their studios in the Twin Cities, and arrived just in time. John Lassman, who scheduled the interview, led me in to the studio and I sat down with Bob Sansevere and Dave Mordal (two of Tom's co-hosts), and we had a little "off mic" banter before the red light came on and we were on the air.

That short little interview, which lasted about fourteen minutes, generated enough cash in donations from listeners to guarantee the ride would go forward. Maybe not comfortably, but it would go forward. It included donations from distant lands – like Kentucky, Texas, and Kansas. Three guys in Louisville worked to collect donations and raised more than three thousand dollars.

Thank you Art, Bill, and Joe.

By the time the interview occurred, we had a couple other volunteers working the phones and social media under my tutelage, and we had small hotels and motels at every stop along the scheduled route. The rooms were all donated. That part was done.

We also had three gas stations and three restaurants every day waiting for us. We wouldn't have to worry about food or gas. Maintenance on the bike was still an issue, but that's pretty small if we have all the rooms, gas, and food, so no one was worried about the cost of an oil change.

Because of the money we raised in that one radio interview, we were able to get the ten year old bike "road ready" or so we thought. My bike went into a local shop that kept it for two days, double checking all the electrical stuff, and finding out why it ran like crap when it got warm. If the bike would only run good for forty-five minutes, I was going to have a heck of a hard time crossing the country – twice.

I learned that because I had installed "slip ons" with the baffles removed onto my exhaust, the pressure inside the engine was off, and the bike needed a "dyno tune." This is a specialized tune up that connects the bike to a computer and makes adjustments taking every possible thing into consideration. This two day tune-up took a full ten percent of all the money we had without the dyno tune.

I learned later that Twin Cities Harley Davidson, which is discussed more in later chapters, has one of these machines, but I hadn't met them yet, just days before the ride began.

The shop I went to wanted more than a grand just for this part of the tune up. We didn't have that much to spare. "How about if I put the old, stock exhaust back on?" I asked, hoping.

"Then it should work fine," I was told. I did that. Then, of course, I noticed the first thing I wasn't going to like about this long motorcycle ride: I was riding a quiet motorcycle.

Part of those repairs included new hand grips, and doing some needed repairs to the fuse box. Two days later, I took the bike for a long ride to test it. It was Tuesday, and the ride was to begin on the following Monday.

I don't remember the exact details of everything that week. I am relatively certain that those six days included at least five more discussions with MSL about why I had to do it.

On Saturday, two days before the ride, we made our third appearance at the thirteenth annual Patriot Ride in Blaine, Minnesota. This is a great event, if you're not aware of it. The goal of this ride is to honor military and first responders in a variety of ways. The primary sponsor is Dennis Kirk, and just so you know, that's a motorcycle parts reseller based in Minnesota. I buy a lot of parts from them.

A few things happened at the Patriot Ride, where I was working a vendor booth promoting the GSRF. First, I unveiled our new T-shirt, which features our logo on the back, but on the front it reads,

MY DD214
CAN KICK YOUR
MBA'S ASS

If you know what that means, it's funny and you don't need an explanation. If you don't know what that means; no explanation will make if funny for you.

Two men walked up to the booth, and I presented the shirt. "Do you know what it means?" I asked. One man nodded and smiled a big smile.

"What if I have four MBA's?" the other man asked.

"Do you know what it means?" I repeated.

"No," he said.

"You need another MBA," I smirked.

The master of ceremonies was Brian Zepp. I knew Brian from other events in other years. He had been a personality on KQRS for more than a decade, but left previous year. He relocated to Bozeman, MT, but was brought back for the Patriot

Ride because he was well known for being the master of ceremonies for this event. It was nice to see him again. He laughed loud when I showed the T-shirt to him. Up to that time, he wasn't aware of the GSRF or that we were leaving in just forty hours. He insisted that I call him when I get close to Bozeman.

The Patriot Ride brought together an estimated (by me) thirty-five hundred bikes which raised money for veterans of all kinds, Gold Star Families, and first responders. You'll likely find me there next year signing copies of this book.

For me, it was another in a long line of fifteen hour days.

The Camera Crew

In February, 2017, the year of the first ride, we were approached by a film crew in Hollywood, California, about recording our national ride for a documentary. This seemed like the perfect vehicle to promote Gold Star Families and the work that we do. In the mid 1990's, I spent three years as a movie critic, and I'd like to think I know just a little bit about movies. I've also penned two movie scripts and a third treatment, and I believed we could make a movie that people would want to see. I was very excited about this prospect. So excited, in fact, that it became part of the work we would do.

We started having weekly meetings on the phone about production ideas, and costs. A year later, they backed out. Of course, this was a response to which I had become accustomed. I did what anyone in my situation would do: I shopped other film crews.

In September, 2017, I rode without cameras to visit a few families between Minneapolis, Minnesota and Cincinnati, Ohio. This trip was not recorded in any way, but it got the wheels turning as to what was required to get the ride accomplished. For this reason, I made hundreds of phone calls to producers, camera operators, production crews, and the like. Everyone I spoke to said something similar: "What a great idea! If only I didn't have to work."

I thought this *was* work.

By February, 2018, I had another production company signed on to record the documentary. By April, they had backed out. I signed on with another company later that same month. They too, backed out. I signed on with another company in May. They worked (it seemed to me) tirelessly. They said they had a financial backer to pay the expenses. All was looking good.

They backed out the end of the first week in June.

I was pretty close to desperate, because I felt that the production of the documentary was the magic key to telling people about Gold Star Families. I kept making calls. The president of the Minnesota Film Society suggested I call the colleges that teach filmmaking and ask if there were students looking for a project.

On Monday, seven days before the ride was to begin, I spoke with a college which put me in touch with the equipment room manager, who heard the story and took my phone number. On Thursday that week, four days before the ride began, I got a call from a student who was interested. He said he knew two other students and the three of them would get it done.

I met with him finally on Sunday, July 1, 2018. We spoke for two hours about every detail I could imagine. We talked about every possible hazard, and we talked about raising money. At 8:00 PM that night, he called me to confirm he and his friends would be at Grumpy's in Roseville, Minnesota at 6:30 AM the next day to film the ride.

That crew showed up at 7:15, and we left Grumpy's at 7:25.

Chapter Two: The Road to Lockport

Sunday, July 1, 2018, was not a day like any other. You just read about some of the things that occurred that day, and the rest of the day was busy with last minute details, like trying to pack the bike with everything we needed on the trip. I had packed the bike with everything because I thought the bike was going alone. Until that 8:00 PM phone call, when the bike was unpacked and all the stuff needed for the trip was packed into the SUV.

Then I set my alarm and went to bed. Sleep was difficult that night. I woke up and looked at my phone for the time at least five times that I can remember. My brain was racing.

Finally the alarm rang, and when it did, I was sound asleep. My first reaction was to try to reset the alarm so I could sleep another ten minutes. I didn't finish that resetting. I realized what day it was, and I was up.

I stopped in the parking lot of Grumpy's in Roseville, because that's where everyone who was riding along was to meet. I got there to see one motorcycle and Dart's patriotic truck. It's a beautiful thing, I'm sure you'll agree. Look at the picture in the pictures section of this book.

Dart didn't have to be here helping us. We hadn't made any formal agreements. Their truck, painted to represent our nation's military and their own patriotism, was a great asset to our start.

Dart offers supply chain capabilities in warehousing services, dry van transportation, transportation brokerage, intermodal and portable storage. Their principle offices are in Eagan, Minnesota. You can see a little more contact information in the sponsors list at the back of the book.

Byerly's grocery store in Roseville donated the donuts for the morning get-together. The manager of Grumpy's was on hand and he made the coffee. Most of both the coffee and the donuts were wasted, though, because there were only a few people there.

When we pulled out, the Dart truck led the way, and

the camera crew followed behind, and we were off at 7:25 AM. Only twenty five minutes late. I should have realized that might be a sign of things to come.

Dart is a great transportation company. I had gone only a week before to see Rockie Lynne, who was playing in North Branch about an hour north of the Twin Cities. I heard some good music, and saw this beautiful truck alongside the park were a patriotic event was taking place. I approached the guys from Dart at that park, and asked them if they'd like to come along on the ride. Remember, at this point, a week before, I was under the impression that eighty or more people who had signed up for the ride on social media would be there, and I had anticipated that the ride would go according to schedule. One of the Dart recruiters told me he thought it was a great idea, and he passed along the information to the powers that be at Dart. The result of his work was the driver and truck showing up at Grumpy's.

We rolled along to Stillwater, when the Dart truck had to pull away. Then, just two bikes and a camera crew turned north and headed for the first stop: The Veterans' Rest Camp in Marine on St Croix, Minnesota.

We were greeted warmly when we arrived, and found another bike waiting there for us. We were surprised to learn about this quite fantastic place. Veterans Campground on Big Marine Lake is a family campground that provides facilities and opportunities for recreation, rest, and recovery for all military veterans who have served honorably in the Armed Forces of the United States, their families, and sponsored guests.

We learned that it was actually the sight of the first VA hospital in Minnesota. The distance from St Paul and Minneapolis is just enough so you can't tell there is a major city in such close proximity. Details of this wonderful place are better learned from their website than this book, but know that if you are a veteran, you are welcome, and anything you want to do in the summer is there; camping, fishing, swimming, campfires, music, and friendly faces. You'll have to bring your own bottle, though, because their liquor license is only for light beer and mixes for your favorite drink.

We spent an hour with the fine folks, met with some kids and campers, shared our donuts from Byerly's then we headed off.

We lost the other bikes while we were here. People have other things they need to do.

MSL and I rode across the St. Croix River to Wisconsin with the camera crew in tow. Our next stop was for food at the Amery Family Restaurant, in Amery, Wisconsin.

They were expecting more bikes, and more people. They had prepared a buffet for about a hundred people so there was some crow served to me before we got to sit down and eat. I was trying to express my regret that eighty people had signed up to ride with us but we were only four people. And only one bike.

As I walked toward the restaurant, I crossed paths with an older woman who struggled with the door. The other members of my group where already inside.

"Thank you," she said as I held the door for her, "it's a nice day for a ride."

"It is," I said, "and today is the first day of a fifty-four day ride."

"Fifty-four days?" she quipped, "where are you going?"

"I'm going around the country," I began what would become a daily diatribe to strangers, "to honor Gold Star Families. You remember that a Gold Star Family is one where someone joined the military and was killed, right?"

"Of course," she said. I was guessing that she was a young woman during the Korean War. "My husband served for thirty-two years."

"Oh!" I responded, "is he here, too?"

"No," she looked down, "I lost him."

"Then, you're a Gold Star Widow in our book," I explained. "Do you have one minute to tell me anything about him?"

She told me of his lifetime of service in the US Navy. She shared with me that Amery was the town where they grew up, and that they were high school sweethearts and married in college. He was a captain in the Navy.

"Thank you," I said, "for sharing your story with me. It is my honor to meet you."

"You're sweet," she said, getting into her car, "thank you for doing what you do." She smiled at me and she shut the car's passenger door, and the car disappeared. I watched it leave the parking lot and went inside the Amery Family Restaurant and met the rest of the Gold Star Ride Crew.

"We had rented the community hall across the street. We have tables set up for all these people," the manager started.

"I'm sorry," I tried to begin. "Maybe we can give all that food to everyone who comes into the restaurant for the next hour or two, and the Foundation will pay for it?" I didn't want it to go to waste, and I didn't want them to lose a great deal of money because they wanted to help us.

"Just sit down," she said to me. "There's a table in the back that is large enough for all of you." I have to admit, I was hungry.

"OK," I responded, "just bring us whatever you have prepared. And by the way, I'm Tony."

"I'm Stevie. Just have a seat."

We all walked to the large booth in the back of the restaurant.

"That was awkward," I said to the group, which consisted of MSL and two camera crew people.

"What else could you do?" she asked me.

"Record all you can," I instructed the camera crew.

We talked and chuckled some as we ate a wonderful meal. We tried to make jokes about the idea that we thought there would be so many bikes with us, and we were all alone. Near the end of the meal, a couple I hadn't met before walked to our table.

"Are you Tony?" the man asked.

"I am," I said, and stood to shake hands with him.

"I'm Chili Illazi, the owner of this restaurant," he said, with a slight eastern European accent. I started to worry about what would come next. Was he about to ask me for two hundred dollars to pay for all the food?

"I'm very sorry our numbers are so small," I tried to apologize and held out my hand to shake his.

"I am from Romania," he said, "and I was rescued by the United States Marines. I was a refugee and they saved me and my family."

"I'm Gzmie. It's nice to meet you," his wife said, holding out her hand to shake mine.

He continued, "I think what you're doing is very important, and I'm very glad that you chose to come to our restaurant."

"Thanks for having us," I said, still a little worried about what would happen next.

"It's my honor to have you here," he continued, "if it wasn't for the US military, I wouldn't be standing here right now. I don't think we can ever do enough for our military and what they've done for us." His accent grew stronger as he spoke. "I'm paying for your lunch, and don't worry about any of that other food that we prepared. I'll find some use for it." I may have breathed an audible sigh of relief at that point.

"And," he said, stretching out his arm, "I'd like you have this also." He handed me a check. "It's not much," he continued, "hopefully, it will help. Now, please, sit down and enjoy your meal."

"Thank you so much," I said, "you know we can't do anything without the help of strangers." I shook his hand again, and sat down as they walked away.

A wonderfully "local" looking woman approached. "Is this a good time?" she asked.

"Sure," I said, then taking a big drink of my iced tea to wash the food out of my mouth. I am always ready to talk to people. At least, I try.

"I'm the editor of the Amery Free Press. I'd like to do a story on your visit here today."

"Great. Have a seat."

That was our first press experience on the road. She asked a few questions about what, where, and why, snapped a picture or two, and left us to finish our lunch.

We left the restaurant with smiles, and an incredibly humble feeling that maybe what we're doing is something that should be done. I felt a little bit important, which is new for me, and I wasn't sure what to do with those feelings.

An hour later, we stopped for gas at a SA gas station in Amery, Wisconsin that was expecting us. The sign outside the door, which is one of those signs that allow you to change the letters and messages, said, "Welcome Gold Star Riders."

I went inside and spoke with the manager. "We don't have all the bikes that we thought we would," I said, apologetically.

"You're doing a good thing," she said, "and I'm happy to buy your gas."

It was at this stop that MSL received a distress message from home, and she had to return. While I pumped gas along with the camera crew, she made arrangements to get on a bus in the next town and go back home.

The next town was Hayward, and after dropping her off within a minute or two of catching her ride home on public transportation, the camera guys and I rode on to find the dinner stop. They were expecting fifty to a hundred bikes also, and the manager there was more than a little disappointed when we arrived.

Now, it's worth saying that the GPS took us to three locations that were not the restaurant, so when we finally arrived, we were three hours late; not just two. I'd like to say this was the only time GPS gave bad instructions, but there are more stories to come.

I told the camera guys to come in a few steps behind me with the cameras rolling, because I thought dealing with an angry manager should be recorded. I was directed to her office in the back, and introduced myself.

"Finally," was the first thing I heard her say, "I've got food prepared for a hundred people. Where are they?" She was not happy.

"I'm very sorry," I began, "but they just didn't show up. I thought they would, but they didn't." I really didn't know what else to say, so I chirped out, "if you'd like to do an impromptu special, I'll buy the food from you and you can give it to any customer who wants it, as long as you tell them it was from The Gold Star Ride Foundation." At that point she noticed the camera guys behind me.

"Turn that thing off," she quipped, noticing the red light on the camera. I nodded to them and the cameras went off. "No," she said, "I won't be doing any kind of special, and I'm not gonna make you pay for it. And I'll buy you guys your dinner, too." Somehow, all her anger had been disarmed.

The next part of the ride became some of the most memorable and enjoyable riding I did throughout the country. For two hours, it was all Chequamegon National Forest in northern Wisconsin. It was here that I saw the second deer of the day, a mountain lion, and an elk. While I did break hard for the mountain lion, I never felt that any of those sightings were really dangerous. Of course, anyone who's ever ridden will tell you, as will I, that any time you see an animal on or near the roadway, the situation can change to dangerous very quickly.

The roads gently curved, the trees were gorgeous, the weather was perfect, and the air smelled of a perfect summer; fresh and clean. I recommend riding the Chequamegon National Forest to anyone with a bike.

Arriving in Hurley, Wisconsin, which is a "twin city" so to speak, with Ironwood, Michigan, we had more interesting issues. The two towns are separated only by a very small river, the Montreal River. The bridge going over the river is so small, that the first time I crossed it, I didn't see it. Hurley had a population of a tiny bit over fifteen hundred in the 2000 census. Ironwood had a population of only fifty-three hundred. Populations notwithstanding, however, we had arrangements to get gas (again, we were two hours late) and sleep in a local hotel.

At the gas station, which was a Cenex branded station, the help was actually waiting for us in the parking lot with their phones set to the camera mode. They actually jumped up and down with excitement at our arrival, and they, like every other scheduled stop of the day, wondered where the rest of the bikes were.

No one noticed me bending over to the right side of the bike, and holding tight to one of my highway pegs with my right hand while my left hand held the front brake tight as I lifted myself off, or more accurately, rolled myself, off the bike. (For those of you who don't ride, the front brake lever is on the right side of the handlebars.) I walked slower than everyone else, but no one noticed. On a scale of one to ten, my pain level was about an eight.

We filled the tanks, took pictures for posterity, thanked them as much as we could, and then they presented me with a gift card. I didn't know the amount, and I thanked them, putting it in my wallet, not knowing or imagining how important that tiny piece of plastic would end up being.

The hotel was only a block away from the gas station, and after again, painfully, lifting myself off the bike, and slowly walking inside, I introduced myself at the front desk, telling the camera guys to just wait a minute.

"I'm Tony, from the Gold Star Ride Foundation," I said to the woman seated there.

"I don't know what that means," she said.

"I had made arrangements with Denise for me and my camera crew to get two rooms tonight," I offered.

"Let me check," she said, turning to her computer. After typing a bit, she said, "No, you're not in the system. And Denise isn't here anymore."

"Is there a chance you could call her and ask her about our reservation?" I hoped.

"No." We looked at each other a pregnant moment. "She was escorted out by the police," she said.

My eyebrows went up into my bandana. I realized I was probably something interesting to see, with a T-shirt, leather vest, bandana, sunglasses, and fingerless gloves, and talking to a person who had never seen me before, and I'm asking for a free room. No, two free rooms. I pulled the bandana and sunglasses off, and began removing my gloves.

"Isn't this the Ramada?" I hoped to keep the conversation going in the right direction.

"It was this afternoon, but that name changed when

Denise left. This is the Snowflake Inn."

I realized there was nothing more I could really do, even if she was the new manager. "Have you heard of the Gold Star Ride Foundation?" I asked. She hadn't. "We're riding and making a documentary movie about Gold Star Families – the ones left behind when someone is killed in the military. We are an official five oh one C three charity. Can you see donating a couple rooms to us? I have a camera crew outside."

She started typing something on the computer. "The best I can do is a triple A discount," she offered, "Sixty-eight dollars per room."

After we settled into the rooms, showered, got some food and I had copied all the GoPro data from the cameras to my computer, the camera guys came in. I was a little shocked by the presence of a third camera guy. They introduced him to me, and told me they had invited him to drive up from Minneapolis to meet here. He wanted to join us on this trip.

After a long "get to know you" conversation, it was agreed that he could come along on the journey, and he would be sharing a room with the other two. It was after one in the morning when they left my room for their own, right across the hall. I knew that too many chefs screw up the stew, so I was a little concerned about the added personality, but I thought I could lead these guys to get the job done. Of course, you've only been reading about this ride for a short time, and I bet you are guessing what happens next.

They left the room, and I opened a bottle of whiskey. I don't remember what flavor of whiskey it was, but I poured it into a plastic cup and slowly sipped on it; thinking about the events of the day. I contemplated the fact that I now had three camera people filming a documentary movie, all of whom were less than half my age. I wondered if I could keep up with three young guys. I wondered if they could keep up with me. I wondered if they were dedicated to getting this job done. They seemed like it, but contemporary twenty-something's are not my specialty. I set my alarm, sent a text saying good night to MSL, turned on the TV for something funny to end my day, and tried to relax in the bed.

I blinked and the alarm rang. As I turned it off, I glanced at the glass of whiskey; still half of what I poured remained in the glass. The TV was still on, too. I guess I was more tired than I had realized.

After realizing how tired I was came another realization: I'm in a very small town and I want espresso. Where will I find espresso in this little town?

I quickly dressed and got my gear together, texting the guys across the hall at the same time. They didn't respond. I texted again, and I called. No answer. I packed the bike and went to the front desk. "Good morning," I said. I had given both keys to that room to the camera guys the night before, so in order for me to go in and get them, I needed a key.

"Good morning. We have coffee and donuts in our breakfast room," the man said. He was about ten years older than me by the looks of him, but I've come to learn that my brain plays tricks on me. I can't tell how old people are anymore with any sort of accurate measure. He might have actually been younger than me. Anyway, he looked about sixty-five.

"Are you running the show?" I asked with as much humor as I could deliver.

"I guess I am," he said, "my name is Tom."

"Hi, Tom. I'm wondering if you can give me another key for room one fifty-nine. I misplaced mine."

"I think so," he said, walking back behind the check-in counter. He immediately started typing something into the computer. "Remind me your name?" he asked dutifully.

I told him. He said, "Oh, yeah, here we are," and he quickly grabbed a new key, swiped it through the machine and handed it to me.

"I wonder if you could help me with something else?" I asked. "You look like someone who's lived here for a while. Can you tell me where I can find espresso in town?"

"Let me think," Tom began to answer, speaking the slow and methodic rhythm of someone from a small town. "Do you know where the Cenex gas station is?" I did. "If you go to the gas station, then, don't turn, but keep on going, you'll see a dog leg in the road to the right. Then at the next corner you keep going straight again, and you come to the light. It's the only light in town, and it's flashing red. Turn left there, and it's right on the corner as you turn. So, you'll turn left, but it will be on the left corner."

"OK," I said, "thanks."

As quick as my little legs could carry me, I scurried down the hall and opened the camera crews' door. We were supposed to start at 6:30 today because we were crossing into an earlier time zone, and needed to make up for lost time. It was already six-thirty.

I flashed the light switch on and off repeatedly and said, in as loud a voice as I could without disturbing the other guests of the hotel, "Get up! Let's go! Get up! Let's go!" They stirred and grumbled a little bit. When I saw an open eye, I said, "I'm going to get coffee. I'll be back in fifteen minutes. Be in the car ready to go."

I jumped on the bike and went looking for a dog leg and a flashing red light. I found them quickly. I parked in the back, and walked around to the front of the store and found a man standing outside the door. He was slightly round, and looked to be in his mid-sixties; like Tom at the hotel, only more round. "Are you waiting to go in?" I asked.

"The doors are still locked," he said, "I come down here every morning to have coffee with a couple buddies, and they usually have the door open, but I guess it's still ten more minutes until they open."

"I think I see someone moving around in there. You don't suppose they're keeping you locked out, do you?" I joked.

"Haha," he chuckled, "I don't think so. I spend money in here every day."

"Oh, here she comes," I offered, seeing someone walk toward the door. She let us in; he got a cup of coffee and sat down. I ordered my espresso, added some sugar to it, then poured it into an empty water bottle so I could enjoy it all day. This "water bottle" was actually a bottle of water the day before. Today, I was recycling it as a coffee bottle. I said my farewell to the guy from outside and went out to get on the bike. It was a little later now, so the camera kids should be ready to go.

I looked at my text messages and was reminded by the volunteers back home that I had a radio interview scheduled for seven-fifteen this morning. I was hoping to do the interview thirty miles down the road, but it was coming fast. "I'll just ride back to the hotel and do it from there," I thought to myself.

The bike started right up, and I let out the clutch. Together, the bike and I rolled about ten feet; then bike died.

It just stopped running.

My shoulders dropped. I sighed a heavy sigh, and looked around for anything that resembled an idea. I hit the starter again. It tried and tried to start, but nothing. No fire in the hole, as I like to say when the engine just won't go. I tried again. I sipped my coffee. I looked around, both distant and local, and couldn't come up with any ideas.

I sighed again. Deep breath in and out. I sipped my coffee out of the water bottle. I looked at my watch, and two things popped into my head: One, why was I wearing a watch? And two, I was scheduled to be on the radio in three minutes.

I called the camera kids, who answered the phone this time, and said, "Bring the cameras and have them running. The bike died, and this should be recorded."

I told them where to find me, but left out some of the more colorful descriptions that Tom used to tell me how to get here. I put the kickstand down, even though I was more in a traffic lane than a parking spot, and walked around the corner of a nearby building to get out of the wind and away from the traffic, little of it that there was, and I called the radio station.

"I'm out here on this bike honoring families that gave up a life for you and me to do whatever you and me do. We would all have nothing if not for them, and they are forgotten or ignored far more than they are remembered. That's why I ride," I said to the radio host. She was polite and treated me pretty much the same as any other radio host ever treated any other call-in interview. I gave her listeners the web address and then it was over. Just like every other radio interview.

There was a time, back in 2016, when doing a radio interview was nerve racking. I would worry for days about going on the air. Now, it's like making a peanut butter sandwich for lunch. Justice and Drew are morning hosts on KTLK in Minneapolis, and I don't remember exactly how I met them, although I'm pretty sure there was a cigar there, but Justice and Drew where the very first talk show hosts to let me come on the air with them way back in 2016. Since then, they've invited me into the studio and done a call in.

I'd like to apologize to them publicly, because the call in occurred while I was in Phoenix. Phoenix is in an area that does not participate in Daylight Savings Time. I was there in the summer, so DST was in effect back in Minneapolis. This means, if you're gonna wake yourself up after four hours of sleep to talk on the radio, you better pay close attention to the time zones.

The short story is, I was scheduled to call in at 6:20 in the morning, and I'm pretty sure I called in at 7:20.

They were consummate professionals, and allowed me to call in and talk a bit, even if I didn't get to the part of the story I was hoping to share with their listeners. While I know that interview occurred, (I have emails to confirm it) I don't remember it at all.

I owe this lack of memory to the fact that I woke myself up after four hours of sleep on a night following my first episode of heat exhaustion; heat exhaustion which occurred two more times but that will come in later chapters.

I don't remember the last time I was on the radio with those two guys, but they are wonderful people who have given the Gold Star Ride Foundation a huge lift when it was needed, starting with an interview almost two years before the ride began. Thanks Justice and Drew, and I'm sorry about the time mix up.

Meanwhile, back in Hurley, Wisconsin, I hung up my phone, turned back around the corner and walked to the bike that wouldn't start. I tried to start it again, but nothing.

I checked my codes. (This is a method that is used to ask the computer on the motorcycle to tell you what's wrong.

There are five areas that codes are reported in, and, once you get a code, you can look up the problem.) The codes said my right blinker didn't work (honest, I couldn't make that up). They also said my crankcase sensor was not reporting.

That's when the camera crew pulled up - in the truck owned by the new guy. "Did you bring the cameras?" I asked, quite frankly, a little afraid of the answer.

"Well, yes and no," Rico said to me. He was the first one to say yes to the trip, so it made sense that he was the spokesperson for the group.

"This should be good," I said.

"We're leaving," he said. "We talked about it, and we decided to go back home. I brought your keys." He held out his hand with a dangling key.

"Well, that's interesting," I said. "Please take that key and go back to the hotel and get my truck. The bike doesn't work and I need to be able to get around from here."

They disappeared for about five more minutes. While they were gone, I thought about my dilemma. "Can anything else go wrong?" I asked myself. "Here I am on day two, barely after the sun came up, and I'm now all alone; with a broken motorcycle; MSL has already dropped out to go back home; limited money; and now the camera crew quit.

"Maybe I should quit, too?" I'm pretty sure I said that out loud, although no one was there to hear it.

They returned with the SUV, and only Rico spoke to me, and I only to him. I didn't care, not really, what their reasons were. I wasn't about to take on the added stress of a hard sell to kids. Yes, they were all in their twenties, but to me, they were kids.

I knew they were close to penniless, so I double checked the contents of the SUV, and gave Rico two twenty dollar bills. "Buy yourself some gas and munchies for the ride home," I said. He took the money and they disappeared, leaving me with an SUV and a broken motorcycle, arguably in the middle of nowhere.

I'm sure there are people in other parts of the country that believe they are in the middle of nowhere, but I felt as close to nowhere as a person can.

I was alone.

I looked around again for anything that resembled an idea. I could see nothing. There was a metal shop about a half block away, down an alley. There was a gas station on the corner, the same corner that featured a blinking red light – the only traffic light in town. There was the back door to the coffee shop that provided my morning espresso, and there was a utility truck parked nearby that looked like it hadn't moved in more than a week.

I was all alone. And nearly broke. And broke down.

I sipped the espresso again, then stopped and looked at the bottle. "That guy who has coffee here every day probably knows everybody for miles," I thought. "He knows who can fix this bike."

I walked back inside to find him, and saw him sitting with eight local men, sharing the insights of how their day was yesterday and how it will shape up today. I approached and looked him right in the eye, speaking loud enough for all nine men to hear me, "Is there any chance you know a Harley mechanic nearby?"

"Well, yes, Bill, right up the hill has been fixing Harleys for a long time. Are you having trouble with yours?"

I thought about being a smart ass with my answer, because why ask for a repair man unless you need one, but I decided against it. "Yeah, I am." I must have looked just a little pitiful.

Then they all started talking almost at once, each trying to tell me the best way to find him. First they suggested calling, because he's probably open by 7:30 every day. I called and got a voice mail. Then they started telling me to go that way, cross the river and stay to the right. He's only three more blocks on the left.

I made a mistake while driving when I didn't see the bridge. Hurley, Wisconsin, where the coffee shop is, is located on the west side of the Montreal River, and Backstreet Cycle and Machine (Bill's shop) is in Ironwood, Michigan, on the east bank. From what I could tell later, the Montreal River is small enough nearly to step over it.

I eventually found Bill. I'm dressed like a biker, with leather jacket and vest covered with patches. I've got a bandana on my head; sunglasses and fingerless gloves. Of course, if you work on Harleys for a living, this is a look you expect. This is Ironwood, Michigan, just over the river from Hurley, Wisconsin. The two towns combined can't come up with seven thousand people. There is a pace. I had to lock my jaw shut because I wasn't on the same pace. I was, however, at his mercy.

Bill is a man who looked to be nearing seventy years of age. He stood about three or four inches shy of six feet and might have weighed a hundred forty pounds after a heavy meal. I could instantly tell that this was a man who had more stories than there were people to write them. In the front of my mind, I was worried about the time. In the back of my mind, I wanted to sit around a campfire with him and listen to his stories for at least a week.

It took Bill nearly three full minutes to walk from where he was in the rear of his repair shop to the middle of his repair shop where he has a desk of sorts, which was a distance of about twenty feet. Not because he was slow of step, but because he stopped to adjust or fix something almost every step of the way. Then he sat down, sprinkled some tobacco into a small cigarette rolling paper, rolled it the old fashioned way, lit it, and listened as I described the problems and the codes from my bike.

He paid attention to every word, as if it were the only thing there was for him to do today. He asked a few questions for clarity, and I could tell by our differing speech patterns that each of us had a speed, and they weren't the same. Then he put out his cigarette, and opened a book. He studied the book while I tried to feel comfortable and not interested in making it to Mount Pleasant, Michigan.

I was still feeling alone when he said, "OK, let's go take a look." He grabbed a few tools (another long process), a part from his parts area, and got in the SUV with me to ride back to the bike.

"When did you start fixing Harleys?" I asked, trying to keep the conversation light while we drove back to Wisconsin.

"1964," Bill said, exhaling loudly. We didn't talk much more. It took ninety seconds to get to the bike from his shop.

He tried a few things, replaced the part, and tried a thing or two more. "I have to get this back to the shop," he informed me matter-of-factly.

We drove back to the shop. He took a call, and did all sorts of other things, while I lingered in his shop. He had a front to his shop which featured about ten motorcycles for sale, a few racks of leather gear, and a wall filled with helmets and boots. It was clear that all this was just stuff. It was not a bright, dust free showroom. His primary business was repairing.

"How is it that you're in town?" came a voice that sounded strikingly like the woman from *Two and a Half Men*, Conchata Ferrell (who plays the part of the housekeeper on that show).

"Bike broke," I said, trying to be witty; it didn't work. She just stared at me. I told her about the Gold Star Ride Foundation, asked her if she knew what a Gold Star Family was, and then said, "I was supposed to head toward the Mackinaw City Bridge at 6:30 this morning."

"That's a ride," she said matter-of-factly, "should take you about six or seven hours," It was clear to me that she and Bill had been together for a while. "How long are will you be staying now?" she asked, but I'm sure she knew the answer as well as I did.

"Depends on when Bill can get me rolling," I said. I didn't try to make a joke anymore, but I was doing all I could to not be angry. This wasn't the way the day was supposed to shape up. I also knew that these kind, small-town people were here to help, not slow me down, even if they did move in a different gear than me. I also knew that if I should be angry, I better find the right person at which to be angry, and I didn't know.

The pain in my lower back was starting to radiate by now, too. I'd been standing for quite some time. "I'm Tony," I introduced myself.

"My name is Mary, but around here they call me 'Ma,' so you can call me Ma."

"Then I'll call you Ma," I said.

"Tom's coming," Bill interrupted, "and he'll take you to go get your bike."

It wasn't long until I found myself in a car with Tom. He was slightly older than me, but I liked him right away primarily because he was faster than Bill. Tom was in a hurry! He sported long gray hair to the lower part of his neck, and drove an unimpressive little sedan. He pulled a flat trailer that looked like it was designed more for snowmobiles than motorcycles, and we stopped to load up the bike.

"Dam!" he said, "I don't have the ramp with me!" We started looking for ways to put an eleven hundred pound motorcycle onto a trailer without a ramp. We stopped looking after about thirty seconds.

"I must have left it in my shop," Tom informed me. "Let's go get it," and off we went, pulling the little flat empty trailer through the very small town to his shop. The trailer was made of mesh steel and with every bump on the road – and there were many – we heard the steel mesh bounce inside the frame of the trailer. The sound likely traveled far and wide. There wasn't a soul within two blocks of our route that did not hear the steel bouncing in the trailer. Both Tom and I knew the sound would be less if there was a load on the trailer but neither of us made a comment on the noise it made.

Noisy trailer or not, Tom was able to tell me about the town of Ironwood while we were on this *ramp finding* mission. "Ironwood," he said at one point while driving, "is the only place I know of where you can pay six hundred thousand dollars for materials to build a house that's worth thirty-five thousand when you're done building it." I was amazed.

"Why is it so depressed here?"

"The iron ore is gone. They stopped mining here thirty years ago. This town went from thirty five thousand people to three thousand over night. There's abandoned buildings everywhere." I could tell by the sound of his voice that it hurt to say it. "Here we are," he pulled into a small car dealership with maybe ten cars for sale and parked near the only entrance. Once upon a time, this was a corner gas station with a single stall repair shop and two gas pumps.

"What are we looking for?" I asked, getting out of the car.

"A ramp," he said, taking all the responsibility of finding it himself. It took about forty five seconds for him to canvas the area and come up empty handed. "Not here. Not sure where it could be. Must be over at the house."

We climbed back into the car, which sat close to the ground. With the aggravation in my back, it was slow moving to climb in. He started driving before I had the door closed or the seatbelt fastened. "How long have you been here?" I asked.

"Thirty years or so," he replied without making eye contact. The trailer behind the car continued to bounce loudly down the road. He navigated a left and a right turn, and stopped the car in a driveway on the right. He didn't pull in, he sort of parked, but stopped the car blocking the driveway. "I came up from Chicago when the town was thriving. Now, I have abandoned buildings over there," he pointed, "and over there," he turned about ninety degrees and pointed again. He stopped pointing and walked around a detached garage and around a small two story house. When he reappeared, he said, "I just don't know where that could be. Let's go look at Bill's shop."

In only a minute and a half we were stopped in the alley behind Bill's motorcycle repair shop. "We need a ramp," Tom announced to Bill, who had stuck his head out the open back door. We had been gone about fifteen minutes.

"Where's yours?" Bill wanted to know, but maybe he didn't really care. He talked as he walked, and both Bill and Tom disassembled the ramp leading up to the back door of Bill's shop, and strapped it onto the flat bed trailer behind Tom's car.

There was an understanding between these two. You could feel their friendship. They appreciated one another, and on some level, could read each other's thoughts.

Tom talked a little more about the town he loved, that he could feel dying around him, and the motorcycle was loaded up and returned to Bill's shop. When Tom was about to drive away, he stopped and gave me a firm handshake. He thanked me for the work I do for the Gold Star Ride Foundation, and insisted that I stop and say so long when it was time to go.

This was only the second day, and by the time we got the bike into Bill's shop, it was nine-thirty in the morning.

The problems with my back were starting to pronounce themselves more and more. I knew I needed to find rest for my back, or I wouldn't be able to go anywhere today. Bill immediately went to work on the bike, and I did my best to let him work without getting in his way.

"I'll check back in a little bit," I said to Bill. I remembered a story from the early nineties, when I had just come home from the Navy. I went to my brother's auto repair shop for help with my car.

Paying for someone to fix my car was a challenge, so I asked him how much to fix the car. He told me a number like two hundred dollars.

"How about if I help you?" I asked, hoping to save some money.

"Then it's four hundred," he said.

I always remember that when someone is working for me.

I'm pretty good at hiding this little piece of information about myself, but I'm self-diagnosed as borderline hypoglycemic. I say this because if I should happen to go without food for just the right amount of time I start to shake. The amount of time necessary for this phenomenon varies from day to day. Given that I've now been up for four hours, I could feel it coming on. "Where can I find a café?" I asked, assuming that "café" would be more appropriate name for a place to get food than "restaurant."

"Right over there," Ma said, pointing toward a six foot high privacy fence that stretched between two buildings – a house and a commercial building – on the opposite side of the alley. "You see that tree?"

"Yes," I said. There was only one tree.

"Just walk to that tree and the door is on the right," Ma was helping.

"You can walk right through there," Bill offered, pointing to the gate in the fence.

"No dogs tied up on the other side of that fence?" I tried to prepare.

"No, that's a city park on the other side of that fence," Bill's voice had a calming effect.

As I walked to the local restaurant, or café, or eatery, or whatever we want to call it, I thought a little bit about Bill. If he was sixteen years old when he started working on bikes, he would be seventy-one years old now. Most people want to slow down and retire by that age. He showed no signs of stopping.

In simple terms, on the motorcycle that I was riding, there is a computer that runs diagnostic scans all the time. If there is a problem with something, the computer records a code for that problem, and, if you flip a switch and turn a key and hold down a button all the exact time, the motorcycle will give you a code which you can look up in a book or on the Internet and see what's wrong with your bike. As I said before, that's how I learned my right turn signal wasn't working.

When I returned after eating, I saw Bill working on my bike, and as I approached I could see that he had been writing down the codes, so he knew what to fix. He had a legal pad on my seat, and at least twenty five different codes were written down.

It was like my bike was very sick and the doctor just wasn't sure which symptom to address. I told Bill I'd be back later.

The town was small, but I wanted to enjoy it if I could, so I just walked, hoping to learn something and hoping even more to stretch out the muscles in my back. As I rounded the first corner, half a block from the front door of Backstreet Cycle, I heard the familiar sound of big twin engine pipes. A block away I could see a couple on a bike rounding a corner.

I walked in their direction because I could see their bike was loaded for a long trip. Maybe they'd like to ride with me across Michigan's Upper Peninsula?

They were unzipping their leather gear when I walked around the next corner. "Been out long?" I started.

"We've spent the last four days in the UP," the man said.

"What's next?" I asked, handing them a brochure about the Gold Star Ride Foundation.

"Lunch," he chuckled, "then we're hoping to make Milwaukee tonight."

"Well, I was going to invite you to ride with me," I said, "but you're going the wrong way."

We talked a bit about the beauty of the Upper Peninsula, how it's great to take time off work and ride, and they thanked me for doing the work of the Foundation. We shook hands and parted company.

I got in the SUV and sat. I looked at messages on my phone, listened to a song or two on the radio, thought about taking a nap, and tried not to feel sorry for myself.

I spent a good deal of time wondering if I should quit.

Although I closed my eyes and reclined the seat, I couldn't find sleep. I drove to the hotel where I had awakened that morning to ask if I could keep the SUV parked there until I could retrieve it in a month or two. They agreed.

I went back to Backstreet Cycle and parked out front. It was a warm day and the windows were open. "Oh, there you are," I heard Ma say from the front door. "Bill says you're done."

I walked in and found that he had the bike parked in the back alley. It was three in the afternoon already. I pulled it around front, and loaded it down with gear – T-shirts and other stuff I thought I couldn't live without – that was packed in the SUV, and I emptied everything from the bike I thought I could live without.

Part of the pile of stuff I thought I could live without was some riding gear that was sent to us from Helmet House (also listed with sponsors in the back of the book). The jacket was beautiful, but designed for someone riding a sport bike, with a long back side. I ride a touring bagger, so the jacket was not comfortable. It was still in the packaging, so I carried it in to show Bill and Ma, and offer it as a gift for fixing my bike with such a short notice.

"What do I owe ya?" I offered to Bill, while he didn't bother to lift his head from his work. His work was now someone else's bike.

"Oh," he started long and slow, "a couple hours labor. How about a hundred twenty?" He asked the question, but it was more of a statement.

"You sure that's enough?" I asked. He'd been working all day and there was a tow involved. "Oh, I want you to have this jacket from Helmet House. It isn't designed for my style of riding and maybe you've got a customer that wants it."

"Oh, you've got gear? Then you don't owe me nothin'. We're even." He was firm.

"That doesn't seem quite right," I countered, "you sure?"

He was sure. I'd like to think we parted as friends, and I wrote them a letter from the hotel I was in almost two weeks later. I drove down the road, constantly wondering if the bike was about to fail. It was an uneasy, nervous feeling. I headed east into the Upper Peninsula of Michigan. It was about four in the afternoon now.

That was Tuesday. On Wednesday, the Fourth of July, I came to realize the bike didn't want to start when it was warm. If I stopped for gas and started it up and started to go right away, it would die after a few feet. I'd have to sit for five or ten minutes, try it again, and off I would go. While I thought this was a little disturbing, I couldn't see why it was doing that. There were no codes to read, and once it started, down the road I'd go.

On Friday, the sixth of July, I was headed toward Lockport, New York, where a Gold Star Mother, who was also a Blue Star Mother, was waiting for me to arrive. Somehow, I got a little mixed up on the road and ended up forty miles in the wrong direction. I redirected the bike, but now I was two or three hours behind the schedule I had planned. Pennsylvania, particularly in the west, is a very beautiful place. I enjoyed the view, the roads, the trees, the hills, and the warm weather on roads I'd never seen before.

I stopped for gas in a small town, and as had become the habit of my bike, it started, rolled a couple feet, and died. I tried repeatedly to start the bike, but to no avail. A kind stranger stopped to help and the two of us pushed the bike out of the way of other cars. Once out of the way, we started talking a bit.

"I've got two college degrees," he told me, "and I work as a train mechanic."

"A train mechanic? You fix trains?" I asked.

"Yeah," he said. His job was repairing the engines of those mammoth machines that pull thousands of tons of stuff down the rails around the country.

"That sounds awesome!" I told him

"They pay me to do that," he continued, "I make nine bucks an hour."

"Nine bucks?" I was astonished.

"They promised me a raise last year, but it never came through."

We talked a while longer, and covered things like Andrew Carnegie's house, which is now a museum, and he pointed out a gas station down the road, and told me, "Up until about fifteen years ago, that station there controlled the price of gas all through the United States."

We talked about a few other subjects, like motorcycles, and then it was time to try the bike again. After we had spoken about ten minutes, I hit the button and it started right up. I waved goodbye and rolled down the road.

I'd been riding all day when I stopped at the New York state line to put my helmet on. While I was there, I had some French fries and a shake to add a few calories to my day – I didn't want to start shaking.

When it was time to take off, the bike died again, ten feet after starting. It was hot, and the bike was dead at the edge of the parking lot, sitting in the sun. I had been riding eight hours already. I was likely dehydrated, and about an hour late.

"Troubles?" came a voice from behind me.

I turned to see a man, a little older than me, with a gray beard and hair, walking toward me. "Mine does that once in a while, too," he said as he approached. "Why don't we push it over there in the shade and try to figure it out?"

I didn't speak. I was angry, sad, tired, and humbled that this total stranger would stop what he was doing to help me. We worked together to push the bike backwards and to the left, and put the kickstand down when we had reached a parking spot in the shade.

"Thanks," I started. "What do you ride?"

"I have an Ultra, like this." Then he raised an eyebrow. "What's the Gold Star Ride Foundation?" he pointed at the stickers on my gas tank.

"I'm traveling the country honoring Gold Star Families."

"What's that?" he asked with a genuine interest.

"That's the term we use to describe a family left behind when someone is killed in the military," I informed.

A sad look took over his expression and there was a long pause before he spoke. "My daughter was in the army. She was killed in Korea three years ago."

"I'm very sorry to hear that. But that makes you a Gold Star Dad."

"I had never heard that. Never heard of that before."

"This is a little serendipitous, but," I said, opening my saddle bags and retrieving a plaque, "I'd like you to have this." As I opened the plaque from its package, I explained how Gold Star Family is a term that's been around for a hundred years, and how I'm trying to inform as many people as possible about it. I shared my own Navy experience, and he told me that he never served, although he lost a lot of friends in Vietnam.

"I've only been doing this for seven years," I offered, "but I'm still not very good at it." Then I read the plaque to him.

I feel how weak and fruitless must be

I couldn't finish the words without tearing up. His name is Joe, and Joe was tearing up, too.

"I know just where that's gonna go," Joe said to me as I handed the plaque to him. He accepted the plaque with one hand, and wiped away a tear with the other. He glanced at the plaque for a long second or two, then, threw open his arms and held me in a long embrace. Neither of us made any attempt to hold back tears.

It seems both odd and a little comforting how quickly our moods changed to sadness.

"I can't believe this just happened," Joe said finally, still wiping the occasional tear. He paused, then added, "Why don't you try this bike one more time, because I have to go now, and I don't want to leave you here."

I buckled my helmet, got on the bike and pushed the button. It started instantly. I shook his hand one more time, thanked him again, and let out the clutch. He disappeared in my rear view mirror as I turned toward the New York state line.

Once again, I was wondering why I do this and once again I was reminded. I did my best to enjoy the ride, but the traffic on I-ninety was heavy, three lanes wide, and fast. It's not as much fun to ride under those circumstances, but I tried. The music was playing loud.

Then the music stopped; then it started. At first I thought nothing of this, because that was common when I was listening to a CD. However, I had the radio on. It stopped again, and started again. I looked at my gauges and immediately noticed my charging gauge was buried to the left. It was under eight volts.

Just to add some information for those readers who don't know, the gauge should be reading somewhere around fourteen point four – or at least more than twelve. I knew I was in trouble, and I knew I had ninety minutes to ride to get to my destination for the day; and that was just to get to the Gold Star Family, not a hotel.

I know that the motorcycle will keep running on the battery until the battery is dead, and I know the engine itself doesn't use that much electricity. I turned off the radio, the spot lights, cruise control and everything I could to save power. I stopped using blinkers and only used hand signals, and lastly, I made the bike go as fast as I could tolerate. I believe the bike would use the same electricity to run the engine at fifty miles an hour that it would at eighty miles an hour, but I would be farther down the road at eighty.

I had turned the GPS in my phone on, and had the headphones in my ears already, so it was telling me where to turn. I unplugged my phone from the charger to save the bike's battery, and kept going.

I was surprised that thirty minutes later I was still rolling. Then forty-five minutes. Then an hour. Then my GPS told me to exit the highway, and I was still rolling.

I turned left, tried to avoid traffic, which was still heavy, given that it was Friday afternoon rush hour. I turned right, following the instructions in my ear, hoping they were steering me the right way.

Then another turn and *oooog*. The bike didn't die, it went into "limp" mode. In limp mode, the computer tells the engine that it cannot go very fast, but it can still go. The intention is so you can get off the road, or, if you're really lucky, you can make it home.

I pushed; not physically, but I didn't want to stop, so I kept going. I knew the bike was in bad shape, with the battery dead and the charging system completely inoperable. I also knew that if I could get closer to my destination, it would be better than being stuck on the side of the road where I was. I made it about another mile, and came to a four-way stop sign. I looked ahead, and to the left and right. I saw a church parking lot to the left about a hundred feet from the four way stop. I pointed the bike that way and rolled through the intersection without stopping. God doesn't seem to be the biggest character in this story, but God is a very important one. There was no other traffic at that corner. God did that.

Just as I pulled into the parking lot, the engine died

completely. I managed to coast to the side of the parking lot away from the church and under a tree which provided a tiny bit of shade. The seventh day in July is pretty warm in northwestern New York.

I got off the bike. Took off the leather coat, vest, and helmet, throwing them to the ground casually, and I laid down on the grass near the bike. I had been riding now for almost eleven hours, and the bike was down hard.

I tried to figure out why I was doing this. I was on a crappy old bike that now has broken down twice in the first week. I've been riding and repairing this bike enough to know that any dealership would charge fifteen hundred for this repair, and up to now, I had not found a single dealership that would donate anything to the Gold Star Ride Foundation. Fifteen hundred dollars was more than the GSRF had left in the bank account.

I laid there on the ground for a long time, with thousands of thoughts running through my head, and the one that repeated itself more than any other, was the video interview of a Medal of Honor recipient, who said,

> *You either get 'em out, or you die tryin', and if you don't die tryin', you didn't try hard enough.*

His name is Dakota Meyer, and he said that after saving some forty men who were under heavy fire in Afghanistan, but he failed to get out four men who were killed. He didn't think he tried hard enough.

I looked up at the blue sky with an occasional puffy white cloud and said out loud to no one there, "I'm still alive, so I better keep going," and I sat up.

After finding my phone, I called the Gold Star Mom who was expecting me, to tell her not to expect me.

What I heard her say on the phone, however, was completely unexpected. "I know right where you are," Katy said on the phone, "I'll be there in a few minutes."

I had only just made it to my feet when a car pulled into

the church parking lot and came to a stop by the bike. Katy got out and greeted me warmly. "What can I do to help?" she asked.

"I'm just not sure yet," I said. I knew that the bank accounts were very lean, and by many standards, I should have never left home in the first place. I knew I couldn't afford the dealership repair. I had to find someone who could fix it in a garage next to a house; not a professional shop.

That's when her phone rang, and she answered a video call. On the other end of the line was her son, who was about to graduate from US Navy training school. I was there to honor her, as she had lost a son, and here was the son's brother calling his mother from the US Navy training school.

When we think about what we do with our lives, not many of us choose to defend our nation. The number of current and former military men and women who are alive in the United States currently is only about six and a half percent of the total population. That's not very many. That means if you see ten people, half of one of them *has ever* served or is serving.

The number of those who is serving right now is really small. If you see one hundred people, half of one of them is *currently* on active duty. Next time you are doing your favorite activity; remember that someone else is doing something incredibly uncomfortable and dangerous so that you can do it.

Here was Katy, with two sons in the military, one of whom was already in the ground.

"I have friends in Hogs and Heroes," she said, "I called them and they'll be here any minute." Almost immediately, a truck pulled up and three people jumped out. The two men slowly walked around the bike, while the woman ran to Katy and hugged her hello.

The tall man approached me and said, "I'm Phil, but they call me Stretch. This is Tom."

"Nice to meet you," Tom shook hands with me warmly.

The Hogs and Heroes Foundation is a Non Profit charity community of motorcycle riders that support Public Safety, the U.S. Military and Wounded Warriors. They sponsor and hold fundraising events for a variety Public Safety, U.S.

Military, and wounded veterans' charities. They perform Honor Missions for fallen Police Officers, Firefighters, Emergency Medical Workers, Members of the Military killed in Combat Operations and U.S. Military Veterans. They plan and participate in fun rides and events and participate in fundraisers, fun rides, and events of other charitable organizations. They strive to set an example of good citizenship for the youth of our nation.

They are made up of awesome people. Three of them showed up to help me on the side of the road on a Friday night. If you ever wished you were awesome, the best way to get there is to join this group.

"I'm Dodie," came the new voice from behind me, "and everyone calls me Stumpy."

"Nice to meet you, too," I said, spinning around to greet her. The five of us continued small talk and serious talk for several minutes without actually doing anything, and the sun was going down.

I asked Dodie if she would run the camera, and with the video being made, and two guys trying to figure out my bike, I presented, in the church parking lot with a broken bike, a plaque to Katy, the Gold Star Mom. I was extremely embarrassed by the entire thing, because Gold Star Moms (as well as sisters, brothers, sons, daughters, and fathers) deserve better than what I was delivering. As filled with doubt about myself and my mission as I could be, I read:

> *...should attempt to beguile you from a loss*
> *so overwhelming...*

As I read the words on the plaque, I occasionally looked up at Katy, who was shedding a tear or two. To this day, I can feel my eyes moisten whenever I read the words on the plaque, because I know what they mean.

The guys had my bike connected to their truck with jumper cables. After about ten minutes I hit the starter button and it started. The voltage gauge was still reading zero, but I had a little juice in the battery. I shut it down and we left the cables connected while we discussed where it would go next.

We talked about the dealer, and I was told about another motorcycle shop, and it was determined that the bike would go there. They would follow me to the hotel across the street to make sure I arrived OK. Oh, and the gas tank was empty, so I'd have to stop and fill it on the way.

Katy and I hugged again, and she thanked me for doing what I was doing. She drove the other way.

After filling the tank, another issue arrived. I was thankful these guys were all still with me. The bike wouldn't start at all – not even with the jumper cables in place.

The four of us fiddled with this and that, changed out fuses, checked wires, added comments, tried to tell jokes, and just as suddenly as it had quit, the bike started. None of us knew exactly what we had done to make it start, it just did.

I rode off, following the truck, into a parking lot of a hotel. I went inside to get a room and asked to have it donated. That wasn't going to happen, but I did get a military discount. It was about a hundred and fifty dollars a night.

I went outside and talked at length with Dodie, Stretch, and Tom for what seemed like a minute but was really more like an hour. We laughed at spontaneous jokes, and they tried to make me feel like being broke down was a good thing. They did their best to cheer me up, and for the most part, they did.

In the morning, my phone started going crazy with text messages from all sorts of people who had learned I was in town and broke down. Katy reached out to me and told me she had nothing planned for the day so she could help me anyway I needed it; and that I was her plan. Whatever I wanted or needed, she was there for me.

I walked to Steve's Custom Cycles around the corner and talked with the guys a bit about my bike. They said get it over there and they'd pull it right in. Steve was quiet and confident that it could happen, even if he was very busy. There were ten bikes, more or less in the front showroom, but it looked like fifty were waiting to be repaired.

I received a text from Katy as I walked back to the hotel. She said she'd be there in twenty minutes.

By the time she had arrived, I had checked out of the hotel and was sitting on the bike. She pulled up, showed me that she had jumper cables, and asked, "You need some of these?" I love a sense of humor, but I was still more than a little embarrassed about the whole thing, and I was worried about having just spent ten percent of my total nest egg on the hotel room for one night.

We jump started the bike and she followed me to Steve's around the corner, and then drove me to downtown Lockport, where I got a chance to understand the city, the important landmarks and meet a few people who shared more stories.

Katy shared with me that the city had allowed a monument to be installed at a place called Veterans' Park for her son, Albert Jex. She was glad that her son was remembered.

I've often said, however, that the best way to screw up something that's working well is to let the government get involved, so too, when the something good is remembering a hero.

The city of Lockport, New York, has a park; a veterans' park. In fact, it's called *Veterans' Park*. I honestly do not know if it is called that because veterans are invited to enjoy the beautiful park or other citizens are invited to remember veterans when they visit the park. I do know, or at least understand, that the city voted to allow a small monument to be placed in the park honoring Albert Jex. While this is a story of the Gold Star Ride Foundation and the mission to expand the knowledge of Gold Star Families around the country and inform people of the sacrifice and meaning of Gold Star Family, it is very easy to understand why all the members of the Gold Star Ride Foundation board of directors and group of volunteers actually like the idea that a "veterans' park" has a way of remembering... um... veterans – particularly those veterans who gave all for the rest of us to enjoy liberty and freedom.

As this part of the story is being added to this book, that is, in early October, 2018, word has come out that the local veterans' fraternities do not like this monument for Albert.

They say the park is to remember all veterans, not just the ones who were killed. They say it's meant for "units" not individual people.

There is an inherent problem with that, and they should be aware of it. There is no such thing, at least not that I am aware of since the Civil War, wherein any "unit" is made up of people from a single town. Considering that, how could they honor a unit in a city park when the unit is comprised of people from other towns and cities?

With a new mayor sitting in office and the mayor who agreed to the monument gone, the local fraternities want the memorial removed. The new mayor seems to be going along with it.

Lockport is a small town, and there were only two people in uniform ever killed from that town, and one of those was killed in a civilian car crash while on liberty, so, I can see their point.

The problem I see is that the point they make is a very small point. While it might be a real reason to not want a small memorial spot for the one local person who gave his life actually in action, the reason to honor that person is far, far more important. Albert wasn't inconvenienced when he volunteered to pick up trash along the freeway. Albert gave his life.

As the volunteer who met with Gold Star Families around the country, I was humbled to honor Katy and present her with a plaque, that while not displayed in public, no one will ever take away.

(We now understand, as we edit this book, that the city decided to keep Albert's monument in place.)

I learned much about the small town of Lockport, New York, and a little about some of its people. The coffee was good, the company was good, and the weather was fine on that July Saturday. Katy dropped me off at Steve's Custom Cycles and we parted company for the last time with a sincere hug and heartfelt *thank you's*.

Steve is a good man. He told me stories of his life in motorcycles, how his father raced, and therefore spoiled him by making him love motorcycle racing. Then Steve introduced me to his "guy." (I refer to him that way because when speaking about him in the third person, Steve always said, "my guy.")

"This is Harley," he said, matter-of-factly. I could see he was waiting for a reaction. After all, Harley is the first half of the brand name of the motorcycle. I raised an eyebrow. "His father was – is – a biker. His name is Dave. Dave spoiled Harley just like my dad spoiled me."

That's right, folks. The technician who worked to repair my Harley Davidson motorcycle was a man named Harley who was David's son.

Harley David's son. Say it fast.

Clearly, Dave wanted his son to be a biker, too.

I wanted to finish my mission to Gold Star Families, and now, Saturday evening was looming, and the family near Syracuse was waiting for me yesterday. Steve and I started talking about costs of repairs and the wonderful way he put others on the back burner while he helped me.

"I appreciate what you've done," I said, "I know you've got a ton of bikes that need fixing here."

"We do it because that's the way we'd hope someone would treat us if we were broke down out of town," his explanation was to the point.

I had explained the Foundation to him already, and I think he understood the work. "What's the damage?" I asked, knowing a new voltage regulator and a stator were expensive parts. For me to just buy those parts, it would cost three hundred to five hundred dollars. I had both the Foundation bank card and my personal bank card in my pocket, and both were in bad shape, maybe a thousand both combined.

"I know what you're trying to do," he said, and I knew he was being genuine – not assuming I was running a scam or anything, "and I'll only charge you cost on the parts, and I have to pay my guy." That, of course, was his reference to Harley, son of David. "I went as easy as I could and we worked hard to get you out of here. I have your total down to eight hundred even."

I swallowed, but not too hard. I knew I could cover that, but only just barely. I handed him a card and said, "Take half from this one, and I've got another one for the other half."

I asked Harley to pose for a picture with me, which he did, and I interviewed him on camera. Then we said our goodbyes, and I saddled up. It felt good to be back on the bike, and with it working properly, even if it had only been a day since I had done it. I gently revved the engine and looked at all the gauges. Full tank, correct voltage, and oil pressure right where I want it to be.

It was just a few minutes after five in the afternoon when I rolled down the road, and right through a green light at the intersection. Another block rolled passed and I turned on the radio. It came on, and within a second or two, it cut out and came back on. I immediately looked to the voltage gauge, which was now buried to the left. My new – expensive – charging system was not working. I was only eight blocks away.

Of course, I turned around and went back to Steve as fast as I could. Steve was pulling away in his truck when he saw me approaching and he immediately backed up and parked to see me.

We studied the problem a little, tried some slight adjustments, but we both knew the truth: Something big was messed up. "Harley's already gone," Steve informed me grimly, "won't be back until Monday." With this news, my heart really sank. I swallowed very hard. I glanced around the shop for a nice place on the grass to spend the weekend.

Steve was visibly upset as well. The sadness in his eyes was unmistakable. He didn't know the half of it. I knew I had about a hundred fifty dollars until I was flat broke. That wasn't enough to return to the hotel from last night for even a one more night.

"I'll drop you anywhere you want to go," Steve offered. We both clearly understood that the problem on the bike was going to wait until Monday.

"Katy told me about a place a few blocks that way," I pointed.

"That's the way I was headed," Steve was and is a good man, doing the best he can.

I wasn't very good company on the way to the hotel. Not that I was bad company, I was just quiet. There felt a melancholy in my mind that bordered on despair. I wondered if this was how Abraham Lincoln felt when his doctors prescribed a dose of mercury and ice baths until his stools were green to cure his sadness.

Chapter Three: More Breakdowns and Rain

At the hotel in Lockport, which was not the same hotel as Friday night, I labored to get my bags through the door to the front desk. My back was an issue as well as the motorcycle. I was only on my sixth day of a scheduled fifty four day ride and I was now, officially, broke down for the third time. I was about to become completely penniless. The outlook was bleak.

I spoke with the owner of the charming motel, which clearly had been around since the fifties, but even with all the charm I had to offer, the best rate she would give me was one hundred fifteen dollars a night. I told her I would stay for just one night, even though I knew it was two days – minimum – until my bike was ready to go. She took the payment from my bank card and gave me a key.

I was depleted. My energy levels were extremely low. Physical pain in my back forced me to walk slowly with an indeterminate limp. I opened the room door, and poured my belongings into the room. Because I'm traveling on a bike, my luggage was basically two plastic grocery bags filled with underwear and socks. I locked the door again, and walked across the street to the discount store. I purchased with my last few dollars a couple cans of generic soup and a bottle of water. The amount of money I had at this point could be counted with only two digits to the left of the decimal. It was not pretty.

I believed what I was doing was the right thing to do, and I believed that God was riding with me, but that belief was weak at best. My thoughts could not leave the notion that both I and the Foundation were broke.

Then the text messages started flying. When I say "flying," I mean, I received seven just walking across the street. MSL was texting from Minnesota wanting to know how things were on the road, and Katy wanted updates right there in Lockport. I also heard from Stumpie and Stretch, and a few new people that I had heard existed, but never had any verification, from the Hogs and Heroes Foundation. They really are great people.

I was as vague as I could be with all of them, except with the reports about the bike. I told them what I could tell them. The guys from Hogs and Heroes offered to come and work on it with me all day Sunday. I politely turned this service down; primarily because the bike was locked up in someone else's repair shop. Most of the time, I was alone, with my own thoughts, prayers, and emotions – and there was no shortage of any of those.

I thought about how happy I was that the weather was perfect. I was looking at the park across the street for the best place to lay my head tomorrow night, when I knew I wouldn't be in this motel anymore. I wondered if the bugs that would chew on my flesh as I slept were the same bugs I'm familiar with in Minnesota? I wondered if I could make a pillow out of my plastic bag of clothes, or if I could take a pillow from the motel room to lie on the ground? I stopped that thought quickly, because I knew I wouldn't take a pillow from the motel.

I ate the soup out of the can, because, well, I didn't have a bowl. I did find a plastic spoon in the motel lobby, so that was good.

I looked at my computer. I looked at my phone. I looked around the room, and mostly, I was depressed about the whole thing. Even if I chose to quit at this moment, I couldn't go home. There wasn't enough money to make it home. I was stuck.

I thought about looking through Craigslist for anyone who needs help fixing a computer. At least that would help me scrounge a couple dollars for a tank of gas, or food for tomorrow. Maybe I could find someone who wanted to buy the bike. Then I could quit and fly home.

I finished the soup and began preparing to take a shower when there was a knock on the door. This was a little alarming, because nobody knew where I was, or so I thought.

I opened the door to a person I had never seen before. She introduced herself, and told me, "I was sent by an angel. A real angel. I don't know who you are, or why I'm supposed to do this, but here," she grabbed the back of my left hand with her right hand and forced it to open, immediately putting a wad of cash in it.

I started to shake a little, and I felt my eyes collect more wetness than usual. The shock of being involved in this was more than I'd ever felt before.

"I've paid for your room for tonight and tomorrow night, and your money will be refunded to your card. I love what you're doing. Thank you."

Now, I've spent twenty-two years as a disk jockey, being paid to talk, and I've written a few books and movies, a crap load of songs, and many dozens of short stories. I've spoken on more than a hundred radio stations and podcasts around the country. Words are my life. I love words and I'm quick with words; but in this instant, there were no words. I think I moved my lips a little, but nothing came out.

"You don't have to say anything," she said, "and my daughter's waiting in the car, so I have to go. Keep me posted on your progress." As suddenly as she had appeared, she was gone.

I closed the door to the motel, sat down in a chair, stared at my computer screen again, then put my face in my hands and cried.

On Sunday, I walked about fifteen blocks to get downtown. I remembered the way because I had gone done that road with Katy only the day before. I found a cup of espresso and walked back. My thoughts were almost always the same:

> *Why am I doing this?*
> *What was I thinking?*
> *This can't be done.*
> *How will I fix the bike?*
> *Should I pack up and go home?*
> *Will anyone miss me when I'm gone?*
> *If I quit now, will anyone notice?*

After repeating those thoughts to myself as I walked

down the street toward the motel room, I remembered the words of that MOH recipient:

If you didn't die trying, you didn't try hard enough...

I spent some time in the motel just being alone, I spent some time sending text messages to anyone who sent one to me, and I tried to get a few things caught up on social media.

I also spent an hour or two talking with my son. It was my time to be something that looks a little like a dad, even though he is thirty years old. I enjoyed talking with him. I always do.

Then my phone chirped. I looked at it to find that someone had made a donation online through the website. My gratitude was huge! This was a three digit donation.

On Monday, I woke up and started working on social media and waiting for the call that the bike was ready. I found time to go to the office to ask if I could check out late. While asking that question, I could see they were struggling with a computer problem. I offered to fix it, and my offer was accepted. I clicked around on the mouse and made it work. They allowed me to have a late checkout time, but never did make a donation and I didn't ask for anything for helping with the computers.

I went back to the room and started calling to get a room donated near the next Gold Star Family. Motel rooms were all set up when I left home, but now the schedule was off by many days. I was calling anyone. Most wouldn't answer, or hung up on me as soon as I said, "Foundation." That's exactly what happened when I called Jeanie's Dream Motel in West Winfield, New York. I had some time, so I called back again, thinking perhaps it might have been an accidental hang up. Same thing.

I looked again online for this little motel, and found an email address. I drafted a quick email describing what I was doing and sent it off. I was completely surprised when my phone rang five minutes later and it was Jeanie's Dream Motel calling me! I heard a heartfelt apology, and an offer of a free room, if I could be there by eleven o'clock that night. I thanked them, and told them I hoped I could, but it depends on the bike.

I was starting again to feel like I was doing something I was supposed to do.

Steve called at about four. "Harley says you're ready to go," he announced, "how soon can I pick you up?"

"I'm ready as fast as you can get here," I'm sure my excitement was palpable.

In the parking lot in front of Steve's Custom Cycles, I found Harley standing next to my bike. He explained that he did this, and that, and that he found out, by accident, that if he pressed down on the seat with his hand, the system would stop charging. He researched that problem, and found the bad wire, and fixed it. Then he pulled a piece of red wire, about an inch long, from his pocket. "Do you want to keep it?" he asked. You could see the burn on one end of the wire.

"I don't keep mementoes of failures," I quipped. Harley chuckled. Steve needed to take care of his "guy," and asked me for another hundred dollars for the work on the bike. I paid him in cash, and loaded up the bike. It was about thirty minutes past four in the afternoon when I rolled out of his parking lot; this time for good.

That was Monday. On Friday of the same week, I woke up somewhere a little north of Charlotte, North Carolina. I had decided to try sleeping early in the evening, waking early in the morning, and driving in the dark at the beginning of the day instead of the end of the day. This was an horrific idea. Looking back, I do not recommend this. I had to get across South Carolina and through eastern Georgia into northeast Florida by the end of the day, so I wanted to cross Charlotte well before rush hour. I thought the road construction would be easier to handle in the early morning with no other cars on the road.

I changed the oil on the bike in the parking lot of the motel on this Friday morning. I was ready to ride at four, so I started the day by first checking the oil, and seeing it was more than a quart low, I pulled off the filter very carefully. I replaced the filter and added oil until it was full. I know, this is not the proper way to change the oil, but all things being equal, it was better to do it this way than to not do it at all.

With that done, I started riding. Within a minute or two, I realized what a huge mistake I had made. It was dark, so it was hard to see. I was riding through road construction, which made it more difficult, and lastly, and most important, the traffic was already heavy at four-thirty in the morning! The cars and trucks were rolling passed me at seventy or seventy-five miles an hour, while I was doing all I could to stay alive at sixty. I pulled off the freeway at the first chance I got.

I stopped at a gas station, thinking I should just kill a few minutes topping off the tank, and waiting for the sun to come up. The events of the day so far should have been some kind of an indicator of how things were going to go all day, but I didn't pay much attention. The gas station was open for business, but the doors were locked. If you wanted something from the store, you had to tell the clerk what you wanted through a small opening at the bottom of what I assume was bullet proof glass. He would then disappear into the store and return with whatever you wanted. He returned with a bottle of water for me, and I saddled up again.

I thought the daylight would make the freeway construction and super high speed traffic easier to deal with, but the sun didn't come up yet. It was still very dark. I pulled off at the next exit. Then, while sitting on the side of the road, an idea appeared in my head.

I put the earbuds in my ears and turned on the GPS in my phone. I set the destination; then I chose the bicycle route instead of the fastest route. The system navigated me through the streets from ten miles north of Charlotte to the freeway on the south side of town. When I got there, the sun was up. The route through town off the freeway at that time of day was much easier to ride. It actually became a bit of a pleasure to ride again.

One of the goals of this ride was to cover the country and find Gold Star Families off the beaten path; and ride on US highways and state highways, not freeways and interstate highways. I was about ten miles south of Charlotte when I turned off the big road. As soon as the rubber was on a state highway, off the freeway, I felt a raindrop.

I'd ridden in the rain before, so that part wasn't so daunting. On July 5th, riding through Ohio, I was wet the entire time. I didn't think much one way or the other with a few raindrops as I crossed the South Carolina state line.

Under normal conditions, I would have stopped and removed the helmet since South Carolina doesn't have a helmet law, but since it was raining, and the small visor on the helmet kept the rain off my eyes (sort of), I kept it on. And I kept rolling.

And it kept raining. And raining. And raining.

And I kept rolling. And rolling. And getting wet.

About three in the afternoon, I had been rolling along for about eleven hours when I saw a break in the clouds up ahead. Then the break became big chunks of blue sky. Then the drops of rain stopped hitting my face just as I passed a sign that said, "Welcome to Georgia." Every inch of riding in South Carolina was in the rain, which stopped the moment I hit Georgia.

I decided to roll through downtown Savannah, Georgia, for a few reasons, and pointed the bike in that direction. All of my instrument gages where foggy because of all the rain, and as they cleared, I saw my voltage coming in at eleven. Not fourteen. Eleven.

There might have been an audible curse word on the street in that moment.

I stopped at the next gas station, where crews were cleaning up a semi truck and trailer that had rolled over, and parked in the shade and slumped in the seat. I might have been soaked from head to toe, but the sun was still uncomfortably warm.

After a few phone calls to local repair shops, I learned that there was only one shop willing to work on my brand of motorcycle: Savannah Harley Davidson. You may remember, I'd had less than good luck with the Harley Davidson dealerships previously. I was not very excited about my prospects.

I rode hard and fast to get the bike into the dealership parking lot and up to the service area. I was afraid again, because even after the wonderful donations I had received the week before, there was no way I could afford to pay a dealer for this repair. My mind was racing trying to find the right idea on how this would work.

> Get it done or die trying. If you didn't die trying, you didn't try hard enough.

The service department checked me in and said they'd have someone start the diagnosis immediately. I asked if the general manager was working today. It was about three-thirty in the afternoon on a Friday.

"I'm the manager. I'm told you wanted to see me," she started the conversation.

"I'm Tony and I'm with the Gold Star Ride Foundation. I'm on a mission to honor Gold Star Families across the United States." I paused. "I'm hoping we can have a conversation that allows me to implore all the generosity available from you about my bike."

"What's wrong with your bike?" she wanted to know.

"I'm not sure yet," I offered, "but the symptoms indicate that it's gonna be big."

"Let's go see," she said, and we walked to the service area sharing tiny pieces of small talk on the way.

The service manager held a two page document in his hands. I held the knowledge that I only had a hundred, seventy-five dollars on the debit card. He approached and spoke to both the manager and me. "It needs a new stator, and we recommend a new voltage regulator at the same time. Also the front brakes need to be replaced; the pads and rotors are shot."

"What's the total," The manager asked.

"Thirteen forty-two," he answered, as if people walk around with that sort of money. "Oh, and the back tire is completely shot."

"Get it done," she said, with the sort of authority you expect from the boss. "We're covering it."

I was floored. I had no experience with this sort of gift in the past. I didn't know how to handle it. This was much larger than the gifts in Upstate New York.

"We don't have the tire in stock," he informed us both. "Can't get it until tomorrow. There isn't enough time today to get that work done."

"Just go." The manager seemed ready to be done with this.

"The least you can do is let me do an interview on camera," I offered. "I'm recording as much as I can to create a documentary. I would like to feature your dealership in that movie."

"Let me introduce you to Rhonda," she said, "she takes care of all our social media and marketing."

I met Rhonda; she tried to show me the Shovelhead and the Panhead motorcycles that are on display in the showroom at Savannah Harley Davidson. Those two are beautiful classic motorcycles. You might want to call down there and see if they're still available. You might want to call there just to tell them thanks for rescuing the Gold Star Ride Foundation at a time when it was desperately needed. The phone number is listed in the back.

Rhonda also showed me the large assortment of clothing they feature, the large assortment of new bikes, the boots, the aftermarket accessories, the party room upstairs, the storage area (people in the military store their bikes free), and the service area. I had already received a pretty good shot of the service area since my own bike was in there.

There were two hotels right across the street, and I walked up to the first one. No, they wouldn't donate a room (this was a question I had learned to ask every stop). I walked to the other, which wouldn't donate a room either, but their cost was twenty dollars less than the first hotel. I checked in.

I woke up without an alarm on Saturday and walked back to the dealership. Rhonda met me almost immediately and invited me to sit in on the Harley Owners Group meeting which was about to start upstairs. I accepted and then went quickly to the bike to get a plaque; the same plaque that I had given to all the families so far on this journey. Then I went upstairs.

The president of the club introduced himself, and Rhonda told him what I was doing. He asked if I'd like to speak to the group. I did.

"Can you make sure the manager is here when I speak to the group?" I asked Rhonda.

"I think so," she said.

I've spoken to groups before. I will again. It's part of the deal. I expected to see twenty or maybe thirty members in this group. I was floored when they announced that there were one hundred, twenty-six people in attendance.

I stood up and told the group how I had met my first Gold Star Family, and how it became the most important thing in the world to me to support them and tell the rest of the world about them.

Then I asked for the manager to come forward, and I announced to the group that Savannah Harley Davidson donated nearly fifteen hundred dollars in repairs to the Gold Star Ride Foundation. I then read the plaque to the group, and presented it to her,

> *But I cannot refrain from tendering to you*
> *the consolation…*

There was a loud applause, a hug from the manager, and then the meeting continued. After the meeting, I sat near the door with my guest book. The members took their turn and their time, and when it was all done, there was another two hundred dollars in cash to carry me down the road. I felt something like my life had meaning. Not just feeling good about myself; but more like the work I was doing *had meaning*.

They say that for every negative thought – which are usually the result of someone telling you something negative about yourself ("You're no good," "You'll never amount to anything," You're such a loser," etc.) – you need ten positive thoughts to correct it. Some of the HOG members asked if they could take a picture with me. Some just said, "thank you for what you're doing." All of them made me feel like I was doing something special. I'm sure I lost a hundred of those negative comments that day. It was a humbling experience.

When the meeting was done, the manager approached me again. "Your bike won't be done for a few more hours," she said, "we're still waiting for the tire to get here. Maybe you'd like to go for a ride and enjoy some wind therapy?"

"Wow," I responded, "is that a possibility?"

"I'll have Rhonda fix you up with a bike. We'll call you when yours is ready."

I pointed the bike in the direction of downtown, and opened the throttle with plans to grab some lunch. I ended up at a place that says they invented the chicken finger. Spanky's Pizza Galley Saloon, on East River Street, is a great place to stop for lunch. Parking isn't easy down there, so go on a bike, but beware of the cobblestone roads to get there. The folks at Spanky's were nice to me, and they're listed in the sponsors' page at the end of this book.

After lunch, I got back on the bike and headed back to Savannah Harley Davidson. My bike was ready to go.

I still get a little choked up when I think of how I was treated at Savannah Harley Davidson. It's still somewhat surreal that other people would think so highly of this mission that I am so desperate to complete.

At about four o'clock that afternoon, I accelerated on my own bike and launched my right hand in the air to wave a final *thank you* to the good people at the dealership, and at about sixty-five miles an hour, they disappeared into my rear view mirrors. I had to make it to Jacksonville, Florida before dark. The news cameras were waiting for me.

Chapter Four: A Few More Issues

The miles were long. My time on the road was excruciatingly lonely. The sun was changing the color of my skin more than it had ever changed at any other time in my life. The wind was beating up my lips and sucking moisture from my body through the pores in my skin. I was becoming dehydrated without being aware of it.

I glanced at the gas gauge and realized it was time to fill up. As I pulled off the highway and slowed for the traffic signal that was in front of me, I heard a *click click click* which repeated itself and it slowed down as I slowed down. It was a faint sound, and I wasn't sure if it meant anything or not, but I knew that it only clicked when the wheels were turning.

I felt good about the bike, though, and rolled along. I stopped north of New Orleans, Louisiana, to fill the gas tank and check in with the volunteers and MSL back home. I'd been riding on this particular day only about five hours to arrive here, and after filling the tank, I walked around the bike to stretch my legs and perform a visual check of the wheels. I didn't see anything, so I saddled up. I rolled slowly in a circle around the gas pumps, listening for the click to reappear.

I was not disappointed. I heard the click. I continued rolling in a slow circle, moving my head from side to side to try to listen for the front wheel or the back wheel. I thought it sounded like the rear wheel.

I stopped in the shade, and studied the back wheel. It didn't take long to find the nail head sticking out of the edge of the brand new back tire, with the sharp end of the nail sticking out the side of the tire. I sank to my knees and allowed my head to fall into the palm of my hand. This was the new tire that was put on in Savannah, Georgia, less than a thousand miles ago.

My mind was racing. How do I get this fixed? I've still got about a hundred dollars, but this is a two hundred, fifty dollar fix. I felt like there was a chance for a simple fix because the tire was still holding air. I also thought that if I pull the nail out, I'd be screwed.

I went inside the convenience store, and started searching for answers, using the Internet on my phone.

"Need some help?" I heard a stranger ask, in a decidedly southern accent. The first thing I saw when I looked up was the name of a very large beer company on his shirt, which signified that he worked for that company. The name wasn't that big on his shirt, but I knew it was a large company.

"Do you know this area?" I answered, "I'm looking for someone in this neighborhood that can look at the tire on my bike."

"No, I'm from Memphis," he said, "but I noticed the patch on your back. Are you a Gold Star Dad?"

"No," I said sheepishly, "but I work for them. That is, the charity I volunteer for helps Gold Star Families. I'm on a national ride for them, and I just found a nail in my tire."

We went on to discuss how much he admires the military, and how sorry he is for those families that lost someone. He wasn't a Gold Star Family member either, nor did he ever serve in the military, but he was happy to discuss it with me. We talked without noticing the time for about thirty minutes before I realized I still had a tire problem, and I'd better get it fixed.

I decided after much self talk to roll down the road to the next Harley Davidson dealership and ask for some help.

Some Harley Davidson dealerships are owned by individuals who have gathered up some fame for one thing or another, and after rolling thirty miles an hour for a little more than an hour, I found myself at one of those that was owned by someone of some renown.

People my age will easily remember a time when there was no Internet, when people didn't have computers, and bikes were repaired only with wrenches and screwdrivers. Now, of course, we need computers to get almost anything fixed. Bringing up technology also brings up web sites. Since the invention of web sites, there have been entities trying to sell web pages to everyone and anyone. One of the most successful of these businesses is owned by a distinctive man.

In the 1960's, the United States was involved in a

memorable military experiment referred to as Vietnam (of course, in Vietnam, they call it the *American War*), which involved hundreds of thousands of US Army, Navy, Air Force and Marine fighting men and women. Bob was a Marine who received a Purple Heart, among other medals and ribbons, during his time fighting in that war. In more recent times, this current multi-billionaire (according to Forbes) was the founding force behind GoDaddy.

No one can ever say that Bob isn't extremely patriotic. It doesn't take long in any of his dealerships to see the presence of all things that show a love for country. So far, however, he has not shown, nor has he asked any employee to show, any special love for the Gold Star Ride Foundation, even though he has donated more than one hundred, sixty million dollars to charity in the last five years. That might be the most in the world for a single person (or couple, since that number is often associated to both him and his wife).

Bob has since sold his interest in the Internet company, I believe, but still owns, among other things, motorcycle dealerships. One of them is very near the state line between Louisiana and Tennessee. It was located forty miles from the gas stop where I found the nail in my tire. The good news is, it was on the same road I was, and it was in the same direction.

The tire expert for the dealership was enjoying a lunch break when I arrived, and the service manager told me to wait. While waiting, still unsure of what we would find with the tire, I tried to start a conversation with the marketing manager at the dealership. I was disappointed to learn that it was all controlled by the team at the Scottsdale, Arizona, location. These were people I'd already met (when I visited there back in 2017) and who had already let me down. That is, they had already shared with me that Bob did not want to donate to the Gold Star Ride Foundation. I made a call to them anyway. I got the voicemail of the marketing person, and for the record, I'm still waiting for her to call me back.

During my trip of over eighteen thousand miles around the lower forty-eight states, I learned that there are three different dealerships of Harley Davidson motorcycles around the country that claim to be the "World's Largest" dealerships. One of them is Scottsdale, Arizona, owned by Bob. I've been to that dealership, and I've spent money there. To their credit, that location has donated a T-shirt to the Foundation.

That Scottsdale location has six motorcycles on display that are worth stopping to see. In fact, these bikes are so wonderfully prepared, it is worth the trip to see them if you are any sort of motorcycle fan. Five of those six bikes are customized to represent the five branches of our military; Army, Navy, Air Force, Marines, and Coast Guard. The sixth is customized to represent Bob's personal dedication to our nation and his wife. It features paint that reminds us of Vietnam, his rank, the US Marine Corp, and an airbrushed image of his wife on the tank. It's beautiful.

Although that dealership in Scottsdale donated a T-shirt, that was not to be the case for the Midwest dealership that shares the same ownership.

When the tire expert returned from his lunch break, we talked briefly about the problem and he walked outside with me to take a look. He glanced for about one and a half seconds and then said, "I'll be right back."

He returned with a pliers and a bottle of water. He poured the water on the nail, and grabbed it with the pliers. He turned it once or twice and then pulled it out.

No problem. The nail had missed the cavity that holds air in the tire, and there was nothing damaged. We talked for a minute or two longer about bikes, and stuff from when we were young, and maybe even a mention of an old muscle car. I liked him. He walked away.

"What do I owe you?" I asked as he was leaving.

"Nothing," he said.

I rolled away, feeling very grateful again, but this time for being lucky. Well, let's face it; this time no one told me they liked what I was doing, but if you're gonna get a nail stuck in your tire, it couldn't have been a more lucky insertion. I was grateful.

Looking back, perhaps I should have purchased a lottery ticket that day.

The Road to Anthony

I finished the month of July rolling into Texas. I woke up on the thirtieth of July in Oklahoma City, and rolled south toward San Antonio. If you're sitting in North Dakota reading this, you might not have a good understanding of what it means to ride into San Antonio on the second to last day of July. Let me try to paint a picture for you.

It's hot.

It's very hot.

It's extremely hot. It's so hot, we should really invent a three syllable word to describe it, because a single syllable, like hot, just doesn't do it. Maybe like *caliente*; which I think means hot in Spanish.

It wasn't, however, as hot as Arizona in August, but the envelope was clearly being pushed in that direction.

I was three hours north of the northern suburbs of San Antonio, which was my goal for the day, when the check engine light came on. I stopped in the shade of a gas pump and checked my computer reports. Then, I took that number and searched the Internet. My phone didn't have service there, so I went inside to see about using WiFi.

The air conditioning inside the convenience store created a temperature difference of at least twenty five degrees from what it was outside. This was a blast of cold air. I purchased a bottle of water and finished it by the time I got to the counter to pay for it.

My research told me there was a problem with the air intake temperature sensor. In other words, the bike thought it was too hot. I drank another bottle of water while sitting in the shade, and then used a broken old coat hanger to wire the vents open on my lowers, which would allow more air to flow over the engine of the motorcycle, which is imperative with an air cooled engine in the heat.

I cleared the computer warnings and hit the road again. The light stayed off almost all the way to Johnson City, the hometown of the man who was president of the United States from 1963 to 1968. I let it cool for a bit, met a local sheriff's deputy and posed for a picture, received a donation of a tank of gas (from the store clerk, not the deputy), and rolled again.

I pulled into San Antonio about an hour after dark, slept, and met with three Gold Star Families the next day. The local news was there to record the event, which I will discuss later.

After lunch, I looked at the bank account balances; I took the call from MSL; and decided it was time to take a break. I spent that day and the next working on computers to raise a little money and talking with MSL.

When I looked back on the bike, I realized I couldn't go any farther without a new front tire. Oh, and I still needed an air temperature sensor.

I spent an hour on the phone with the various Harley Davidson dealers in San Antonio and the surrounding area, when the Alamo City (Cowboys) Harley Davidson Dealership came to my rescue.

"I'm going to pass you on to Alexandra," he said, "She'll take care of you."

"Thank you," I said. I could tell that he felt strongly about Gold Star Families.

"This is Alexandra," the voice said, "How can I help you?"

"I need a tire and the computer tells me I need an air temperature sensor."

"How soon can you get that bike in here?" she asked.

"Thirty minutes," I said, optimistically.

"That's cutting it close," she said, "we close at five."

When I arrived at Cowboy's, I was met at the door as soon as I pulled myself off the bike. "Hi, I'm Shelly," she said, "You must be Tony?"

"I am," I said, "I thought I was going to meet Alexandra?"

"Alexandra runs our service department. Follow me and I'll show you the way. I take care of media and marketing."

"So, you're the one I get to interview on camera while magic is happening with the bike?" I asked as we walked into the service department. I was feeling like a smart ass, I won't deny it. I mean, I was still feeling mostly like I didn't deserve a donation, but I've always been a smart ass, so I didn't see a need to pull back on that today.

"I guess," she said, "but I don't photograph well."

"Don't worry," I said as we approached Alexandra, "I'll take the pictures."

Alexandra was more of a smart ass than I was, so when you stop in with a service request, be sure you bring your happy face. She is a lot of fun.

Shelly and I toured the facility with the camera rolling while Alexandra and her team worked on the bike. In similar fashion to Savannah, the dealership was full of beautiful bikes. She estimated that there were two hundred-fifty to three hundred bikes in the store. There were two floors, which seems to be more and more popular with the dealerships. The clothing area seemed to have more T-shirts than the other stores I had seen, and Shelly was quick to provide a nice white one with red prints (we need RED to Remember Everyone Deployed) and handed it to me.

We finished the tour before the bike was ready, so Shelly invited me to sit in the lounge upstairs and wait for it. I had a little work to do on the phone, so I accepted. I was sitting for just under two minutes when she approached and said, "I'm feeling like the work you're doing is extremely important, and a tire just isn't enough, so please take this," and she, like the woman from upstate New York, took my hand and opened it, placing wadded up cash inside.

Choking was my reaction, as I tried unsuccessfully to be stoic as I thanked her. She asked if we could have a picture together and then the bike was done.

Alexandra informed me that they did not have the temperature sensor for my bike in stock, however, "This is a list of all the dealerships you will pass between here and Phoenix," she said, handing me a two page document, "I've highlighted the dealers that have the part in stock."

If you need a break from reading, and you'd like to say thank you to Cowboys, the number is listed in the back.

I left Cowboys about five-thirty and rolled toward the

sunset. I rolled about fifty miles staring straight into the sun before I stopped for the night. I'll discuss hotels a little later, and this one is worth discussing.

The West is big, and maybe I can help you understand just how big it is, starting with West Texas.

I woke and packed the bike at the crack of dawn, (since I had already learned the lesson of riding before the sun comes up) and prepared to ride west. I stopped at the front desk to see what they may have for breakfast, but there wasn't much – just a pop tart. As I swung my leg over the seat, an old pickup rolled in to the parking lot. A woman in her late sixties jumped out of the other side of the truck and ran inside. The driver, who hadn't had the benefit of a hair cut or a razor for many years, had his window open and his seventy-year-old left elbow hanging over the door.

It only took seconds for me to notice the very large dog and the young person who looked to be about thirteen or fourteen sitting in the back seat. My own experience with running away from stuff at a young age had me thinking that this may be one of those situations where someone was taken without their consent.

"Been on the road long?" I asked, "You look tired."

"Yeah, I started in North Dakota," the old man driving the old truck spoke with a raspy voice. For the record, the closest point in North Dakota to the spot where he and I were sitting is about *fifteen hundred* miles. "We love this motel," he continued, "we stay here every time we come down."

"No rooms," the woman said, returning to the truck and jumping back in on the other side.

"They have at least one," I offered, "I'm leaving." The old man chuckled. We began talking about the Gold Star Ride Foundation, and he shared that he had spent time in Vietnam. I told him about the bottle of Cuban rum I keep in a saddle bag, but he wasn't interested in it.

He did thank me for the offer, "But," he said, "haven't had a drink in nearly two decades." That earned a little more respect from me. I know how hard it can be, and I immediately imagined the challenges that this man has had to endure to stay alive this long.

While we spoke, the young person in the back seat jumped out with enormous amounts of energy, investigating this and that. The dog came out with him.

"That's Schnook," he said, introducing me to the dog. "He's a full bred wolf."

"A wolf?" I asked with a little shock.

"Yes, I've had him since he was a pup. He's thirteen now." This was an incredibly beautiful animal which, I'm guessing, weighed over one hundred pounds, and when he put his paws on the shoulder of the boy, the wolf wasn't even trying to stretch to his available height. He could have put his paws on the shoulders of someone seven feet tall. He was a very impressive creature.

We talked a little about the wolf, and the boy told me the story of winning his black belt in Karate and Judo. He said he owed it all to his grandparents, who have been raising him.

I felt honored to have met them. They went to the next motel on the street, and I rolled west all day.

There was a time on this road, and I'll use no exaggeration in the telling of this, while I was rolling toward New Mexico, when the only things you could see were cacti. Not the big beautiful ones you see in books, these were short; most only a foot tall. There was no ditch along the sides of the road, only flat land that rolled out into the fields of cacti. Every now and then, there was a mountain in the distance, but mostly it was flat, dry, and very hot.

During one sixty minute period, I did not even pass or even see a car on the road.

I had plenty of time to not be distracted by anything. I was able to speak to God in complete sentences. Not all of those were filled with flattery, but they weren't filled completely with complaints either. I think I've already mentioned that God and I have had differences in opinion along the way.

There's something indescribable about being alone for that long. About being *that* alone. I mean, we've all had moments when we were alone. Hopefully, it happens every time you go into the bathroom; but this is different. This is so alone, that there is not a living person within fifty miles, and you can feel it. You can feel the fact that even if you wanted to come in contact with another human being, you'd have to travel a long time to get there. Distance adds something to the alone factor and it's palpable.

This road, in the end, looking back, now that I've been all over the country, was the single, most lonely place I have ever Ridden the motorcycle. I rode a full hour, rolling along at eighty miles an hour or faster the entire way, without any sign of *breathing life* at all. No snakes, raccoons, porcupines, or even mice could be found. Oh, sure, there were long stretches like this in Montana, South Dakota, and Wyoming, but those places all had, at the very least, other cars on the road.

For those who think the world is overcrowded, go take a trip down this road, and you'll see plenty of space for all the people on the planet and then some.

The temperature on this road was over one hundred degrees all the way. I stopped to cool off in a little town called Marfa, Texas. At first, I thought it was misspelled. As I explored this little town, I encountered the very first person who flatly refused to accept anything in the way of information from me. Let me explain.

When I stop for gas, I usually invite the employees and management of the gas station to donate the gas. Well, in addition to that, it was not uncommon for me to strike up a conversation with whoever is filling their vehicle on the other side of the pump. In this case, a woman of about thirty years was filling her car at the same time I was filling the bike. I finished and returned the hose to the gas pump, reached into my pocket and produced a brochure, which I handed toward the woman saying, "Here. It's a shameless plug which discusses my favorite charity."

She shook her head.

"It's just some information," I added, in the most polite voice I could find.

"No, thank you," she said, and returned the hose to her side of the gas pump. She quickly and quietly got in her car and drove away. I walked around the pump and looked at her purchase. She had stopped the pump at four dollars and eighty-eight cents. Not even two gallons of gas.

That was not the only time that my gesture to expand the knowledge base of people who understand, or at least know about, Gold Star Families was rejected, but it is the first one I remember. I found a taco stand in Marfa and enjoyed a locally made taco before rolling down the road some more.

Incidentally, Marfa is also well known for mysterious "lights" that occur in the evening on the hillside. I didn't wait around to see them.

Las Cruces, New Mexico, has a Harley Davidson dealership, and its name and address was highlighted on the two page list of dealerships which had my temperature sensor in stock. It was necessary for me to stop there, and in order to get there, I had to go through El Paso, Texas. Barnett Harley Davidson was located on the freeway when I entered the town, so I stopped to say hi. While I was there, which was after they had closed for the day, I noticed their very large billboard depicting that location as the world's largest Harley Davidson dealership. This was the third one.

No one was there when I took the picture of me standing in front of that billboard, so I couldn't confront anyone about it, nor could I walk around inside to see just how large it was. I'd already been in the Scottsdale, Arizona location and the Daytona Beach, Florida location, so I had a little knowledge of those two "World's Largest" dealerships, but I just couldn't see it with this one.

I woke up in Anthony, Texas, and given the name, it was imperative that I should stay there. The motel room was not donated, so I had some ill feelings waking up with less than a hundred dollars remaining in the bank accounts, but still, it was Anthony. There were letters twelve feet high spelling out the name of the town just across the street from my hotel room, so you know I had to get a picture of that.

It didn't take long to arrive at the second Barnett's Harley Davidson, this one in Las Cruces, New Mexico, where Denny and I got off to a very slow start. We circled each other while we spoke in short sentences, trying to feel each other out. I was trying to learn about his generosity while he was trying to figure out my scam. Looking back, I don't remember the exact sentence that kicked it off, but I sat with him at his sales manager's desk for about an hour reminiscing about things neither of us knew about the other, but we shared the stories like we knew each other our entire lives.

Steven Wright, the comedian, said, "I like to reminisce with people I don't know." That's what we were doing.

Denny was from "Jersey" as he put it, and he had had a colorful past. He felt himself lucky to have survived it all, and he loved having a home in New Mexico. He was quick to laugh, and smiled often, whether it was an old biker joke, the likes of which should never be in print, or any number of politically incorrect statements that carried a twinge of humor. He was the sort of guy you wanted on your side during both the good times and the bad times. He was that sort of person.

I shared a few of my own stories, including some bad run-ins with sales managers at Harley dealerships, which he seemed empathetic to hear.

"Wait here," he said suddenly, and got up from his chair. I assumed he had to assist a salesman with a customer or something similar. He walked briskly across the showroom floor and returned with a plastic bag. "Here," he said, passing ownership to me.

"Thank you," I said, still feeling awkward about receiving donations and gifts.

"I think that'll fit you. It won't make up for the guy who threw you out of his store, but you'll always know you're welcome here."

We walked outside and got a few more pictures of him and me together in front of the sign. "Don't go anywhere," he said, again, suddenly. He disappeared into the showroom, leaving me standing in the heat of the parking lot. It was close to noon, and the temperature was stretching up toward a hundred-ten degrees already.

He returned in less than two minutes with a small white box. "What's this?" I asked, truly not knowing the answer.

"That's a temperature sensor for your bike," he said, smiling, "I'll take some heat for it tomorrow, but you'll be long gone by then, and you need it now. I don't have a tech who can install it, but you should find one of those down the road."

The sun was high in the sky, and I was unaware of what lay ahead of me as I pointed the bike toward the hot part of the dessert and rolled on.

Wall? What Wall?

It was a Friday when I woke up in the Rocky Mountains of Colorado, north of Denver about a hundred miles. I had finished my business there, and it was time for the next family visit, about a six hundred, seventy-five miles away. I'd been riding without a problem for a couple weeks, and felt pretty comfortable on the bike. I woke up a little late, and spent more time with the families this morning than I had planned, then got a little lost coming down the mountain and rode about an hour in the wrong direction, so the day got long quickly.

By two in the afternoon, I was already tired when I passed the sign that said, "Next Gas 68 Miles."

"Shoot," I thought – or maybe even said out loud – although I knew I was talking to myself, "that's only an hour. I can do that without music!"

An hour later, when I awoke from a nap on top of a picnic table at a rest stop, I was still thirty minutes away from that gas pump. I rode on, stopped to fill the tank, and rode on some more, then made it to the next gas stop about an hour south of Rapid City, South Dakota, filled up again, and rode on again.

I was on the edge of Rapid City, South Dakota, approaching a traffic light that had turned red. I looked to my left and saw the sun, about an hour up from the horizon. I pulled in the clutch and pushed down with my foot for a lower gear and ...nothing.

Nothing. There was nothing there. The shift lever had disappeared under my boot! I pulled in the clutch, made a mental note of the fact that I was in fourth gear, and found a

---

way to coast into a gas station at that intersection.

I came to a stop, and looked at the sun again. There may have been some exchange of words and ideas with God, since God was my only companion for this ride, and then I looked down.

The shift linkage consists of a shifter that runs parallel to the ground, a vertical shaft near the engine, a horizontal shaft that connects to another vertical shaft that comes out of the transmission. The shift lever had disconnected from the first vertical shaft. "I can fix this," my optimism returned, but it was guarded when I looked back at the sun again, which was racing toward the horizon. No matter how many times I looked at the sun, it was still sinking.

It was another day of long riding, spending nine hours in the saddle so far, which is not easy for anyone, but this was day forty-eight in a row for me. The good news about the ride thus far is, the part I thought would be next to impossible at this stage had actually become the easiest part.

That is, my back, and its degenerative condition. On the third day of the ride, I could barely get off the bike. Now, after forty-eight days of riding, I was nearly pain free.

It took a little to empty the saddle bags and find the tools I had buried on the bottom, but I did, and with those tools, I managed to put the linkage back together without having to call another dealer.

I packed up and down the road I went again, this time with the big ball of red half hidden by the edge of the earth containing the Black Hills. I rode thirty minutes, and with the sun down completely, stopped for a hotel and gas, in a very cute little town, not that I could see it through the darkness, called New Underwood, South Dakota.

"I'm sorry," she said, "we don't have any rooms. The rally was just two weeks ago, and we haven't had a chance to clean yet."

"I don't need much," I thought, but then kept that thought to myself.

"Where ya from?" an older man with dirty fingernails, calloused hands, and worn cowboy boots asked.

"I'm from Minnesota," I answered, "but I've been all over for Gold Star Families."

I told him a tiny bit about the work I do for the Foundation, and the woman behind the counter with no rooms in the motel listened intently, as did the rancher, as I went on.

"I'll buy your gas," she said, "just pump it and go."

I thanked her.

"Which direction you going from here?" the rancher wanted to know.

"East," I said.

"How far?" he continued.

"I want to stop as soon as I can find a room," I said, "I don't like riding in the dark."

"Go to the motel in Wall," he said. "Tell them I sent you. They'll take care of you. They all know me in Wall." He was talking of course, about Wall, South Dakota.

I rode about thirty minutes and arrived in Wall. I arrived a minute later at the motel he sent me to, and found myself talking to a woman who had no rooms. "Go just up this road to Fourth Street," she instructed, pointing to something off to her right side, "turn right and you'll see Hillcrest. He's got cottages there, and he'll fix you up with a room for the night."

I walked outside and could feel my body start to shake. I thought about the day, and the food I ate that day. I started with coffee and a sandwich at a national chain which shall remain nameless for this moment, at about noon, then only a granola bar on the South Dakota state line – only about four hundred, fifty calories today. I should probably eat something.

I swung my leg over the seat and started the bike. It was as dark as night gets now, and I had fourteen hours of experience on that day alone. I let out the clutch and rolled toward the street. Everything happened so fast, it's difficult to remember exactly.

There was a slight incline to the left in the parking lot, and as I came to a stop after rolling only about four or five feet, the front wheel was turned into the incline and my balance was thrown to a place I could not recover. The bike went down to the right. I managed to throw myself or jump out of the way so the bike didn't land on my leg, but I hit my elbow pretty hard on the pavement. I rolled a bit and saw my phone and a handful of stuff from my pockets strewn across the parking lot, and as soon as I could realize that I had fallen, a young man of about twenty-five years was there asking if I was hurt.

"Just my pride," I said, full of embarrassment.

"You sure?" he asked, "You took a pretty good fall."

I felt old as I got to my feet. "I'm OK," I repeated. "You think you can help me get this thing up?"

The two of us lifted the bike up and I sat there on the bike with both feet on the ground as he drove away. I sat there for a long time – or at least it seemed like a long time.

I hit the starter, let out the clutch and down the road I went.

A few blocks later, as I approached Fourth Street, I put my foot on the lever to down shift and found there was no lever there. The linkage had come apart again. I was in second gear, and I knew it, so I just worked it like an automatic until I arrived in front of the Hillcrest Cottages.

I got the room, and once parked, I tried to call for a pizza or a sandwich to be delivered. I was still shaking and needed food. No signal. I couldn't order anything. Plan B was finding food in the bags on the bike, which, once I emptied, produced four bags of peanuts and a bottle of water. Good thing I don't have a peanut allergy.

In the morning, I pulled out my tools again, and put the linkage back together. I didn't have the proper tools to tighten it down, so I stopped at the hardware store and purchased what I needed. I tightened the screw that held the linkage together, and today as I write this, after nearly four thousand miles, it still has not come apart again.

I had been resting at home for a week or so, when it came time to hit the road again for the last families. The route had been restructured at the end of July to make up for the times the bike broke down, and since there was a motorcycle event in Fayetteville, Arkansas in September, that's when it was time to go there and see those families. In order to see those families, I had to do some work on the bike.

I had traveled more than ten thousand miles since Savannah, Georgia, and the back tire was tired (pardon the pun). I couldn't very well take another twenty-five hundred mile trip on a bald back tire, so I stopped in to the Harley Davidson dealer in Blaine, Minnesota; Twin Cities Harley Davidson.

The sales manager at that location was far more receptive than I had imagined he would be. He listened with great attention as I explained what the Gold Star Ride Foundation is all about, the work that had already been completed, and the work that was left to do. I thanked him for his service to our country and he said he'd call in a day or two when the general manager had come back from his own ride across the country, and give me an answer. While he had made me feel welcome while we spoke, I left without much hope. I'd been told that I would get a call from other dealerships, and I'm still waiting.

Five days later, he proved me wrong when he called, and on a cloudy Thursday in September, I rode the bike into the shop on Central Avenue in Blaine, Minnesota, for a new back tire.

As was my practice, while the bike was receiving professional care, we made a movie in the dealership and I learned all the great things about this dealership and its new location.

For example, not all dealerships feature a "dyno tune" bay, but this one does. Dyno Tuning is essential for bikes with exhaust other than stock. Because the pressure on the engine from the exhaust pipes is so sensitive, a tool like this is critical for optimum performance. This was a lesson I learned the hard way earlier in the summer, when I slipped off the stock mufflers and slipped on some mufflers that had the baffles removed. My bike ran like crap until I put the stock mufflers back on. I know where to go when it's time for me to have louder pipes on the bike.

We all know, even if you don't like the loud motorcycles, loud pipes save lives.

When the bike was done, I saddled up for the ride back home to finish preparations for the journey to Arkansas and southern Missouri. As soon as I hit the start button, the clouds opened up and the rain came down. This wasn't a summer rain, like before, this was September in Minnesota.

I've already written about rain, and I'll write more later. Right now, the only thing I want to say is a brief comparison between the rain in Minnesota and the rain in South Carolina. I rode for something like six hours in the rain across South Carolina. When the rain stopped, and I opened the small leather card carrier that I call a wallet, all the contents were still dry. When I rode the five miles from Twin Cities Harley Davidson in Blaine to my home in northeast Minneapolis, Minnesota, in the rain, all those same contents, while wearing the exact same gear, were soaked.

Chapter Five: Tails and Tales, Hot and Heat

Name an animal that roams the wild in the United States. Go ahead, name one.

Yep, I saw that one, too.

The first day of the ride was in Wisconsin. If you who live in Arizona or Florida, and you're not sure what life is like in Wisconsin, well, most of Wisconsin is a national forest. Sure, you have national forests in your state, too, but Wisconsin is filled with thirty-eight different species of needled – Christmas – trees, and two hundred, thirty-eight species of trees that lose their leaves every fall. Well, that last part might not be exact, there are a few broad-leafed trees that keep their leaves through the winter.

Not many of the roads are straight in Wisconsin, which makes for wonderful motorcycling. Is it any wonder why Mr. Harley and the Davidson brothers decided to build motorcycles in that state?

With all these trees and so many national forest acres, come animals. Before noon, I had danced with two deer in the road. By the time the day was done, I had danced with an elk, a moose, a black mountain lion, a small black bear and a skunk either on the road or alongside the road.

I was fortunate not to see any snakes. Incidentally, snakes never appeared anywhere on the trip. There may have been a person with a pet snake who engaged me in conversation along the way, but if that was the case, no one ever told me. I've been told by other riders that snakes can pose a special problem on the road. I'm glad I don't have that experience.

Come to think of it, I didn't see any crocodiles or alligators either. I'll call that luck.

After the first break down, I started riding east into the Upper Peninsula of Michigan and I had one thought: How fast can I make it to Mount Pleasant? Given that it was roughly a ten hour drive from my location to Mount Pleasant, holding that thought made it difficult to enjoy the ride.

I found myself in a small town stopped at a traffic signal, wishing the light would change. Of course, I was rolling along with two US flags on the trunk of the bike. The flags serve two purposes: patriotism and visibility.

Being a patriot means something. It means you know your country is flawed, but you love it anyway. It means you never disrespect the commander in chief, even if you disagree with him (or her, in the future). It means the country and those things that represent the country – like the flag, the Pledge of Allegiance, and the National Anthem – are all to be respected. Disrespecting any of those things is disrespecting the country. Just as I wouldn't disrespect my spouse when I believe she is making a choice different from a choice I would make, I cannot condone disrespecting the country for a choice the country is making that I would not personally choose to make. In my opinion, disrespecting the country, if I were the commander-in-chief, would be a punishable offense.

This does not mean that I don't believe in free speech. I do. Free speech is allowing me to write everything I'm choosing to write right now. Free speech may be the greatest of our constitutional rights. I just do not believe that free speech and disrespecting people or countries are synonymous. If you don't like something the country is doing, say so. There is nothing wrong with that. If you don't like the way one race of people is being treated by the system, then say something about that. Kneeling or sitting during the National Anthem is not the same as saying there is something wrong with racism in this country; it is simply disrespecting this country.

Whew! I'm glad I got that out of my system.

The secondary reason for my flags, and much less important generally, but very important personally, is visibility. I believe people can see me better on the motorcycle with two flags proudly displayed on the bike. Case in point, which I started to describe several paragraphs ago, is this traffic light in a little town in Michigan's Upper Peninsula called Iron Mountain.

I wanted the light to change. I was concentrating on the

light, thinking about how I would make it to Mount Pleasant before dark. It was five in the afternoon and I was still about three hundred-sixty miles away, and I was already tired, so there was really no way I could make it, but that's what I was thinking about at this traffic signal.

"I hate this fucking country!" I heard the masculine voice from behind me and to the right, but I didn't understand why I was hearing it just then. I turned to my right to see a small pickup truck come to a stop at the red light, right next to me.

I just looked at him; about sixty-five years old, straggly beard, torn, red and blue plaid, long sleeved shirt covering his left arm, elbow exposed through a hole in his sleeve, arm hanging out the window. Rust covered almost every inch of the bottom of the vehicle and the two wheels I could see did not match each other.

"And I'll tell you why," he continued, looking directly at me, "'Cause they can't get these stupid traffic lights synchronized!" he said as the light turned green. I accelerated to remove myself from that spot, and as I did so, I realized he was joking. I found myself laughing out loud as I rolled to a stop at the next block. He was right, you know. That town did not have its traffic lights synchronized. He had turned right the block before, so when I was poised to make a comment to him, he was gone.

The road changed quickly enough, with that small town disappearing in the rear view mirrors. Within minutes, or it seemed minutes, perhaps it was closer to an hour, the road became this incredible view of summer in the north. Woods appeared and disappeared, the road gently curved to the left and the right, the sun appeared in all its brilliance in my rear view mirrors, and Bob Seger's *Roll Me Away* never left my mind.

In case you're not familiar, Bob Seger is a singer and songwriter in the rock and roll genre who wrote the song *Roll Me Away*. It's a wonderful biker anthem which includes the lyrics that were motivating me that day:

Took a look down a westbound road
Right away I made my choice
Headed out to my big two-wheeler
I was tired of my own voice
Took a bead on the northern plains
And just rolled that power on

Twelve hours out of Mackinaw City
Stopped in a bar to have a brew
Met a girl and we had a few drinks
And I told her what I'd decided to do

Why this song? That's a question worth answering. Mr. Seger was heard on a radio interview (with the aforementioned Tom Barnard, actually) during which he discussed getting on his motorcycle and riding twelve hours. His home was north of Detroit at the time, and he rode (according to his own account) across the Mackinaw City Bridge in northern Michigan, across the UP (where I was in this story), then across northern Wisconsin and south along the St. Croix River, which separates Minnesota and Wisconsin. When he stopped, he was in Rochester, Minnesota, and according to the song, that's where he met a woman.

I don't remember ever learning that any other part of the song is actually a true story, but I was in the U.P. headed straight toward the Mackinaw City Bridge. This song, which was also on the CD in my CD player, was constantly in my head.

It's also worth mentioning what there was to look forward to when I would arrive at the Mackinaw City Bridge. The Straits of Mackinac connect Lake Michigan with Lake Huron, two of the five Great Lakes. These Straits provide a major shipping lane, connecting Chicago, Illinois and Duluth, Minnesota with the other Great Lakes, and on to the Atlantic Ocean. In the early history of our country, these were main highways connecting things like coal and iron ore from the upper Midwest to the east. The European influence in the area dates back to 1671 (at least) when the French had a Catholic

Mission on the north side of the Straits at a place that was then and is still called Saint Ignace.

The bridge itself is about five steps short of a five mile span, which by today's standards is still impressive, even if longer bridges are easy to find. Its nicknames of Big Mac and Mighty Mac might just tell a story that's not all that compelling.

That notwithstanding, it is still the longest suspension bridge between two anchorages, and rather than turn this into a bridge history narrative, I will just add that this bridge was open in 1957. Eisenhower was president of the United States, and John Kennedy was still a senator. Edward Kennedy was still just a troubled youth, and Ronald Reagan was still an actor. Marylyn Monroe was still struggling as an actress, and most roads in the country were not freeways.

I was really excited about arriving at this bridge, and actually thought I could make it there by dark. Of course, I had to cross the bridge during daylight to capture it on the cameras on the bike.

My excitement about crossing this bridge became palpable when I rounded a curve to see the trees to my right disappear to show me a vast expanse of water. I was riding along Lake Michigan.

This is where I was, awestruck with the view of the great lake, when up ahead I saw something very dark near the side of the road on the north side. I thought at first it was just bushes or small trees near the side of the road, since there were so many along the road, then I saw the right side of this "bush" move toward the sky, and I knew I was looking at a moose.

I released the throttle and hit the brakes to slow down, but he was close and he was massive! Just as I was about to lock up the brakes completely, he turned and disappeared into the trees. I looked down at the camera and started to audibly share my disappointment. The cameras were not recording.

The road continued and the lake continued. My false belief that since I was near Lake Michigan the Mackinaw City Bridge would produce itself around the next corner also continued. I found myself drifting into the serenity of rolling passed the giant lake. I rode for another half hour and realized it was getting dark.

The road curved to the left, and Lake Michigan disappeared behind the trees, and I knew I wouldn't have much more light. I glanced at my gas gauge and realized I needed that, too, so I pulled into a gas station on the north side of the road. I was getting tired and hungry, too. I pulled up to the gas pump and used a debit card to pay at the pump, then went inside for a pee and a snack.

Once inside, I quickly spotted two employees who were cleaning up because closing time was near, and I approached one and handed her a brochure. I told her what I was doing and excused myself to the rest room.

When I returned, I was surprised to hear her say, "Did you buy gas already?"

"I did."

"Well, I was gonna buy it for you. Can I go online and make a donation?" she asked.

"Of course," I said. "How much farther to Mackinaw City?"

"About an hour and a half," she said, which was news that I wasn't particularly pleased to hear. I thought I was much closer. I paid for a bottle of water and a granola bar then made my exit.

As I pulled out of the gas station I realized that from that moment onward, if I was to finish this mission of Gold Star Family visits, I would have to get into the habit of asking for a tank of gas before I paid for one.

I only just shifted into fifth gear when I saw the motel lights, so I pulled in. I was surprised to ring the bell outside the door that said, "Office," and then be greeted by a woman who was old enough to have retired fifteen years ago. And she was wearing a worn out bath robe.

"Do you have a room for the night?" I asked, as politely as I could through the screen door.

"Yes," she said, but she didn't move or say anything more. It was then I realized that just as she looked like she shouldn't be greeting people at a motel, I looked like someone she didn't want to greet – with fingerless gloves, a vest filled with biker patches and a dirty bandana on my head. It was also ten at night, another little fact I was ignoring. The sun goes down late this far north.

After a pregnant pause, she invited me inside. It was a very small room with a counter along the left wall, which she quickly put herself behind. I leaned on the counter with my elbows as we talked.

I told her about my mission and invited her to help with a room. I explained that I had a donated room waiting for me in Mount Pleasant, but I couldn't make it there tonight.

"That's about five hours away," she said. "You'll make it by tomorrow night."

I didn't have the heart to tell her there were people waiting for me tomorrow night in Ohio. She charged me fifty dollars for the room, and I'm not sure if that was regular price or a nice price for the charity work I was trying to do.

The WiFi didn't work and my cell phone didn't have service. I sent a text to MSL and hoped she would get it eventually, which she did – the next morning. I showered and went to sleep.

I knew that sunrise was about six, and I had people waiting for me in Mount Pleasant, and I wanted daylight for the ride over Big Mac, so I set the alarm for four forty-five and I was loaded and riding by five, a full hour before sunrise.

The beauty of the ride along Lake Michigan that morning was lost on the incredible dampness of the air, and the multitude of bugs offering their life in exchange of poor visibility on my windshield. There were hundreds and hundreds of bugs, and they came in all sizes. My windshield took the lives of moths, bees, mayflies, grasshoppers, and butterflies, and those were the ones I recognized. There were more than a few that gave up their lives to add color to my leather jacket and vest as well. The fireflies were the most fun, because after they gave their life to the dirtying of my windshield, they continued to glow. Little green lights dotted my windshield in the predawn darkness.

Riding in the dark is never my favorite thing, although I can remember a time in my youth when it was a favorite activity. The traffic was quite light, and there were only occasional cars that didn't know how to use their low beams to meet oncoming traffic, or maybe what was true during the day was true during the dark hours also – that my "super power" of invisibility is applied. (I always assumed I became invisible when I swung my leg over the bike. It's my super power.)

With full leather, from chin to toe, I Rolled into the very humid, pre-dawn air collecting dead bugs, bright lights, and condensation on every part of me that could feel the wind. Just like when the afternoon sun is high in the sky, and you try to see it move, I was unable to see the sun come up. I just kept riding east, knowing I would get there and the sun would get there with me. I pulled off the road just before taking the Interstate seventy-five south ramp, and found myself in Bridge View Park, even though I never knew Bridge View Park existed.

An hour of riding in the dark, and I pulled into this very small park in full day light. I snapped a couple pictures of myself with Mighty Mac in the background, and got ready to ride over the much-anticipated bridge. I paid my four dollar cover charge for the experience and accelerated toward the Lower Michigan.

The center of the bridge is a metal grate, which I was rather surprised to learn. I realize that if I just keep going, the bike will keep going, too, but it still felt like I was being thrown around on this impressive bridge. I managed to change into the right lane, which was concrete and continue rolling over the bridge.

I'm not going to lie to you. I looked at the water and decided then and there that I would do everything in my power to stay *out* of that water. I know it is three hundred feet deep. That's the bottom of the water from the top of the water. The top of the water from the bridge deck is two hundred feet. The top of the towers extend more than five hundred, fifty feet. It's an impressive structure.

In about the time it took you to read the last paragraph, it was over.

While I haven't looked at all the video footage of the

trip (and there are over three hundred hours of video to look at) I did record going over that bridge.

There was another bridge here and another bridge there along the way. There was the London Bridge in Lake Havasu City, Arizona. There were dozens of large bridges in Jacksonville and Pensacola, Florida, but nothing had the reputation and buildup that Big Mac had. It was over too quickly.

Not Quite Hot Yet

I pulled into a motel in Oklahoma City, Oklahoma, in the seedy part of town (like I always choose) and I was unable to persuade the young woman in her early twenties to donate a room two days before July ended. I paid the fifty-nine dollars and parked in front of my motel room. I couldn't help but notice the incredibly bad shape the place was in, considering curb appeal. The parking lot had pot holes scattered throughout, and paint was chipping off the doors and door frames to all the rooms. For the first time in a month of staying in the worst hotels and motels I could find (that one night in upstate New York being the exception), I actually worried about being someplace I didn't want to be. I felt concern over the bike. I was never concerned about my own safety. Not ever. I found myself giving some thought to rolling the bike into the room with me to make sure it was still there in the morning.

In the parking spot adjacent to mine, was a truck. Being from Minnesota, I'm used to seeing old trucks with more rust than metal, but this was Oklahoma. Trucks don't rust here, at least not much. This was an old truck, with the most obvious problem being that it was missing a wheel. Remember now, this truck is parked less than ten feet from the motel room door where I'm sleeping this hot July evening. I looked over my other shoulder and saw a twenty-year-old Cadillac with too many people in it, none of whom are wearing new clothes, all of whom are yelling at the others in the car. I didn't know how they could communicate, but they were trying. All this and I was still in the parking lot.

Back to the truck parked next to me with a wheel

missing. There isn't a straight piece of metal in the entire body of the vehicle. The missing wheel is, well, missing. The truck is being held up by an hydraulic jack; the kind often called a "bottle" jack. You pump a little lever on the jack and a steel shaft comes straight up from the middle of the cylinder to lift an object.

In the box behind the cab, the truck is filled with tools. Well, not just tools, tool boxes. The largest tool box in the truck has replaced the tailgate. It's held in place with a variety of bungee cords and nylon "ratchet" straps. My first thought was, "I hope I never follow this guy down the street." Honestly, I'd be worried those drawers would come open and tools would launch themselves at me every time the truck hit a bump.

As always, I made several trips into my room, each time passing the truck with a missing wheel. I set up shop as I do every night, connecting my laptop to the WiFi and downloading all the videos from the day onto my computer so I can record more videos tomorrow. The download process takes about twenty minutes per card, and there are five cards. By the end of each day, all five cards are full. I usually shower while the first card downloads.

Then, after the shower, I find something to eat and check email while the other cards are downloading. After exiting the shower on this night, I heard excitement right outside the door. I immediately wondered what sort of person owns that truck with the wheel missing and I dress to go outside.

I made up something that I forgot on the bike as my reason, so I stepped outside and started fiddling with latches on the trunk and saddle bags. The two men working on the truck are in their sixties and they immediately ask me about the stickers on my gas tank.

Of course, I shared with them that I'm on the road taking care of Gold Star Families, to which they both offer their respective thanks for the work I'm doing, then they take turns telling their own stories.

"I was in the Army," the first man says, who is doing more supervising than working on the wheel-less truck.

"I was a Marine," the other man says through his labor as he attaches the wheel to the truck. He's as dirty as any mechanic I've ever seen and he works with just a white T-shirt which is saturated in dirt, grease and sweat. His face has dark streaks of grease from trying to wipe the sweat from his cheek with the back of a greasy hand. "I was sent to Germany and I re-enlisted after four years,"

"When were you in?" I asked, thinking that they were both really close to Vietnam era, but I wasn't quite sure.

"Eighty-two to eighty-six," the first guy said.

"Seventy-seven to eighty-three," was the reply from the guy putting a wheel on his truck.

"That's an odd number of years," I did the math quick in my head. "Why'd ya get out?" I figured there was a story. Why would someone do a four year enlistment and then re-enlist for two years?

"Funny story," he says while tightening the nuts on the wheel. He grunted, "Well, I was a Marine."

"Yeah?" I offered

"And they sent me to anger management," he continued, "but I was a fucking Marine!" we all chuckled just a little bit. "I mean, I got mad a few times, and found myself in fights with some of the guys, but you know? I was in Germany..."

"Where beer is a food group," I offered.

"Exactly," he continued. "But I was a Marine, and they didn't want me fighting. So, they kicked me out."

"O T H?" I asked, spelling out the letters for Other Than Honorable discharge.

"Yeah, but," he had more to the story, and I hoped it went well. After all, he gave six years of his life at a time when being in an American military uniform wasn't thought of the way it is today. "I got mine back after the bombing."

The bombing he referred to, I assumed, was the Oklahoma City Bombing, when a domestic terrorist exploded a truck filled with fertilizer in downtown Oklahoma City, Oklahoma. The bombing actually occurred on April 19, 1995 and is still the largest ever domestic terrorist bombing in

United States history. In the explosion, more than three hundred, fifty buildings were damaged in Oklahoma City, one hundred, sixty-eight people were killed, six hundred, eighty were injured, and the blast damaged property in a sixteen block radius.

"Thee bombing?" I asked, pronouncing both E's.

"Yeah, you remember?"

"Of course I remember!" I said, "McVeigh, right? I don't remember how long ago it was, though."

"I don't remember the exact month," he continued to work while he talked, letting the truck down off the jack. "It was in the springtime in 1995."

"I just remember it was on the anniversary of Waco," I said, referencing the Branch Davidians of Waco, Texas and the FBI turning that standoff into a tragedy.

"That's right, McVeigh was retaliating about Waco," the Marine continued his story. "I lived around here then. I'm on my way to do a new job in Vegas, but I was here then, and I was unemployed. They came and asked me if I would go do security at the bomb site."

"You mean, after they got all the victims out, during the reconstruction?"

"Right. They needed somebody to do security and they came to me and said, 'you used to be a Marine, right? Will you come down and do some security?' and I said, 'sure!' and I worked down there at the bomb site for about six months."

"I bet that was intense. A bomb like that goes off in your home town and you – a Marine – get to go down to work at the scene for all that time." I tried to imagine what it might have been like.

"That's right. I was glad to do it! This is my home town, and I was glad to protect it. But you know what they did?"

"No."

"They gave me my discharge back." He stopped working, stood up straight and tall, looked straight at me and said again, "They changed my discharge to honorable."

"That's awesome!" I was really excited to hear that.

"And then, they paid me! They gave me my honorable

discharge for doing what I was willing to do anyway, and I thought I was volunteering to do security down there, but they paid me and gave me my honorable back." The dirty, sweaty financially struggling sixty-something man stood proud for this part of the story, and I was proud of him in that moment.

We talked a little more about where I was going next, and his new job in Las Vegas, but most of those details blur with the passage of time. I was able, however, after talking with him, to find the good that comes with the bad in regards to the Oklahoma City bombing.

Incidentally, the part of town where we were is on the south side. I planned it that way so I could get a good jump on Monday morning riding toward Texas without dealing with traffic. Downtown, where I did not go on this trip, is the site of the Oklahoma City National Memorial, which has been built on the exact site of the bombing, and was opened to the public exactly five years after the bombing. While I did not make it downtown on this trip, I have been downtown Oklahoma City, and it is truly one of the greatest places in our country. Oklahoma City carries both a small town feel, and a big city experience, and the people there are some of the kindest, most honest people in the country. It is one of my favorite places in the United States.

Oh, and for those of you who have no access to history books at all, there were two people who were complicit in the bombing, Timothy McVeigh and Terry Nichols. McVeigh carried out the deed, while Nichols designed the explosive. McVeigh was put to death in 2011, and Nichols is serving a life sentence. Two other accomplices in the bombing were Michael and Lori Fortier. Michael served twelve years for not reporting the terroristic activity and Lori received immunity in exchange for her testimony that sealed the fate of McVeigh and Nichols.

I guess it's true what they say in those signs by the airport, "If you see something, say something."

We are all in this together

After riding from Oklahoma City at first light all the

way to San Antonio, Texas, where I arrived after dark, and then the lonely riding across the southern highway of Texas all the way to Anthony, Texas, and another day crossing New Mexico and Arizona, and falling to the ground three times in two days from heat exhaustion, I found myself in Lake Havasu City. (Boy, that sentence was so long, Earnest Hemmingway would be proud of me for constructing it!)

In the first half of the twentieth century, a wealthy family produced a son named Robert. Robert Junior, actually, who, in order to keep the story short, because his life could make a book of its own, got involved with the Briggs family and started making internal combustion engines. His name became synonymous with chainsaws, moving away from boats and airplanes. Robert McCullough grew his family's fortune to previously unseen heights in the chainsaw engine business. The first chainsaws with the McCullough name were marketed in 1948.

Ten years later, in 1958, McCullough purchased a crap load of land on the east side of the Colorado River. Five years later, he named that chunk of land Lake Havasu City, and fifteen years after that, the city was incorporated.

McCullough is an interesting man. He was laughed at wildly in 1971 when he announced he would purchase the historic London Bridge, which was slated to be torn down and rebuilt in, of course, London, England. He purchased the London Bridge for two and a half million dollars.

Today, Lake Havasu City and the London Bridge attract, according to the concierge at the London Bridge Resort and Hotel, more than double the city's actual population of fifty-two thousand people as tourists. On the first Monday of August, 2018, MSL and I were two of them.

Getting to the city was not easy. I had arrived in Phoenix Sunday evening, after falling down at a convenience store between Tuscan and Phoenix and spending about half an hour regaining my composure. I spent the night in a cheap motel by the airport, doing laundry and trying to recapture fluids my body had lost in the previous days of riding in the heat.

I had scheduled a radio interview at six-twenty the following morning in the Central Time zone, so I set my alarm and fell asleep. I woke to the alarm, called in to the radio station, we talked for a few minutes about what I was doing and where I was, I hung up the phone and went back to sleep. When I woke up again a few hours later, I realized that I had actually called in an hour later than the scheduled time!

I'm going to share too much information with you now. I did not find a recording of that interview anywhere, and I did not record it in the room, and I'm not really sure of anything that I said.

When I woke up again, loaded the bike and proceeded to go visit the Gold Star Widow in Phoenix, Arizona. We had set up a time and a place to meet, and I went there with no problem. Sure, it was warm on the bike, but only about a hundred and five degrees. Not the super hot of one-nineteen from the day before. Not yet, at least.

MSL was flying in to the Phoenix airport to spend a day or two with me. We finally had a schedule that allowed us to do that. By that I mean, she had two days she could take off work. That meant that I had to pay close attention to the time, which was not something I usually did when meeting with Gold Star Families.

I parked in the parking lot of the strip mall very close to the coffee shop where I was to meet the GSW. I tried to put the bike in the shade, because even in Phoenix, were I'm sure they make the asphalt different than the rest of the country; I was worried the pavement would get too hot and the kickstand would sink into the hot asphalt and the bike would fall over.

I walked up to the door of the coffee shop, and saw a man in his late sixties sitting at a table all by himself just outside the door. He was in the shade, but even in the shade the temperature was already over one hundred degrees.

"Nice enough day," I said.

"It is!" he said with some enthusiasm. "It's a hellavolot better than that winter up north!"

Well, see, now he was baiting me, and I was falling for the bait. I don't think I looked like someone from Minnesota anymore. My skin, that part of it you could see at least, was dark now. The sort of dark you get from thirty days in the sun. Of course, I looked rather silly when I removed my sunglasses, which were always on my face when I was in the sun, and rarely on my face when I was not. The white skin around my eyes was something like a raccoon: very pronounced and you could see it from a long distance. Even I would look in the mirror and say, "Whoa!"

I stopped and said, "You say that like someone who's lived through a few winters up north."

"Oh, yeah, there's nothing like the cold winter wind of Nebraska!" I heard what he said, and quite frankly, didn't think much of it, given that I'm from Minnesota.

"Nebraska is home for you?"

"I live here. I lived there when I was young; before I joined the Navy." Somehow, I knew he was a vet.

"When were you in the Navy?" I wanted to know.

"I signed up in 1956," he said, "I got out in 1960."

"So you didn't go to Vietnam?" I knew it was happening then, but not many of ours were going during that time; just a few advisors, or so the history books tell us.

"No, I went to the *USS Ticonderoga,* but I spent most of my time in her belly," he informed me. "After working in the fields of Nebraska, when that cold wind would come up out of nowhere and chill you to the bone, I was glad to work in a warm environment."

"You were a hull tech on a WesPac ship?" I asked. "WesPac" was the abbreviation for Western Pacific, which was a popular place for US Navy vessels after WWII all through Vietnam, and although not talked about as much today, still a popular location for ships. "And the *Ticonderoga*; wasn't that nicknamed the *USS Never Home?*"

"Yeah," he chuckled, "Or the *USS Always Out*. We used both of those names. But I had a good time in the Navy. It was a lot better than the farm, I'll tell ya that."

"Thank you for your service to our country," I said, with all sincerity. I handed him my card. "I'm actually here to visit a Gold Star Widow. She's supposed to meet me here."

"Well, thank you for your service, and the work you continue to do." I think he understood that I was former Navy as well, because of my comments on the ships.

"I could probably sit here and talk to you all day, but I think I'm already late." He smiled warmly and shook my hand using both of his. I walked inside the coffee shop.

Before the door closed behind me, and before my eyes could make the adjustment to the dark coffee shop, I heard a woman's voice say, "You must be Tony."

"I am," I said, turning to look in the direction from which the voice came. "And you must be Cathy." She stood to shake hands with me and we immediately began to talk. "I'm doing my best to beat the heat," I offered.

She looked at her phone. "It's only a hundred-thirteen. This is easy."

One thing she had on her mind was to ask why I was there. She was dumbfounded by my very presence.

"I do this for a couple reasons," I began, "on any given day, I talk to twenty people. Of those twenty people, nineteen do not know what a Gold Star Family is. I think that's wrong. Everyone should know. Everyone should have an understanding that freedom isn't free, and someone paid the price for everyone's freedom. Maybe it's because I'm a card-carrying member of the disabled vets club, but I think this is the most important thing I can possibly do with my life. I want you to know that there is at least one person who hasn't forgotten that you live without someone, you live without your husband, so the rest of us can live."

She smiled, and wiped away not a tear, but just some extra moisture in her eye. We talked about her husband, and how he didn't have to go back. He had served three tours in Iraq, and he was home. "But," she said, "he just couldn't leave his guys."

"I hear that a lot," I offered.

"He said he didn't think they could live without him."

"But now we all have to." We talked for about two hours about how he was such a great dad to her kids, even though they weren't his kids.

I presented her with a plaque, as I do with all Gold Star Family members, reading it to her as I presented it:

But I cannot help but to tender you the consolation...

I introduced the idea that I was expected to call into a podcast and asked if she'd like to be a part of it. She was reluctant, and I understood. It's difficult to be asked to be in public.

The podcast was The Tom Barnard Podcast, as you likely guessed, and I told Tom (while we were live) I was sitting with a Gold Star Widow, I asked if he wanted to talk with her. He did, and I handed her the phone. You can still hear this podcast at this website: http://www.tombarnardpodcast.com/2018/08/06/. Cathy is on the third episode, number 1435-3.

Say whatever you want to about Tom Barnard, but he somehow gets people to say things that you wouldn't expect, and the deep story gets told. Cathy explained to Tom that every day while her husband was deployed she would drive home from work and carefully look up and down the street where her home was, and if she didn't see any strange cars, she knew he was still alive. Every single day, holding the steering wheel so tightly that her knuckles would turn white, she would drive home and if she saw no unrecognizable vehicles; she knew she was in the clear. She knew he was still safe.

One day, he wasn't, and she is still a widow. A Gold Star Widow.

Our time came to an end, and it's worth mentioning that in our time together, I consumed two bottles of water and a fruit smoothie. I was still a little worried about the heat and its affect on me. We hugged a log time with moist eyes, she walked me out to the motorcycle, and I headed toward the airport – a forty minute ride from where I was.

In the heat, back on the bike, it seemed like I just couldn't make it go fast enough. The air was so hot, it was hard to breathe. I found myself breathing in very short breaths through my nose, and when I rolled under a bridge, I would inhale deeply through my nose, taking in air that was cooled by the shade of the bridge. The official temperature for Phoenix that day was one hundred, fourteen. I just felt so incredibly hot.

I pulled into the airport, which can be tricky when you've never been there before, and managed to navigate the bike to the correct door to pick up MSL and I put the kickstand down. I climbed off the bike and walked toward a concrete bench only a few feet away and saw her walking toward me before I could get my phone out. I felt a complete weakness take over me. I struggled to lift my phone back into my pocket.

"Come on, let's go," she said with excitement.

"I need to catch my breath," I said. I was hoping just a minute or two in the shade would be enough. I saw the security guard walking toward me.

"This your motorcycle?" she asked. "Oh," she said, not waiting for my response, "you don't look so good. Why don't you go inside the airport for minute to cool off? Or do you want me to call a paramedic?"

"I'm sure I'll be fine in a minute," I said. MSL just looked a little sad.

The door to the baggage claim area was only ten feet away, and once inside, I pulled off my leather vest, my bandana, my gloves, and dropped to the floor. Once on the floor, I pulled off my boots and just sat as motionless as I could.

MSL said, "You want me to get you some water?"

"Yes."

She walked away and returned with a wet paper towel. I used it to wipe my face, then held it between my wrists, crossing my forearms on my lap. The security guard came in and walked directly to me, although I wasn't far from the door.

"You want me to call the paramedics?" she asked. It almost did not sound like a question.

"No."

MSL said, "Would you like some water?"

"Yes."

"You can find a vending machine over there," the security guard offered, pointing in the direction of the machines. She stood nearby and watched me as MSL left and returned in less than a minute with a bottle of cold water. Upon her return, the guard asked again, "Do you want me to call the paramedics?"

"No, I think I'll be fine," I said, taking the bottle and drinking a lot, then pouring some over my head and down my back.

"OK," she said. "Have you been riding long?"

"I started Saturday morning in San Antonio," I said. "I've been riding all day every day since then."

"Oh, then you are definitely dehydrated." I had actually not thought of that: dehydrated. I should know better. "If you don't stop shaking in two minutes, I'm calling the paramedics."

I breathed deep through my nose. I didn't want to be there. I kept thinking about MSL arriving to ride with me for two days. I kept thinking about how I was going to get to Lake Havasu City to meet the Gold Star Mom up there. She was expecting me that evening. My mind was racing. I was also thinking about how I would pack the bags on the bike that MSL carried with her? Too many things were going through my mind.

Then, I asked myself why I would sign up to do this job?

Get 'em out or die tryin'. And if you didn't die tryin', you didn't try hard enough...

I took a big drink out of the bottle, finishing it. I remained seated, but I put my boots back on, then my bandana, then my gloves. MSL and the security guard helped me to my feet, and I started walking out to the bike. I'd be lying if I didn't say I was afraid to breathe that hot air again, but I had a mission to accomplish. And I wasn't dead yet.

Honestly, I wasn't working very fast, but I was working. I imagine I stopped shaking, because that guard did not call the paramedics. MSL had two bags. I told her to pack light because we were on a bike that was already loaded. She packed about eight newspapers, a dozen magazines and two books – so she would have reading material on the plane. I managed to strap one backpack onto the trunk and I tried to tie the second one to the gas tank. It wasn't very stable, but under these circumstances it seemed the best choice. I started the bike, MSL climbed on, and I started down the road.

I made it to the end of the passenger pickup lane at the airport which was the distance of about a block and a half, and realized there was no way my packing was safe or going to make it any father. I stopped the bike to repack – in the sun.

MSL threw the backpack around her shoulders, letting it rest on top of the trunk and the other backpack. That seemed safe enough, and down the road we went. A half mile later, we were stopped at a fast food joint, sitting inside with air conditioning, drinking water and sipping on a shake.

"Why don't we rent a car?" I asked.

"I did not fly all the way here to rent a car! I came to ride the motorcycle."

I took another large drink of water. We busied ourselves by checking our phones for local hotels, the distance to Lake Havasu City, and the cost to rent a car.

"OK," I said after an hour of memorizing the highways to Lake Havasu City, "let's go."

"On the bike?" she asked.

"Yes, on the bike. How bad can it be?" I had swallowed two bottles of water and a shake while we were sitting there, and we were sitting in air conditioning for more than an hour.

I wasn't as slow as I was at the airport. I loaded up the stuff and we walked out to the bike. Just like at the airport, I found myself afraid of the air as I pushed the door open. The heat was like a wall that hit you as you opened the door. I swung my leg over the seat and backed the bike up, then stopped so she could get on.

The heat was hot and the sun was dry, just like it says in the song, *Horse With No Name*. I managed to pull the bike out into traffic, but once there, I could feel the weakness that had set itself into my body.

I made it out to the freeway where I was able to navigate into the HOV lane, which allowed me to go almost thirty miles an hour. At least we had some wind.

Each breath on that highway was difficult. I knew my breathing was shallow, because I was trying to make it shallow. A deep breath in that heat was very painful.

I saw a sign that said there was an exit in two miles with gas services. We didn't need gas, but I knew that a gas station would have shade. Traffic was heavy at that spot, with nothing moving faster than about twenty miles an hour in four or five lanes. I managed to dodge the cars and exit the freeway, and sure enough, the gas station was right there. I pulled into the shade next to a gas pump and put the kickstand down. Neither of us spoke. She climbed off and waited for me to do the same. We slowly walked in silence inside the convenience store.

I walked straight toward the coolers in the back, found water, grabbed one, stepped back as I opened it, then sank to the floor. I sat there without saying a word to anyone, and with no one saying a word to me. MSL was walking around in the store, and every couple seconds I heard her voice, but I didn't have any idea who she was talking to. Then I saw her feet approach.

"So we can pick it up now?" I heard her say on the phone, "and drop it off tomorrow?"

I looked up at her from the floor, "ask them if we can park the bike there," I said.

"Can we leave our motorcycle there?" she asked, then nodded to me. "OK, we'll be there in a few minutes." She disconnected the call and looked at me, still sitting on the floor. "I'm so glad you stopped," she said. "I knew I couldn't ask you to stop, since I wanted to ride so much, but that's hotter than anything!" said the woman who grew up in a tropical climate. "It's like sitting in your favorite chair in the living room and having a hundred hair dryers pointed at you!"

"Where is that car rental place you were calling?"

"They said they were only three blocks from here."

"Do you have an address?" I asked.

"Yes. I'll GPS it.

I struggled to get to my feet. The water I took from the

cooler was now all gone. I made it to my feet. "Show me the map," I said, looking at her phone to see where I had to ride the bike. I made a mental picture of it and walked to the counter to pay for the water. She carried two more bottles, unopened.

We turned together to leave, and both of us stopped at the door and looked at each other. "Ready?" I didn't wait for the answer. Her look suggested to me that she was quickly coming to understand a little of what I was going through. I pushed the door open and we stepped out into the sunshine.

The ride to the car rental office was truly only three blocks away, but it was some of the most memorable riding I had done. Weakness was taking over and breathing was truly difficult. I found a shaded spot next to the door of the hotel and we walked inside. I would have been so happy to stop right there. The beautiful hotel had a large fountain in the indoor pond in the center of the lobby and the air was only about eighty degrees and easy to breathe. I did so slowly and deeply. MSL approached the car rental office and I waited near the door in a high back chair that reminded me of old England. Well, it would have if I had ever been to old England.

It was only moments until we were rolling down the road in a small, air conditioned sedan. I tried to make light of our situation, and the challenges we faced, by making as many jokes as I could. MSL smiled every once in a while, but she never laughed. Most of the jokes were in reference to the heat. I took a picture of the dashboard readout. It said the outside air temperature was one hundred, fourteen. We drove for an hour staring at the sunset.

Arizona is an interesting place. It's my constant habit, wherever I am, to imagine life two hundred years ago. It's sort of my go to move. I just think about Billy the Kid riding his horse through this incredible countryside – trying to beat the heat.

We pulled off the interstate highway and turned north on a state road – Salome Road. The name reminded both of us of the story of John the Baptist and the young dancing girl who asked for his head on a platter. MSL was driving, and I was still feeling weak, although I felt I was recovering in the air conditioned car.

It wasn't a busy road and only had one lane going each direction. This is the sort of road I wanted to ride on the bike; but not in this heat. The towns we passed through were small; maybe a thousand people in each one, and there weren't very many of them. Both MSL and I enjoy observing these little towns; it's almost like the very charm of doing things by hand and not having access to the Internet makes them more welcoming; more friendly.

We drove through the barren land, both of us amazed that anyone or anything could live here. We were surprised at each little ranch we passed, most of which had what looked like broken down vehicles parked in the yard, if you can call what they had a yard. Being from Minnesota, even the poorest houses and homesteads have something that looks like grass growing around the broken down buildings that are used as homes. Here, it was dust and dirt. It was easier to understand how someone could be tracked (like Billy the Kid) in this environment.

The houses, because I don't know what else to call them, disappeared by for many minutes. We didn't see another car on the road for what seemed like a half hour. The sun was still eight or nine fingers above the western horizon, (it's an old Boy Scout trick – you stretch your arm toward the sun and count how many fingers fit between the bottom of the sun and the horizon and each finger represent fifteen minutes until sunset) so I knew we had more than two hours of daylight, but it felt desolate. I wasn't feeling lonely here, MSL was with me, but there was something a little eerie about the setting.

Suddenly, and neither of us saw this coming, there was a small hand painted sign on the right side of the road that read, "Little Road Side Chapel." Both of us said, "Let's stop!" at the same time.

Again, my thoughts were rolling along ideas like, "I wonder if Pat Garret stopped here to pray?"

The pavement disappeared into the hard earth of a baked western Arizona landscape as we rolled up to the Little Road Side Chapel. I wondered if the Chapel came first, or did the highway? A cloud of dust enveloped the car as we came to a stop, and MSL was out of the car almost before it had dissipated. I was riding with my boots off (still trying to beat the heat) so I took a moment to put them on while she entered the wide open, little building.

The little white rectangular shaped chapel was maybe eight feet wide, and maybe twelve feet long. The doorway had no door that I remember, and the windows had no glass. Once inside, it felt, well, safe.

Along one of the long walls was a bench, suitable for maybe four or five adults to sit, and the opposite wall featured a handful of wooden folding chairs. Near the door is the podium with a guest book, and the far end was something that resembled a pulpit. Three crosses adorned the wall opposite the doorway, which seemed symmetrical to the giant cross atop the buildings' steeple, which towered twelve to fifteen feet into the air.

Aside from the picnic table that separated the parking lot from the building on the hard Arizona earth, the Little Road Side Chapel offered little. No rest rooms, no snacks, no convenience store. There was no farm or other residence within view of the building.

Just a little – very little – road side chapel, pretty close to the middle of nowhere.

We signed the guestbook and made our exit and we did so with a new issue: We had to find a rest room.

Back on the road, the little town of Salome, Arizona, arrived in the windshield only a few minutes after starting. We felt relieved that we had found a town – any town – so quickly.

Salome, Arizona, is a cute little town and I'd like to say it was in the middle of nowhere, but that's not really true. I did joke when we arrived in the town that while it was not the middle of nowhere, you can see it from there.

It's an old town, and a small town with less than fifteen hundred residents. Its smallness made itself known right away. We stopped at the only gas station we could find in the town, hoping for empty bladders and some snacks and beverages for the rest of the drive.

We parked off to the side of the building, avoiding anyone who might want to buy gas, and slowly walked in. The main door to the building had a sign written by hand in red marker, "USE OTHER DOOR," so we walked around to the shaded part of the building. The doorway featured a beat up, half off the hinges screen door, just like almost any thirty-year-old trailer house in Minnesota. Once that door was opened, there was a wooden door with a large glass center. I pushed down on the small thumb lever only to realize I didn't have to. The door didn't latch.

We walked in and immediately I felt the pull of gravity to the left. The entire floor sloped downhill in that direction. I told MSL I'd be right back and went for the restroom.

When I returned, I knew we needed to be in a hurry, and I knew our urgency was about to become worse. I grabbed a Gatorade and a candy bar with chocolate and nuts, while she had assembled a couple chimichangas – made fresh right there at the gas station. I told the attendant about the ride, what we do, and how we were on our way to visit a Gold Star Mom in Lake Havasu City, and how much farther was that?

MSL excused herself to use the restroom, coming out quickly, "We have to go!"

I knew this was going to happen. I'd seen the restroom before her. I knew she wasn't about to loosen any clothing in there.

Twenty minutes later, we found another, more modern, place to stop and she did her business. I was taking my turn behind the wheel now.

I was surprised and slowed the car when we rolled passed another small town called Bouse. It rhymes with blouse, the woman's top. In Bouse, which seemed like a town of fewer than five hundred people, we found Monument Row.

This area of land, less than half the size of a football field, along the right side of the road, was bookended with tanks, and featured monuments for military and Camp Bouse, which, upon closer examination, was extremely fascinating.

Camp Bouse served as an internment camp for the Japanese during World War II and is considered the second most highly guarded secret during that time. The camp was actually started by General Patton as a tank training compound, where a new defense mechanism called a *Gizmo* was created and tested. This fancy little devise acted sort of like a strobe light, mounted on top of a tank's gun turret. The idea behind it was that during night tank encounters, it would temporarily blind the enemy, or at least leave them disoriented.

The camp was opened primarily for desert training or DTC (Desert Training Camp) to prepare tank squadrons to fight in Africa during the Second Great War. It was closed after African fighting had ceased in 1944, just a few months before Germany surrendered.

Just another one of those things we would have never seen if we were still on the bike.

The Memorial salutes those tank squadrons which trained there, in secret. So secret, most historians, when telling the stories about that war, skip this camp altogether.

With the sun only three fingers above the horizon, the landscape started to change. I was driving now, while MSL was repeating the word, "wow" over and over again. The mountains took our breath away. Each view of a valley surrounded by peaks was more beautiful that the one before, and each view of the mountains from the bottom of the valley was more exhilarating than the one before it. We drove along the winding Colorado River for many minutes, maybe a little jealous of the California campers we saw on the other side of the water.

The road continued to wind until we made it to Lake Havasu City just as the sun disappeared behind the mountains and we made our way to the prearranged restaurant meeting with the Gold Star Mom.

After the casual dinner and discussion, we were told that the hotel across the street had donated a room to us, and we were to go there for the night. This was a total surprise. I had planned to just go door to door to find a hotel room.

I walked into the lobby and was completely shocked at the sight of what appeared to be a solid gold carriage, the sort that would have carried the king of England two hundred years ago.

"That was a gift," said the desk clerk, who, it turned out, loved to talk about the hotel where he worked, "from the queen of England. She gave it to Mr. McCullough after he purchased the London Bridge for two and a half million dollars."

I introduced myself while MSL waited in the car.

"Oh, we've been expecting you."

"I'm glad I could make it. Tell me more about this place, because until about ten minutes ago, I didn't know it existed."

"Maybe you've heard of the chainsaw king, McCullough?"

"I know the name," I said.

"Everyone laughed at him when he parlayed his chainsaw wealth into a tourist hotel. Then when he purchased the London Bridge, they laughed even more. Who's laughing now?"

I was tired, and I wanted to get to bed, so I accepted his literature for future study and accepted the room keys.

The next morning, with a little more spring in my step, MSL and I walked about the place, snapped a few pictures, and enjoyed breakfast. The place was magnificent. So much better than the places I was used to staying. This hotel room had a bedroom separate from the living room, and it featured a kitchen and a bathroom with two sinks! This wasn't a hotel room; this was a really nice one bedroom apartment with maid service! I wish I was in better shape physically and prepared to enjoy it. Alas, I had no swim suit, nor time to stop and smell the roses.

We enjoyed our time at the London Bridge Resort, but I had work to do, and MSL had a plane to catch later that evening.

We returned to the room to pack. I sat at the kitchen table with my laptop and started looking up a few things, making sure my plan was ready for another day, when it hit me.

I remember studying first aid my first year in college, and learning the difference between heat stroke and heat exhaustion. My teacher in that class, some thirty-five years prior, said to remember that heat exhaustion is like exhaust on a car. Everything comes out. With heat stroke, nothing comes out. Well, sitting there, thinking I had recovered from the heat, everything started to some out.

I ran to the bathroom and found myself drooling, crying, emptying fluids from all over, sweating intense amounts. It was not a fun thirty minutes for me. Thirty minutes later, I stepped out of the shower, and started again to pack up to leave.

Once outside, the heat was in full force again. The overnight low for the night we were there was ninety-eight. We quickly got in the car and enjoyed the incredibly scenic drive back to Phoenix. The mountains and Colorado River made us feel small in the universe.

Back in Phoenix, we enjoyed dinner together and then rode the bike to the hotel for the night.

The ride from the restaurant to the hotel was hot, even though the sun was touching the western sky, and it was still uncomfortable.

I parked the bike and unpacked the daily stuff. Just as I walked through the door to the hotel, the sky opened up. I set our belongings on the floor and the two of us walked back outside. I do not ever remember feeling this much relief because of the rain. It cooled quickly and it really poured! Low spots in the parking lot were immediately made into small wading pools. Lightning lit the air with incredible flashes. The downspouts were overflowing with the water running off the top of the building.

We stood and watched in silence for a very long time.

The room wasn't nearly as nice as the accommodations we experienced at the London Bridge Hotel and Resort, but it was better than my usual fare.

Together, we sat in silence in the hotel room for a few minutes, then MSL got up and grabbed her backpack. I walked her downstairs and out the front door, where the shuttle to the airport was waiting. We hugged a long time, then she boarded, and the bus disappeared.

The rain had slowed to a sprinkle, but it was still steady, and it seemed appropriate that we would part company while it was raining.

I didn't realize it at the time, but it would be the last time I would see her until the ride was finished.

I was alone again.

It's Not Always Lonely

Days later, maybe ten, I found myself on Highway Three-Ninety-Five in Washington, when I stumbled into Rattlesnake Mountain Harley Davidson. I'd been riding alone for two days when I arrived there, and was feeling a little small and uncomfortable around people. Smoke from the fires in the Rocky Mountains had been entering my lungs every day for the last eight days, and it was still hanging in the air, even if I couldn't see the fires anymore.

Rattlesnake Mountain Harley Davidson was delighted to provide me a T-shirt for the collection, and off I went, feeling a little stronger knowing that I was actually pointed east, and home was only a couple more weeks.

Sometimes, when you feel lonely, almost anyone you see who has anything in common with you is a delightful and refreshing site. That's what I was experiencing while eastbound on US Highway Twelve, along the Columbia River, headed toward Lewiston, Idaho. The road was one of those that you wished the entire ride was. It was smooth with rolling Rocky Mountains on the south and a winding Columbia River on the north, and the sun in the western sky. This part of the world is rather sparsely populated, which means the highway didn't have much traffic. For nearly two hours, I rode along, wondering if there was another motorcycle anywhere.

Nearly in Clarkston, Washington, about three hours east of Kennewick, Washington (the location of Rattlesnake Mountain Harley Davidson), I saw a single headlight in my rearview mirror. A bike was catching up to me.

In Clarkston, which is on the eastern edge of the state of Washington, the traffic lights slowed my progress considerably, and the other bike quickly caught me. Just before crossing the river into Idaho, we found ourselves abreast on the road, stopped, waiting for the light to change.

I looked over his bike quickly, and saw he was riding an old Shovelhead, loaded for the road. I could make out a small tent, a frying pan, a shovel, and a backpack filled with his personal belongings.

"Where you off to?" he asked me above the sound of our bikes.

"Sun Valley," I said, adding, "Looks like you live on that," nodding toward his bike.

He was older than I am, with far more gray hair, a thick, rounded gray beard and mustache. All of his hair was wiry and unkempt from the wind. He looked like he had seen neither a toothbrush nor a shower in a long time.

"Try to," he said; smiling and showing me how many teeth were missing. It was more than one.

The light turned green and we both accelerated. The GPS had me turn right, and he turned left as soon as we crossed the river into Idaho. I stopped a block or two down the road to realize that the GPS took me the wrong direction once again. I turned around and went back the way he had gone, but I never saw him again.

Chapter Six: Let's Call This Utah

To say the ride was intense would be an understatement. Sometimes it was brutal. Sometimes it is pure pleasure. Pulling out of Moab, Utah, for example, was some of the greatest pleasure I experienced.

The night before, I had stopped to fill my tank just as the sun set behind what I would later learn was a "hill" on the west edge of the town, and met a young man who, at first glance, gave the appearance of someone I didn't want knowing where I parked my bike at night. His hair was uncombed, his shirt was wrinkled, he hadn't shaved for more than a few days, his teeth were crooked, and he was missing one or two of them. He worked at a gas station. I suppose, in hindsight, I should have immediately allowed him more credit because he was working.

As I spoke to him, however, my entire first impression was not only thrown out, it was tossed out a fifteen story window, crushed by a passing truck and flattened by an oncoming steamroller! This young man told me his name was Jeffrey. He then introduced himself to me in Spanish, then French, then Italian, then German, then Russian.

Moab is a tourist community. People come from all over the world to climb the hills in Jeeps, on dirt bikes, mountain bikes, and on foot. Because it's a place people come to from all over the world, speaking different languages gives you a talent which is in demand. Jeffrey was one of those.

I told him about the ride and the Foundation, and he pulled five one dollar bills out of his pocket. "How many gallons to fill your tank?" he wanted to know.

"No more than four."

"Jamie," he turned to the other person working at this gas station, "loan me six dollars."

"What for?" Jamie wanted to know.

"I'm going to donate to this guy's foundation," Jeffrey explained.

They teased each other.

"You still owe me for the pack of cigarettes from

yesterday," Jamie quipped as she approached.

"We don't get paid until tomorrow," Jeffrey countered.

"Who is this guy anyway?" Jamie gave me a suspicious look.

"Just give me the money," Jeffrey pleaded.

Jamie didn't take her eyes off me, moved slowly toward the cash registers, reached down under the counter, pulled out her purse, dug up some cash, and handed it to Jeffrey – not once taking her eyes off me. Ironic right? My first impression of him and her first impression of me.

"I should get myself something to drink, too," I added, walking to the water cooler.

They started ribbing each other some more. I thought Jamie was teasing me by the way she was staring at me as if I were a criminal. I couldn't be sure, and I didn't ask, but it's my story and I'm sticking to it.

"You know, this guy's the nicest guy you'll ever meet!" Jamie instructed me.

"I thought that was me," I joked.

Two other young men walked through the door and up to the counter. They were riding mountain bikes, which I could see right outside the door. "Can you help me?" the taller man asked Jeffrey. I could hear a thick French accent in his speech.

"Comment puis-je vous aider?" Jeffrey spoke very quickly.

"Can you help me?" the man asked again.

"You're from France?" Jeffrey asked in English.

"Yes, I am," the man answered.

"Parle couramment le français," Jeffrey explained.

The man changed from English with a thick accent to French and carried on a conversation with Jeffrey about the location of something or other. I could tell it was directions, not because I understood a lick of French, but because Jeffrey was pointing out the window to different things.

The Frenchman smiled a big smile, shook hands with Jeffrey and made his exit.

"He speaks six languages," Jamie boasted about her co-worker.

"That's pretty impressive," I said to Jeffrey. He shook it off like it was no big deal. "Can you help me find a hotel?" I asked both Jeffrey and Jamie.

"What kind of hotel would you like?" he asked.

"I want the most flea bitten place in town."

"Yeah. If you go down the road, maybe three or four stoplights, on the right, no, wait, maybe…I think it's three stop lights. Go see Kent at the Slippery Stage, er, I mean, the Silver Sage Inn."

"Kent, huh? Silver Sage Inn, huh? How will I know it?" I asked.

"It's the first place passed El Charo Loco," Jeffrey clearly liked his home town.

We shook hands, hugged in a brotherly fashion, and posed for a picture for Instagram. His picture is still there. I walked out to fill my tank.

As I hung the hose back on the pump, I heard the all too familiar sound of a V-Twin engine. It was already dark, and I knew I wasn't going to leave town tonight, so I waited and said, "Hello."

"Good lookin' bike," he said.

"Not as pretty as yours," I offered. "Where are you from?" I knew he would say something other than Moab.

"Jacksonville," he said, uncapping his tank.

"I was just there a few days ago," I said with some excitement, "No, wait, what day is it today? Maybe it was last month I was there; sometime around July twentieth or twenty-first."

"Yeah, that was last month. What's that sticker on your gas tank about?"

"Gold Star Families are what we call those families left behind when someone gets killed in the military," I explained.

"I know what they are," he said, "I spent thirty years on the police force in New Jersey."

"New Jersey? I thought you said you were from Florida?"

"I'm retired now," he pulled the gas hose from his motorcycle tank. "So, what are you doing? Where are you from?"

"I'm covering the country meeting Gold Star Families, helping them with anything they want or need. I met a Gold Star Dad just south of here earlier today."

"Well, that's pretty cool what you're doing," he said.

I never get tired of hearing that.

"So, how'd you land here?" I asked.

"Well, the wife planned it all out with another couple. I worked with him on the force. They've been family friends forever. I've got a Mack fifth wheeler pulling a forty eight foot camper. The bike rides on the truck between the truck and the trailer."

I imagined a semi truck pulling a camper instead of a trailer across the country.

As he spoke, we heard another V-Twin engine pulling into the station. The retired police officer moved his bike out of the way so the new arrival could park at the pump.

"I better get running," he said. "Nice talking to ya."

"Looks like you just washed it," I said to the replacement rider.

"I did," he said with a smirk, "and it looks like you need to wash yours."

"I wash mine when I'm riding in the rain," I joked.

"What's that sticker on your tank about?" he asked. I told him. "Times are a lot different now than they used to be. Did you serve?" he wanted to know.

"I'm a card carrying member of the disabled vets club," I said with a tiny grin.

"Me, too. When did you serve?"

"I just had my twenty-seventh anniversary of my honorable discharge. How about you?"

"I got out in 1972. Navy. I remember coming home in my dress whites," he replaced the gas pump hose and turned very somber. "We were walking through the airport in our dress whites and came passed some protesters. We didn't think much of it as we did; they seemed like they would stay out of our way, but then a couple of them came out of the group with syringes."

"Syringes?"

"Yeah, syringes. Syringes filled with blood. They sprayed us down in our dress whites with blood. I never did know where they got it, but they destroyed my dress whites."

"I've got something for you," I said, walking to the back of the bike and opening a saddlebag. I have a friend at a really nice steak house in Minneapolis who gave me this, and I keep it here on the bike just in case I meet someone who served during Vietnam. I think you qualify."

"Oh, I qualify," he said quickly, following me to the bike, "but what is it?"

"It's a bottle of rum from Cuba," I said, lifting the bottle out of the bag.

"Oh, that is nice," he smiled, "but I gave that up about ten years ago."

"Well, it's my way of saying welcome home. It's been a long time coming, and I think you've waited long enough."

"That means a lot."

We both looked at the bottle of rum in silence for a moment.

"It's not much," I broke the silence, "but it's all I have, and I want you to know that I'm thankful for your service." As I put the rum back in the saddle bag, I pointed to the sticker that says, "We [heart shape] our Vietnam Veterans."

He smiled again, "Thank you, brother," and pulled me in for a hug. "You don't know what that means."

We broke the hug and I held out my hand. "I'm Tony," I said.

"Call me Doc," he said, "they always have."

"Were you a medic in country?"

"No, I'm a drummer. I fix guitars and pianos. And bikes."

"Where are you from?" I asked.

"Here. I've lived here a long damn time, but I've been everywhere. I toured with a couple bands. Here," he gave me a business card. I gave him one of mine. "I gotta run," he said, "but I'm real glad to meet you. Keep up the good work."

I never get tired of hearing that.

I rode south on highway one-ninety-one and pulled into the parking lot on the right side of the road, just passed El Charo Loco, and parked in the only parking spot the motel had to offer, and walked passed the "vacancy" sign in the window, pulled the door open, and heard the chime caused by the door.

The lobby was extremely cluttered and small. There was only room for one other person in there. I walked one step up to the desk, which had no one sitting behind it. I glanced around at the display cases with brochures from what seemed like a hundred different caves, resorts, hiking tours, biking tours, and other tourist attractions.

"Can I help you?" came the voice from a man entering from another room.

"I was told to talk to Kent," I said, then, taking the risk that someone might not understand my sense of humor, I added, "You look like someone who could be a Kent. Are you Kent?"

"I am he," he replied, and a tiny sign of a twinkle in his eye helped me understand that he knew I was in a good mood. "Why were you told to look for me?"

"Well, Jeffrey told me I should talk to you. Jeffrey just donated a tank of gas to our cause," I said, handing him a brochure. "If you look here," I started, taking the brochure back from him, turning it over and pointing to the map on the back, "this is what I'm doing. I started in Minnesota and rode this way." I pointed along the line on the map, showing I've been around the country already. "And I do it all for Gold Star Families."

"I just bought this place six months ago," he said, "and I've only got one room left tonight, and it was reserved." He paused. "But it's after ten, so I'll give it to you. If they show up, I'll just explain that I had to let it go."

"That's a pretty awesome thing you're doing," I said, always a little bashful when someone makes a gift to the organization. "We don't have any light left, but if you're around in the morning, I'd like to make a little video with you. Maybe someone will stay here 'cause they saw how good you were to the Gold Star Ride Foundation."

"I'll be around in the morning. Here's the key."

In the morning, I slept until I wasn't sleepy anymore. Sure, I had places I had to get to, but I was tired. This was only the second day out of Phoenix. I slowly packed the bike to head out. I was feeling better than I had in a long time. It's amazing what a good night of sleep can do for you. Kent made his way over to say good morning as well. We did a short interview on camera about why people should stay at The Silver Sage Inn, and I made a joke about the mountains to the west of Moab.

"Those ain't mountains," Kent corrected me. "Those are hills."

Being from the upper Midwest, I often joke that I have to ride five hundred miles in any direction to get to the really good riding places in the US. That is, I have to ride *at least* five hundred miles. I was standing in a parking lot on a gorgeous summer morning, staring at a rock coming out of the ground that stretched something like ten miles from the north end to the south end, and jutting something like (and this is a total guess) two thousand feet into the air. I thought I was looking at a mountain.

"People come from all over to climb our hills," Kent told me, "and we don't have the best hotel, but I just bought this place six months ago, and I was born here, went to school here, and I'll probably die here. And this hotel is a work in progress. I make changes every day. We're getting better and better every day."

The Silver Sage is likely the least expensive motel in the small tourist town of Moab, Utah, and if you're in that area, stop in and say hi to Kent. There's a chain of motels that says they have clean comfortable rooms at the lowest price of any national chain. I've slept in those motels; and I've slept in the Silver Sage Inn. As I grow older and wiser, I'll take the latter every time I'm given the choice of those two.

With a good night sleep, and plenty of fluid in me to stave off the dehydration, and the extreme heat of Arizona behind me, I headed north from Moab. The "hills" as Kent had informed me changed to mountains, then back to valleys, then hills again. I sat in the saddle in total awe of my surroundings until the gas gage said it was time to stop. This was a part of the ride that was pure pleasure.

I was still on highway One-Ninety-One when I pulled into a beautiful mountainous town called Price (no relation). In Price, I started looking for gas. I'd been sitting in the saddle without a break for about two and a half hours. It was time to stretch my legs.

Once in Price, I followed the "business" route and stopped at a Maverick convenience store and gas station. I parked by the gas pump and slowly walked inside. Because summer was everywhere, my riding gear consisted of a T-shirt under my vest, faded blue jeans, boots, fingerless gloves, and bandana, and I'm sure that made an immediate impression on the help in the store that day. I walked up to the cashier, noticing that there were five women working that I could see, and I gave her a brochure. "This is what I'm doing," I said, and before she could say anything, I added, "Which way to the little boy's room?"

I think, now that I see that in writing, that I'll never say that again.

"Right there," she said, pointing to her left.

When I came out of the rest room, I was checking my phone for information like weather, and looking at maps to see how far I'd come, and how far I'd have to go.

One of the employees approached me holding the brochure I had left on the counter. It wasn't the same employee I left it with, "Is this you?"

"Yes."

"You'll want to talk to Judy," she said, then turning her head away from me, "Judy!" Come out here and meet this guy."

A woman in her mid sixties approached from an area I can only describe as either a pizza kitchen or a chicken kitchen. The place sold both of those. "How can I help you?" she said to me.

The other employee spoke up, "He's doing this ride for veterans," she said.

"Veterans' families," I corrected. "You don't want to be

in the group that we help. We only visit families after they've had a funeral."

Judy studied the brochure with intensity. "This is you?" she asked.

"It is. And if you turn that brochure over, you'll see my map."

She turned it over. "Oh, my goodness! Where did you start?"

"I started in Minnesota, and I've already covered all the area to the east of the Mississippi River. I'm headed into Oregon from here. I already stopped to visit a Gold Star Dad in Utah."

"Well," she started, then turned her head to the cashier area, "girls! Do any of you have any cash you'd like to contribute?" Then she looked back at me, "I want to help you, but I can't do anything with the store, itself."

Several of the "girls" said they had some cash. It's funny to call them girls. I was the youngest person in the store.

The girls swarmed, if I can use that language, and produced some cash, and handed it to me. I counted out a couple dollars for the drink I had already finished, and then counted out twelve dollars for the gas. We posed for a picture or two, and Judy suggested I look up the fires in the area.

"If you're going on Highway Six, they were talking about closing that," offered one of the girls from behind the counter.

"Right," Judy offered. There's a website you can look at to see where the fires are." I didn't have the heart to tell her I can't very well search the Internet while I'm riding the motorcycle. I did pull something up while I was standing there that showed me a map of Utah with little flame pictures in the areas that were on fire. I was about to be very close to at least one of them.

This was troubling because the primary reason for being in this part of the country was that the trip was re-routed to avoid the fires in California.

I said my thank you's and my goodbyes, and headed out to the bike, filled the tank, and headed west.

It was then that I remembered, I hadn't had breakfast yet, and I was hungry.

Balance Rock Eatery and Pub in Helper

Just west of Price, Utah on Highway Six is the quaint village of Helper. Helper was a Wild West town with a little twenty-first century sprinkled into it. The icon of Helper is a mysterious mountain formation that the locals refer to as Balance Rock. This is not the same as the natural formation referred to as Balanced Rock, which is about twenty or thirty miles south of Price. This is a rock that sits on the southernmost ridge of the top of the mountain, on the western edge of the town of Helper, Utah.

When I saw the name of the town, I knew I wanted to stop there, just as I knew I wanted to stop in Price before. As I pulled off the road, I learned right away that this was an old west town with incredible charm. I rolled slowly passed the old post office, which looked as though it had two employees, and slowly passed the local hardware store, passed "Marsha's Home Bakin and Sammich Shop" (that's not a typo) and pulled into a parking spot in front of an eatery called, "Balance Rock Eatery and Pub."

I immediately felt like I wanted to stay here.

The front of the restaurant was glass from top to bottom and from left to right. The entire front was glass. The door was also glass. Once inside, I felt as though I had stepped into the saloon of every western movie I had ever seen, but missing the swinging doors. The floor was open and made of wood. The sort of floor that announces every placement of every heel that advances across it. Big wooden planks made up the floor, which featured a scattering of tables throughout the large room. My guess is that this floor was twenty feet from left to right and forty feet from front to back.

Along the left side, as I walked toward the rear, I saw the staircase that led up to the balcony area. There was no seating up there, just a wrap-around balcony that covered three sides of the room.

Off to the far right side, as I walked toward it, was the bar, which is where I bellied up.

I sat down, placed a brochure on the bar, and waited. A young woman approached as said, "How ya doing?"

"Hungry," I said.

"You've come to the right place," she said, reaching for a menu and placing it in front of me on the otherwise bare bar. She was a young woman of maybe twenty-three years, and while she was young looking, she also looked a little bit tired, as though she'd already worked through a lunch rush.

"Thanks," I said, looking over the menu.

A few minutes later, another waitress came along with the first one. "I'll take this," she announced, "You can go," and with that, I had a new waitress.

"I saw the brochure," she said to me once we were alone, or at least as alone as you can be sitting in a large restaurant that seats a couple hundred people. "I'm buying your lunch today."

"That's very kind of you," I said sincerely. I was now about six weeks into this project, and every day was still a struggle to pay for everything. "I hope you'll let me interview you after I'm done eating."

"Me? Why would you want to interview me?" She was a strikingly memorable waitress. Actually, she was a strikingly memorable person. Her appearance said *Marylyn Monroe* more than anyone I'd ever met in my life. She was robust, full of life, wearing her hair like Marylyn; dressing in the style of the early 1960's, and even trying some sort of California accent. Her question was serious.

"You strike me as the person who knows more about this place than anyone else," I explained. "And I think you might be very photogenic. What's your name?"

"Well, I have worked here a long time," she said coyly, "I'm Debbie."

"And are you the owner of this wonderful eatery?" I asked, not remembering that *eatery* was actually a part of the name of the place.

"Oh, heaven's no," she sounded shocked that I would

ask that.

"Usually it's the owners that step up and by my lunch when they learn about the work I'm doing. I don't often have employees taking money out of their own pockets," (I misspoke. Looking back, it was far more often employees taking their own money than it was owners making a donation).

She made sure I had plenty to eat, told me about the Balance Rock on the top of the mountain peak on the west edge of town, and she told me about the history of the eatery itself.

Located in Utah's Castle Country, the scenery around the Balanced Rock Eatery and Pub is as wonderful as anything that can be seen outside of Monument Valley. The history of this particular eatery is as old as the town of Helper, itself. While they feature "down home cooking," I'm not sure what I ate could be found *down home* in another part of the country.

"And when you live in a town named Helper, it's pretty natural to help people," she said.

Mother Teresa is quoted to say that people may not remember what you say to them, and they likely won't remember what you did for them, but they will always remember how you made them feel. I don't remember everything about that day, that stop, or that visit, but I do remember she made me feel like I was the most important person who ever walked through her door.

Maybe it's the way I was raised, or maybe it's the luck I've experienced throughout my life, but for the most part, I've not felt that my presence in the world is necessarily important. I didn't die defending America. None of my kids or parents or brothers or sisters did either. Those are the important people. My job is simply to tell people about them. I'm not sure that makes me important.

"Be careful," she instructed as I was leaving, "the smoke is everywhere, and they say the fire is gonna jump Highway Six today."

"I will," and with that I made my exit. I spent a few more minutes going up and down Main Street taking in all there was in the beautiful little town, and stopped to mail a letter to MSL at the local post office. I thought it would make a good post mark.

Twenty minutes down the road, at seventy miles an hour, the taste of the forest fires' smoke was starting to irritate my throat. I found a place to pull over, dig up a bandana from the saddle bags, drench it with water, and tie it around my face, covering my nose and mouth, before continuing down the road.

The fires didn't disappoint - which is very strange language - because it was only about six more miles when I slowed to fifty-five miles an hour to watch the helicopters load the bucket of water to fight the fire. Another half mile, and I saw the flames towering above the trees on the south side of the road. I had the cameras rolling and there's a picture in the pictures section of this book featuring that helicopter.

The smoke was thick on that part of the highway, and to say the least I was glad I stopped to put the bandana on my face. It was surreal to see. The motorists were all obeying the signs that said, "Do Not Stop In Smoke."

I had chosen this route specifically to avoid forest fires which seem to be at an all time high this year. As eerie as it was to drive passed this one, there was more to come.

Once I passed the fire, the air stayed clouded with smoke, but the beauty of riding in the mountains returned. For those of you who actually live in the mountains, it may be boring, but for the rest of us, well, riding in the mountains is so wonderful, it's hard to describe. The mountains are so big, I couldn't help but feel very small.

I found myself rolling through these spectacular pieces of land and imaging how Brigham Young must have felt leading all those Mormons through these mountains. How did he know when to stop? Each valley seemed as spectacular as the one before it.

I found myself riding through Provo, Utah, thinking it would be better to stay off the big road of Interstate Fifteen, as I headed north toward Salt Lake City. The heat was not anywhere near what I felt in Arizona, but it was still hot, and sitting at stop lights in heavy traffic got old pretty quick. I felt my inner thighs burning from the heat of the bike's exhaust. Freeway it is.

Once on the freeway, I was quite amazed. The other drivers on the freeway seemed like they could see me. Even though the traffic was extremely busy, with cars filling five lanes, I wasn't crowded on the bike like I am in every other city I've ever been in.

By comparison, I remembered driving south of Washington, DC, in heavy traffic, when the traffic came to a stop. I stopped behind a car in the far left lane. I saw in my mirror a car approaching too fast, and navigated the bike in between the two lanes, moving to my right in the stopped traffic.

No sooner had I nestled myself into that non-lane, on the stripe between two lanes, that the car approaching from behind me hit the brakes hard. It steered a little bit to the left, so the two left tires were actually skidding on the shoulder of the road, and it came to a stop with its front bumper only inches away from the car I had stopped behind. Had I not moved in between the lanes, I would have been hit by that car.

The entire thing only took about five seconds to complete, and when I looked at the absent minded driver, I saw a twenty-something woman who was still holding her phone in her right hand!

Back in Utah's heavy traffic, and this was my first experience with city riding in this state, it was different. No one got that close to me from the rear, no one changed lanes in front of me, no one cut me off, and everyone seemed like *they could see me*! This was a pleasant and needed surprise, since I'd now been riding about seven hours.

I felt it was okay to take another break, and I had visited Salt Lake City before, so I took the exit to downtown. Even downtown, Salt Lake City is one of the cleanest cities I've ever visited. Every street corner looked like it was manicured or swept just before my arrival. I stopped to ask someone for directions on a corner, who informed me that he was homeless. Even the homeless people in Salt Lake City are prettier than any other city I have visited. While his clothes were worn, they were clean!

Stopping in Salt Lake City was motivated by my past visits to this amazing city. Say whatever you like about opposing religious viewpoints, or contradictory religious viewpoints, it's still a magnificent city. It's clean; it's well planned; its structures are works of art; and the traffic is the nicest in the United States.

Growing up Catholic, I usually look at places I visit from that perspective. Salt Lake City is no exception. On my first visit to the city, several years ago, I found the Cathedral of the Madeleine, where I stopped for another visit. The building was and still is, amazing. No expense was spared in the creation of this work of art. This is where I wanted to stop this hot afternoon that started way far away in Moab about seven hours ago.

Being on an eleven hundred pound motorcycle has its own challenges, and after riding for so long, I was tired, and the Cathedral of the Madeleine, like almost everything in Salt Lake City, is built on a hill. Managing a heavy bike on hills requires a little extra, and doing it tired, well, that is just dangerous. I managed to get the kickstand down and park the bike on a steep side street, with the bike rolling downhill backwards into the curb. I walked up the forty or so steps to the massive entrance while slowly removing my bandana and gloves.

Once inside, I sat in the very back of the cathedral, not wanting to be noticed, since prayer is a very personal thing no matter who you are. Sitting there, I slipped my boots off and leaned forward, crossing my arms on the back of the pew in front of me and resting my forehead on my forearms.

Some time had passed, and I was feeling like it was time to get back on the bike. As I slowly put my boots on, collected my gloves and bandana, I noticed the triangle-folded flag on display near the front of the church about a hundred-fifty feet from where I was sitting. This sort of flag is only found at military funerals. I did see one once that was a former military base flag, which was presented to the base's Chaplin upon retirement, but otherwise, this flag represents a military funeral.

I stopped a young priest walking in from the back of the church, "Excuse me, Father," I said.

"Yes?" said he.

"Are you having a funeral today?"

"Yes," said he again.

"Was it someone killed on active duty?" I wondered.

"Actually, no, he was an Army corporal at the end of World War II, and he served this community for the last fifty years. His son is our parish pastor, Monsignor Mayo."

"I wonder if I could ask you to deliver something for me to the family?" I asked, and immediately saw the look of fear sliding across his face. I was, after all, standing in front of him with a leather vest, motorcycle boots, and gloves with the fingers cut out of them while standing in the entrance to one of the largest and most magnificent Catholic cathedrals in the western hemisphere. "I'm with the Gold Star Ride Foundation, and it's quite by accident that I'm here, but my job is to help Gold Star Families anyway that I can. I would just like to leave them a plaque honoring their father's service."

"Oh," the priest nodded, "that might be nice. I think I can do that."

I excused myself and ran back to the bike to get a plaque. Of course, I hadn't carried one in with me because I didn't know I was going to meet a Gold Star Family in the church at their father's funeral.

I walked quickly to the priest I had been talking to, who was now speaking to another man in a dark suit with just a hint of white near his throat. "I'd like you to meet someone," he said to me as I approached, "this is Monsignor Joseph Mayo. His father is Deacon Silvio Mayo, the decedent."

"Please accept my condolences for your loss," I squeaked out.

"Oh, thank you so much," the Monsignor said, shaking my hand.

"I know it isn't much," I offered, "but as the executive director of the Gold Star Ride Foundation, I'd like to present this plaque to you in honor of your father's military service." I removed the plaque from the thin cardboard package and handed it to him. He spent a long moment reading the inscription.

> *leave you only the cherished memory of the*
> *loved and lost...*

He reached out his hand again, said, "thank you," with moist eyes. "I'm very sorry," he continued, "I wish I had more time to talk with you, but the Mass is about to start, and..."

"Think nothing of it," I interrupted, "I came without an invitation and I have to go myself. Thank you for taking a moment of your day for me." With that I made my exit and walked out to the bike.

The sun was still high in the sky, and the temperature was still hot as I made my way down the forty or so steps from the Cathedral of the Madeleine.

From a distance of about twenty feet, my heart started to sink. There was a dreaded puddle under the bike. Every rider of motorcycles has dreaded this happening to them, and almost all of them have had it happen to them. Today, it happened to me.

Normally, this is just part of riding. You just figure it out; but here, I'm on the road; I've been on the road for almost six weeks. I'm two weeks from home, and I've discovered an oil leak.

Usually, a genuflection is reserved for inside the church, but I was with one knee on the ground outside the church trying to figure out why I've got a leak. I quickly diagnosed it to a leaking clutch cover. This told me two things: first, I've most likely been leaking fluid since San Antonio, Texas, which was the last time that cover had been removed, and second, my primary fluid must be quite low by now. I was in Texas a long time ago; two weeks and nearly two thousand miles.

I quickly ran through a list of options in my head, including find the local dealership and spend the last money I had; find a local mechanic on Craigslist and spend a little less; or fix it myself. It was certainly something I could do and have done myself before. I chose the last idea, and with the help of the GPS program on my phone, I headed for the nearest auto parts store.

The store clerk gave me a rag and loaned me the torx bits I needed to open the cover. I purchased the extra thick primary oil and went to work. It was easy enough, but it took some time. The primary case was a half quart low, which is to say it was nearly half empty, so I got there just in time. I should be more optimistic and say that it was half full. That is, I wouldn't have wanted to find out what happens when you ride long distances in the heat and the primary is any lower than that.

After assembling the bike, I started it and let it idle in the parking lot for two full minutes. No drips appeared under it. Now I had a different problem. I had only two fingers of sunlight left.

I was starting to understand this routine I was on, so, I shut off the bike and opened my GPS on the phone, looking for nearby motels. I called three different places only to discover that there was only one room between the three of them, and it was two hundred dollars for a single night's stay.

With hotel-hopes dashed, I got back on the saddle and headed toward Oregon, not knowing what was next. By the time I was on the highway, the sun was down, and the road became dark quickly.

If you didn't die tryin', you didn't try hard enough

After being on the highway for thirty minutes or so, I pulled off the highway and followed the signs to a motel with such a local name, I knew it would be nasty; one or two stars at best, and I knew I might have a chance to find a place to sleep.

The Charin Inn, somewhere south of Ogden and north of Salt Lake City, turned out to be the perfect place. On a street lined with payday loans, auto title loans and pawn shops, I pulled into the incredibly dark parking lot and turned off the bike. I reminded myself that to the people here, I was the scary creature, and I hobbled, with extreme exhaustion and some pain, up to the office which was locked, and I rang the bell.

A younger man in his late twenties or early thirties came and talked with me through the window. "I need a room," I told him.

"How many?" he asked. They always ask me how many people I am. I found this odd, because he could see the bike (I think – it was dark, so maybe he couldn't see the bike), and he could see me.

"Just me."

"Let me check," he walked behind a desk that was a few feet behind him, shuffled some papers here and there, then walked back to the door and opened it. "How did you find us?"

"I just followed the signs from the freeway."

"What brings you here to this part of the world?"

"I'm glad you asked," I answered slowly. I was really tired. "I'm honoring Gold Star Families across the country," I handed him a brochure. "If you look at the back, you'll see my map. I'm doing that now."

"Wow," he sounded impressed when he looked at the map.

"It'd be a big help to our organization if you could donate a room."

"I have one room left," he said, and then added, "I've seen this organization before."

"Thanks for remembering us," I said humbly. My thought was that he probably did not really recognize us, but that was okay with me.

"I can donate the room," he confirmed, "what else can I do for you?" he handed me a key.

"A shot of whiskey if you've got one," I said, trying to be a little funny.

"I'll see what I can do."

The Charin Inn is like a small strip mall, without the lights and fan fare. The parking lot is large enough for twelve cars, parked diagonally, and it features twelve rooms. I was in number nine, which is a number I associate with since I'm the ninth kid born to my parents.

I've always liked the Beatles song *Number Nine*, too.

The room was about the size of a king sized bed, with a queen sized bed in it. The bathroom had a toilet and a shower, but there wasn't enough room for a sink. That feature was under the TV.

The window air conditioner was stuck in a hole in the wall that had been made for that purpose. Silver duct tape accented the edges, keeping the heat out. I didn't use the air conditioner that night.

I began my nightly ritual of downloading all the days video onto the computer so I'd have ninety-six gigabytes of free space to record movies tomorrow, and while that was downloading, I stepped outside the door to take a deep breath and relax. I called MSL to let her know about the day, and while I was talking with her, the motel clerk walked up to me and handed me a glass of whiskey.

"It's all I got," he said.

"It's all I need," I answered, "thank you very much!" If I had to guess, I'd say it was three shots.

I showered and climbed into bed, which was a box spring and mattress on the floor. It felt odd to sleep so close to the floor without actually being on the floor. I double checked my alarm so I could start at dawn tomorrow and lay there, motionless.

The Charin Inn is a place I may return, simply because they were so generous and understated. I wouldn't recommend staying there if you're driving a brand new Cadillac or Lexus, but if you're in a five year old Chevy, it works.

Chapter Seven: Some Gold Star Families

Monticello, Utah

Tom was a mountain man from the old days, but now he was a little more cautious. He didn't know me, nor did his wife for that matter, but his wife set up a meeting with the Gold Star Ride Foundation, so I was happy to be meeting him.

It was in a part of the Rocky Mountains where my telephone didn't work, which helps very little to pinpoint the location, since my phone is how I found places I needed to go. While riding north on a state highway, hours after nearly colliding with a herd of wild horses (that's right, I said horses; I said herd; and I said wild), I stopped and asked the gas station attendant if I could use their landline to make a call.

"Is this Tom?" I asked,

"Yes," he replied with a little hesitation.

"I'm here to meet you."

"I'm at the grave site twenty miles south of you. Do you want to come here or do you want me to come there? Where are you again?" I had rolled right passed him.

"I'm near the veterans' memorial," I said, "calling from the gas station across the street."

"I'll come there," he said.

"I'm doing my best for Gold Star Families," I said, when we were finally face to face.

"Well, it's nice to meet you," Tom said to me.

He was still a little stand-off-ish, so I talked about stuff that didn't really matter. He was a little shorter than I was and wore a floppy hat with a brim that went all the way around his head and a loosely fitted chin string. He was old enough to remember to remember Eisenhower, but maybe not remember him well. His round face displayed memories of good times as well as bad. "Is it always this hot in August?" everyone knows it is. "Did you grow up here?"

"I grew up in the mountains over there," he pointed west. "I was something of a trouble maker," he said with a shy, yet all-knowing sort of tone in his voice. "Me and my friends used to take a shot gun shell and tape it to the end of the BB gun barrel."

"A live shell?!" I asked with more than a little shock.

"Yes, we didn't have a shot gun, but we had shells. So we taped the shell to the end of the BB gun barrel and fired the BB gun."

"And that would fire the shell? Isn't that more than a little dangerous?"

"Oh, yeah, I wouldn't recommend it at all now," he said, still calm and confident. Almost like a dry sense of humor, but he wasn't making jokes. "I'm a retired school teacher, and folks wouldn't want me talking about those things."

The more he talked, the more comfortable he was talking, and the more fascinating things became. He told me of stories in the classroom; he shared that all the names on the Veterans' Memorial wall, which was only about thirty steps away from us, were students in his classroom at one time or another.

It was after about fifteen minutes of us getting to know each other when I realized my boots were parked on top of an army ant hill. Those ants didn't like my boots! He suggested we walk to the wall.

"We paid for a brick," he said, "that was supposed to have our son's name on it, but it never appeared. You see all these names?" he swept his hand wide to show me the red bricks that lined the edge of the sidewalk around the memorial. Each brick had the name, rank and year of each life lost to the military.

"My wife teaches, too," he explained, "she's got one year left until retirement. We have seventeen kids, eight were adopted. Nathan has two brothers still over there fighting."

"Did he know he was adopted?" I asked.

"Oh, of course he did. He was Korean. The other kids were from here, so he knew he was different the whole time. We never hid the fact that any of our kids were adopted."

"Did you teach your kids to fire a shot gun shell with a BB gun?" I tried to make a little joke.

"No, if they did that, they learned it on their own. I

wouldn't be surprised to know they did it, but I never heard about it." We took another step toward the Veterans' Memorial. "Well, I never saw that before."

"What's that?" I asked.

"Nathan's name has been added to the wall," he paused.

We sat down on the base of the memorial, he on my right. "I have something for you," I said, producing the plaque just like all the other plaques for all the other families around the country. "I'd like to read it to you," I was both asking and telling at the same time.

...and the solemn pride that must be
yours...

When I finished reading, there was no hiding his tears, or mine for that matter. We both paused a long time before he said, "That's beautiful," then after two short breaths, "We will treasure it." I put my arm around his shoulders and let him know I was there. We didn't speak for a long time.

"Nathan was always good at what he did, no matter what it was. He decided right out of high school that he wanted to join the Army. He earned the Green Beret from the Army Rangers."

"How long did he serve?"

"Fourteen years."

"He must have really liked his job to have advanced to so far in only fourteen years," I opined.

"Well, he was a Korean, and he was an adopted son, and he wanted to repay the country that gave him the freedoms that he had and wanted to make sure that the rest of the world could stay free."

No one spoke for a moment.

"He did that, didn't he?" I broke the silence.

"Yeah, I guess he did. He set a good example, that's for sure."

"Was he married?" I asked.

"Yes, and he has two kids. They live in Canada now. He

was nominated by his men to have a clinic named after him, too. That says a lot about how his men felt about him. They named a clinic in Washington at Joint Base Lewis-McChord, since he was a medic."

"So, not only was he a great soldier, everyone knew he was a great soldier," I offered.

"Him and his men just finished their duty, they had been on patrol for two days, and they just went to sleep. It was Nathan's turn to stay awake and they all went to sleep when the call came in from the MP's in the area. The MP's were pinned down, so Nathan woke up his men and they went to get the MP's out.

"Nathan was the one who took out the sniper's nest. They thought they had cleared the area, and pulled their vehicle up to the MP's and as soon as he got out, he was driving, he caught a bullet in the only place he wasn't wearing Kevlar. They shot him in the throat.

"And the report said that he lived for about twelve hours, but I talked with the guys on his team. The other guy in the vehicle with him was the one who grabbed him and drug him out of the line of fire. He told me that Nathan was probably dead before he hit the ground. So, that made me feel a little better."

"He won the Bronze Star, Purple Heart, and the Meritorious Service Medal."

There was another long pause. Tom wiped away another tear or two.

After about a minute of silence, I broke it by saying, "This is why I do this. So you can be reminded that you are not the only one who is grateful for your son's life. Even if the country doesn't say something to you every day, I remember."

"Thank you, Tony," he said, calling me by my name for the first time since we met.

"Didn't your wife tell me your daughter was coming to meet with us here today?" I asked.

"Well, she was supposed to. And she was coming with a couple bikes from the Patriot Guard Riders, but they were in an accident."

"Is she ok?" I asked with some excitement. How could we go so long without mentioning his daughter was in an accident on the way to the meeting?

"Oh, she wasn't in the accident. The motorcycle was involved in an accident," he explained. "The only thing I know is they air lifted him from the scene."

"Ouch. It's always difficult to hear about those stories. I hope he's OK. So, your daughter went to the hospital to see about the guy on the bike?"

"Yes, but she was looking forward to meeting you."

We didn't say much more after that. Slowly, we stood; slowly we walked toward the intersection, across from which my bike was parked. We stopped at the traffic light and thanked each other. We hugged each other. He said, "I'm really glad; really glad you came," and I knew his sentiments were genuine.

I felt like I was doing the right thing when I climbed on the bike and pointed it north.

Harrisburg, Pennsylvania

Billy was everyone's friend. His was the sort of heart that just didn't quit. Maybe it was the way his heart presented itself that made it susceptible to the hidden danger that took Billy, no one can say for sure.

Billy served in the United States Coast Guard, and when he wasn't in his Coast Guard uniform, you could find him wearing a shirt with "Swatara Fire – Rescue" on the front left breast. Billy worked for the York Ambulance Association, the South Berwick Fire and Rescue and served as a volunteer for the York Village Fire Department as well.

Billy was as much at home working as an EMT with Swatara Fire and Rescue as he was on a Coast Guard Cutter. It's their firetruck in the pictures section of this book.

I'm getting ahead of the story.

When Billy was very young, he could be found playing with fire trucks like most little boys. Just playing with trucks was never enough for the size of his heart. He also loved the

Teenage Mutant Ninja Turtles when he was little and he would demonstrate this by pouring rice into the gutters on the street to feed those turtles.

Billy was not just his name. It was his father's name, too. His grandfather also lived with that name. His great-grandfather did, too. Billy was William the Fourth.

There was much more to Billy's heredity than his name. Both his father and his grandfather made careers in law enforcement, and Billy had applied to the Massachusetts State Police Academy. His father also served as a Marine, and his uncle was a Commander of a ship in the US Navy, so there was no shortage of examples for him to follow into the military.

He signed up for the Army while still in high school, and went to boot camp between his junior and senior years. After graduating he was off to medic school and then the Middle East, which he handled with stoic charisma. When it was time to re-enlist, he chose a different uniform, and became a member of the US Coast Guard stationed in Boston.

By the time he got to Boston, he had married Tara, and was madly in love with her. When the couple produced a daughter, his heart grew a few more sizes. His heart must have been too large, because he was diagnosed with high blood pressure.

No one in their twenties is diagnosed with high blood pressure, right? Billy wondered about that, too. Billy remembered that application to the Massachusetts State Police, so he worked to control his high blood pressure without medication.

The locals like to retell a story of Billy in his EMT uniform. There was a call and Billy rushed out to the scene of a single car crash. The accident was bad, and the driver of the car was killed on impact, which was a significant number of minutes before Billy arrived. There was nothing that could be done for him.

It turned out that the driver was not alone in that car on that day. The driver's companion was a golden retriever who was quite badly injured and lay motionless and crying in the back seat of the car. Billy jumped to help the pooch, and after additional help arrived, excused himself to take the dog to the animal hospital. The dog survived.

His heart may have grown a size or two that day as well.

Billy was gifted and rose in rank quickly. This was demonstrated with his advancement in the Coast Guard to Second Class Petty Officer. His father, William III, was at the ceremony, and pinned the advancement on his son in what must have been the most proud moment of either Billy.

Moments like those are the sort of things that make caring for a terminally ill father so much more bitter-sweet. Billy took care of his father until his father's death.

From July, 2013, until December, 2013, just six short months, Billy was the proudest papa on the eastern seaboard, doting on his baby daughter every day. For those who were fortunate enough to see them together there was no doubt.

As for me, I do not, nor will I ever doubt it or any other part of this story. I woke early in a tiny village in upstate New York, which is discussed in a different part of this book, and started riding south toward Harrisburg, Pennsylvania. The ride that day was as perfect as can be. The sun was shining and only the occasional puffy white cloud casting a shadow on me rolling through the hills and woods around the lakes, with the big twin engine humming along like nothing else mattered.

I rode that day for a long time. I was on small highways that often would go no farther than the next village or town. I was stopping to look at maps often, but never did I wish to be somewhere else, and I had little knowledge of what was in store.

The minutes of riding were placed one in front of the other until I had well over five hundred minutes stretched end to end when I drew near the prearranged meeting spot on the northeast edge of Harrisburg.

I ride for two very distinct and separate reasons. One is because I enjoy leaving my stress in the wind. For this reason, this was a perfect day. No one could add to it, or in any way make it less than perfect. It was the sort of day and the sort of roads, and the sort of weather that makes everything just, well, perfect.

I pulled off the road and into a parking lot that, like nearly every road and parking lot, I had never seen before. I found a place to stop and put the kickstand down. I spent a moment breathing deeply; recovering from the journey I just completed which burned through two full tanks of gas and half of a third. I was exhausted, but I knew there were people waiting to meet me, and this visit to see a Gold Star Mother had been waiting a long time.

I didn't think anyone was paying attention to me, so I quickly changed into a fresh T-shirt, slipped the vest back on and walked toward the door. I pulled the door open with one hand, and immediately knew all the stories about Billy were true as I stepped in and found myself face to face with the other reason I ride. I met Patti, a Gold Star Mom.

This restaurant had seating for about eighty people, and every seat was taken. Well, sort of taken. Every person there was on their feet, applauding my arrival.

In years past, I had been an entertainer, and I had heard applause before, but this was different. I was there to honor a Gold Star Mom, but they were applauding *me*. Like I had done something special, and I had not. At least, I didn't think so.

I was greeted at the door by the Gold Star Mom, who held my arm until the noise stopped.

"I didn't do anything to deserve that," I said to the crowd, "I'm here to honor her."

Patti introduced me to fire men and women, fire chiefs, and EMT's that had worked with and known Billy for a long time. Each was very excited to tell me their personal story about Billy.

There were some more introductions and talk of the high school football team. The crowd was kind to me and remained silent while I read the plaque to Patti.

> *I feel how weak and fruitless must be any
> words of mine...*

Billy was standing a routine watch onboard the US

Coast Guard Cutter that was his Coast Guard home, when his oversized heart stopped beating. His daughter was one hundred, seventy-eight days old. One week later his acceptance letter to the Massachusetts State Police arrived in his mailbox.

The world will not have a William V. And we are all sorry for that.

While his widow and his mother will cherish his memories for the rest of their days, each and every one of us can be grateful that this big heart was there for us.

Mebane, North Carolina

The Clinton Administration doesn't seem like it was that long ago. Bill Clinton is still in the news once in a while, so was it really that long ago?

Phil was the last son born to Christy and Dave, and he went from toddler to tween while Clinton was president. During that decade, fishing became his favorite pastime. Dave would spend a day preparing to fish by taking his young son's hand the day before and going out to the backyard to dig up worms. The prizes were the night crawlers, which is a lesson Phil picked up quick.

The catching of the fish was always exciting. Even at eight, Phil understood that when the line went down, there was a fish eating the worm, and there was some sort of seafood for dinner. You don't have to be a child to remember how good fresh fish can taste.

The nighttime worm hunting was the best. Phil would be allowed to stay up a little later than usual, and go outside with his dad to get the big worms. On rainy days, the knowledge of the big worms coming to the surface was enough to inspire a day of fishing the very next day.

Christy would always bite her tongue when young Phil would come into the house exhausted and covered with dirt and mud from his nose to his toes. After being tucked into bed and drifting off to dreamland, Christy would turn to Dave and offer a less than gentle reprimand for letting Phil catch worms wearing his pajamas!

As he entered puberty and teenage years, the three brothers would constantly try to outdo one another. Phil was the youngest, and as such, was not quite as boisterous as his older brothers. They were typical of three brothers, even becoming almost cliché with bicycle stunts, fishing expeditions, football prowess, golf, and looking out for one another. Golf was the game that Phil liked most, because he could out perform his more athletic older brothers.

Phil, even more than his brothers, developed the sort of personality that was keenly aware of others. Not just people, but animals, too. His kindness was felt by many people and many animals.

It was not unusual for Phil to adopt a stray pet until he could find the rightful owner, even if that meant five days of cleaning animal feces several times a day.

Phil outpaced his older brothers for the last time when he came home from the US Navy recruiter's office with the documents announcing that he had enlisted.

As with everything he did, Phil excelled in the Navy, rising to the rank of Second Class Petty Officer within just a few years. His ability to feel for others was not lost on his seemingly meteoric rise in rank either. Both the junior enlisted and senior enlisted praised Phil, and all loved serving with him.

He was serving at his second permanent duty station during the summer of 2013 in Naples, Italy, when he found a stray kitten. Unable to find the correct owners, the kitten was then named Pickles. Pictures of Pickles became the most celebrated pictures among family and friends. Pickles was inspirational in motivating Phil to get a home away from the base, which is not what most US sailors do when stationed in Naples.

Pickles became, and by many respects, is still, the star.

Late that summer, in early August, even driving to the base just before the sun came up was a warm activity. Southern Italy in summer can be very hot. Phil had his windows down and was nearly the only vehicle on the road in the still dark morning. It's a safe bet that Phil thought he was the only vehicle on the road, too.

He wasn't.

Christy and Dave earned their Gold Stars August 3, 2013.

I rode through Mebane, North Carolina, in July, 2018, and was fortunate enough to meet Christy. During this visit, I learned first that the name of the town is pronounced Meh bin, and almost a single syllable. It's important to learn how to pronounce the name of the town. This is important to me because I come from a state with many Native American town names, many of which are difficult to pronounce.

Another important lesson of the visit was finding on the menu something called *chicken fried chicken*. Of course, I ordered that.

"Philip was a wonderful young man," she told me, "and you'd think the pain would be easier with the passage of time, but most days, it seems to be more painful."

"I have never buried a child," I said, "but I understand how the pain of the child being gone does not get easier. And if you'll let me," I continued, "I'd like to offer that it is wrong for a parent to lose a child. I mean, we have a word for it when a child loses a parent: orphan. We have a word for it when we lose a spouse: widow. But in the English language, we do not have a word for it when a parent loses a child."

We paused for a moment.

"I'd like to tell you a little story," she broke the silence, "about how Philip still shows me that he's around. Last week, Dave was getting ready to spend some quality time fishing," she began, "and I told him I wanted to go visit Philip.

"When I got to his gravesite, I sat down on the grass, and almost immediately I found a worm on the ground. I looked over and was like, 'Really Philip?' and then there it was; a second one! I told Philip that no one would believe me and it would never show up in a picture. I told him if he wanted me to take a picture he needed to show me a stick 'cause I sure wasn't going to pick them up with my fingers! Well, I glanced around and there was a stick! I shook my head and took the stick and used it to pick up the first fishing worm, placed it on

Philip's headstone and then began getting the next one up.

"Then I took the picture."

"That's amazing," I said, "and I'm glad he still communicates with you."

"Some people may think it's strange," she said, "but it helps."

"You know," I offered, "I don't have much to give you, but I'm here to give you all I can. I think Philip gives you all he can, too."

After a short pause, I added, "and I'd like to give you this memorial plaque, reminding you that there are others who would like to support you, and help you through the difficulties that come with having a hero like Philip in your family."

...words of mine which should attempt to beguile you...

We talked more about his service, and Pickles, and I enjoyed my chicken fried chicken.

Riding to the next stop, and still to this day, I remember Christy, Dave and the difficulties of losing their *youngest* child.

Jacksonville, Florida

An airplane rolls into the wind in order to leave the ground. This is an interesting thought. In the navy, we used to say, *A smooth sea never made a skillful sailor*. These are examples of how difficulty in life is necessary to excel. "Flight or Fight" is how the psychologists describe difficulty inside the human body. Another common word to describe it is stress.

A quick Internet search returns a list of things that cause stress; and it's worth mentioning that everyone is a little different, but odds are, you can relate to these stressful things. First on the list is death of a loved one. Second on the list is divorce. Third is moving your home.

Chris took stress in stride. Even before he made it to double digits in age, he was already holding onto the responsibility of his three younger sisters. He was quick to stand in between trouble and any one of them. He was quick to help them any way an older brother can help younger sisters.

Chris liked to do things without any help. He was a take charge sort of young boy, even developing a paper route when he was ten. A paper route. Most young people today have no idea what that is. At ten years old, he managed to persuade people in his neighborhood to start receiving printed daily newspapers which he would personally deliver to their doorstep. He was a take charge boy.

Chris was someone who quickly took charge of every situation and found a way to change things for the better. The family joke has always been that he would go to summer camp with a few dollars in his pocket for incidentals, and always come home with more. Chris was a creative kid who knew how to take control of the situation. It was nothing for Chris to move; although the other two top stress factors did not present themselves to Chris.

Chris knew what he wanted, and he knew how to go get it. Sarah recognized pretty early on that this was a quality she was attracted to in a man. No one can say it was love at first sight. In fact, Chris chased Sarah five years before the two young adults decided it was time to tie the knot. They weren't the sort who needed a great deal of fanfare either. They quietly got married in Las Vegas when no one was looking, then made the announcement to friends and family later.

Chris was on his second enlistment by then, and he knew he was off to medic school for Special Forces. They would start their new life together as soon as his orders came in to move to California for the training. Sarah patiently waited in Nevada for the moving truck which would take them together.

The moving truck didn't come. Instead, two Marines in dress blue uniforms came carrying a flag folded into a triangle.

I never met Sarah, although I'm certain that when I do, I will like her. I met Chris's mom Lori, and through her, I met Chris, and armed with the knowledge I have of Chris, I'm certain I would like the person with whom he chose to share his life.

Lori called me when I was on my way out of Florida.

Even though a local TV station did a short story about my travels, she didn't see that. She found me on social media and asked via email what The Gold Star Ride Foundation was all about. I rearranged the schedule of leaving Florida – a decision that would hit me hard later – and went back to Jacksonville to meet her.

In November the year before, she had moved to Texas. That's number three on the human stress list – moving. Almost sixty days later, her mother died. That's number one on the stress list. Two and a half months after her mother died, her divorce was finalized. That's number two on the stress list. Ninety-five days after that, Chris was killed, making her a Gold Star Mom. That's number one on the stress list.

In nine months, Lori had to deal with the top three most stressful things four times.

Being pregnant with quadruplets would be less stressful for nine months.

We struggled to meet. I texted her and told her I was coming to see her after she invited me to visit – at the cemetery. GPS horror stories are listed in another chapter, but they play here. I was supposed to be there by two in the afternoon. I arrived about five-thirty.

Lori wasn't sure what to expect, which was quite common among the Gold Star Families that I visited along the route. We sat down and started talking. Not about anything specific; just talking.

"Sometimes," Lori said somewhere in the conversation, "people will come and talk to me, and try to help me get passed the fact that my oldest child is dead. But that won't ever change."

"I've never had a child die," I offered, "but I've lost my children, and I know that you're a Gold Star Mom, and that will never change. Blue Star Families are only Blue Star Families while that person from their family is serving. Once they come home, they are no longer a Blue Star Family. Gold Stars are forever. I don't want to try to take that away from you, I just want you to know that when it gets heavy, I'll do all I can to help you carry it."

"I don't think they mean to be hurtful," she said, "I just think they don't know any better. If they did, that means they went through it, too, and I wouldn't wish that on anybody. But sometimes, it really rubs me the wrong way."

"I hope I'm not doing that; I certainly don't want to be rubbing you the wrong way."

"We were planning to go to his wedding reception," she changed the subject, "when we got the news that we were going to his funeral instead."

"That's not an easy thing," I offered, thinking that my visit wasn't as productive as I wanted it to be. "I do have something for you, and if you let me, I'd like to read this to you."

"Oh, please do," she said.

> *...consolation that may be found in the*
> *thanks of the Republic they died to save...*

"Those are the words of Lincoln, who incidentally, said we were to 'care for the widows and orphans,' of the war. He was talking about the Civil War, but I think he meant it for all time."

She wiped her tears away carefully.

"You know," she started speaking again, "Chris died accidentally. I know that. Everyone at Camp Lejeune knows that. But I feel for the driver of that other vehicle. I know he had a young family, but I never met him, or talked to him. I just feel for him."

"I bet he would really like to know that," I offered. I really didn't know.

"You know, you being here – it's important," she turned the subject to me.

"I'm not here for me, so, I'm here for you. Your sacrifice is the important one," I countered.

"I hope your wife knows – I hope she realizes – how much your visits mean to us. I mean 'us' as all the Gold Star Families."

I looked down at the table.

"I feel so honored," she continued, "just to have met you. You are kind of bringing him back to life."

I slowly spoke, "The honor," I said sincerely, lifting my eyes back to hers, "is mine."

The camera that was recording us beeped to break our train of thought. She laughed. I understood that I had done as much as I could do on that visit, and suggested that I start riding west.

"How far will you go tonight?" she asked as we stood and started walking toward the door.

"Don't know until I stop," I said. There was something a little wonderful in letting the open road be my guide for such things. I guess it helped me tolerate a GPS system that took me twenty miles in the wrong direction.

"Thank you so much for coming," she hugged me at the door for a long time. "Can I give you a bottle of water for the road?"

"Sure," I said, taking the water and stepping outside into the Florida heat.

I rode a few more hours before stopping for the night at a wonderful spot that I'll share more information about in a different place in this story. I slept, and woke and started riding at dawn. Around lunchtime, I stopped at the Naval Air Station Pensacola to watch the Blue Angels practice. I still like to think that they decided to practice when I got to town *because* I arrived.

I know that's not true.

I looked at my phone messages before going farther down the road to find this message from Lori:

> *My heart is so full! I hope to eventually find the right words to express all that has been running through my head and heart in the last 12 hours. Ride easy Tony. Keep safe. I feel all those warriors whose families you're honoring are present with you. Really. I felt that last night. There were more people in that room last night than just us! Have a beautiful day!*

A Little Summation

I rode for the Gold Star Ride Foundation for fifty days, then after three weeks, I got back on the road for another nine days.

I met too many people to include them all in this collection, and many that I met asked me to leave them out completely. They thanked me for what I was doing, but didn't want anyone to know their story.

There was the young man whose father was killed while serving as an Army Ranger. That dad managed to win the hearts of so many of his fellow soldiers that his son now has his own personal army. They don't follow him around and make sure he stays safe, but that young man receives emails and texts from the Army Rangers who will always be there if he needs them. The stories you've heard of brotherhood within the service are true, and in this case, there's a team of Army Rangers taking care of an eighteen year old kid.

There was a Gold Star Widow whose husband served twenty years, most of them during Vietnam, who came home and entered law enforcement, serving as a county sheriff's deputy for another ten years, then was elected to the position of sheriff, and was re-elected twice. He died as a result of illness derived because of exposure to Agent Orange at the age of fifty-six. She didn't want me to tell his story.

There were multiple stories of soldiers (this word is used to represent sailors, Marines, airmen, and soldiers alike) who did not have to go back. They had served their time and were offered an honorable discharge. They kissed their wives goodbye and went back. They loved their country, but that's not why they did it. That's not what I was told. I was told they went back to take care of the men and women in their charge. They went back to take care of "their guys." They went back to continue the friendships that were far too strong for something like a discharge to separate them.

None of the stories of our nation's heroes are the same as any other story, but it is possible to see the common thread among them. All of our heroes will go to the very ends of the earth for the other guys they serve and who serve them.

You either get 'em out or die tryin'...

I learned about accidents and acts of valor, none that were not worth discussion. All of the stories remind me of the Battle of Shiloh, during the Civil War. Casualties mounted because fathers, sons, and brothers would march into battle elbow to elbow, none flinching for fear of losing the other; ultimately all receiving the fast end of a hot ball of lead.

The current attitude is the same, whether it be from SSG Paul Smith from Illinois or any of the three Tony's whose families I met along the way. (Believe it or not, one was Tony, one was Anthony, and one was Antoine.) "He didn't want to leave his guys," they would tell me over and over.

I was asked in an interview once what I thought was a great question. If the soldiers who came home damaged (the disabled veterans) knew they would come home injured, would they do it again?

There is no doubt in my mind.

They would all do it again.

And if you didn't die tryin', you didn't try hard enough...

Chapter Eight: It's Not Easy at Home, Either

"Why don't you come home?"

"I've got a job to do and it's not done yet."

"But you're only eight hours away."

"But I'm three days behind, and that eight hours is only one way. If I come home even just to have dinner with you, it'll add three days to the total mission."

"Mission?"

"Yes, I call it a mission. I know I volunteered. I know it was my idea. I know it was me that made this difficult for you. I know. I know."

"Why do you want to leave me?"

"I don't want to leave you."

"If you don't want to leave me, why are you gone?"

"I'm not gone. I'm just working."

"Why can't you work around here like normal people? Why do you have to leave me?"

"I don't want to leave you. This is just something that has to be done, and no one else is doing it."

"So you can be some sort of hero?"

"No. I'm doing it because it needs to be done."

"Why can't someone else do it?"

"I suppose because no one else wants to have this conversation with their wife. Or husband."

"So, you do want to leave me."

"No, I don't want to leave you. When I promised to be with you for the rest of my life, I meant it."

"It sure looks like you're trying to leave me."

"I'm not trying to leave you."

"So, is this some sort of mid-life crisis?"

"It's not a mid-life crisis. It's just me doing something that I think needs to be done."

"So, you met someone new?"

"Well, I meet new people every day, but no, I'm not looking to replace you."

"Don't you miss me?"

"Yes, I miss you very much."

"Why don't you come home?"

"I have a job to do."

"Why don't you come home, and fly to those towns, rent a motorcycle, and go visit them then fly back home?"

"Because no one will take me seriously, first, and second, because the Foundation does not have the money for that."

"How much money would it cost?"

"No one would take it seriously. Who will pay attention to me if I just fly in and fly back home? Then I would just be another eccentric trying to meet people. I would be a weirdo."

"I think you're a weirdo now."

"I know you do. But I was a weirdo when you met me. This shouldn't be anything new."

"That's not funny."

"Well, you know me. I know in my heart I'm funny."

"I don't know if I'll be here much longer."

"That's a strange thing to say. It's your house."

"Well, I'll start moving your stuff out tomorrow."

"Do you have that sort of time? You can stop everything you're doing so that you can move my stuff out?"

"If that's what it takes."

"That's what I've been trying to tell you. I have to do whatever it takes."

"Where are you today?"

"I'm outside of Cleveland, Ohio ...Nashville, Tennessee ...Buffalo, New York ...Jacksonville, Florida ...Hattiesburg, Louisiana ...Peoria, Illinois ...Oklahoma City, Oklahoma ...Estes Park, Colorado ...Rock Springs, Wyoming ...Burns, Oregon ...I think it's called Biggs Junction, Oregon ...Grangeville, Idaho ...Wall, South Dakota ...Hondo, Texas ...Moab, Utah ...Believe it or not, this town is called Anthony, Texas ...Madison, Florida ...Covington, Louisiana ...Salt Lake City, Utah ...seventy-five miles from Syracuse, New York ...Harrisburg, Pennsylvania ...Baldwin, Florida ...Salem, Oregon ...Sun Valley, Idaho ...Cameron, Missouri ...San Antonio, Texas ...Uranus,

Missouri."

"How far is that from here?"

"I don't know."

"I think you're crazy."

"I think we've covered that."

"Why don't you want to see me?"

"I do want to see you. What I don't have is an opportunity."

"Why do you have to do this?"

"In order for me to have the success that I wanted, it had to be done this way."

"I don't see why you can't fly."

"If I fly, all I'm doing is spending money."

"I don't think anyone will know the difference if you choose to fly."

"I'll know the difference."

"I don't like you being gone so long."

"I don't like being without you either. And I don't like riding motorcycles fifteen hours a day either. I don't like sleeping in cockroach infested motels. I don't like living out of a suitcase. I don't like eating dinner made of gas station sandwiches. I don't like two hundred fifty degree heat crawling up my pant legs every time I come to a stop light. I don't like waking up with an alarm every day."

"Every day you get to be out there having fun."

"I'm not having that much fun."

"Then why are you doing it?"

"I do it because it's hard. It's very, very hard."

After a long pause, she breaks the silence. "Why don't you come home?"

"There was a goal. And the only way to accomplish the goal is to do the work. And the only way to do the work is for me to work my ass off."

"I don't think you want to see me."

"I do."

"Then why can't I see you?"

"As long as you refuse to fly out to see me on, it has to happen this way."

"I don't know if I want to see you."

"It's insulting to both of us when you say that you don't want to see me."

"You don't want to see me either."

"I don't know when you learned to see my thoughts – which means you're calling me a liar."

"This is all against my will."

"Actions have been planned for two and a half years against your will."

"I didn't want to do it."

"You've heard me say for a long time – certainly more than once – because otherwise we'll never know what could have happened."

"So now you're blaming me for us being apart?"

"I'm not blaming you."

"Now I understand your ex."

"Really? You want to bring up my EX wife?"

"Why didn't you do this with her?"

"It wasn't the right time for me to do this ten years ago."

"Lucky me."

"Yeah, lucky me, too."

Long pause. She breaks the silence; "Why do you have to do this now?"

"I don't know how else to explain it. I feel like I'm repeating myself over and over again – which is redundant, I know."

"But if you were here, you could fly in, and they would never know."

"Today, I met the family and said, 'I rode five thousand miles to get here' and tomorrow I see a family in the morning and say, 'I rode fifty-one hundred miles to get here,' and in the afternoon I'll get to say, 'I rode fifty-two hundred miles to get here.' I can't say that if I don't do that."

"Well, you're out there doing this fun stuff, and I'm not so sure I want to wait for you to come home."

"I guess I don't understand what you're trying to accomplish with this sort of talk."

"You get to be out there being the hero for other people."

"I used to be your hero. Now you're telling me I'm everyone else's hero?"

"I just can't see why you're doing this."

"I don't say shit like that to you when you're doing your work. I never say anything to you unless it's a positively reinforced statement. When it comes to you doing your work..."

"Well, I just can't wait around for you to finish your gallivanting around."

"That's what you said yesterday, too, and the day before that. But we found a way to deal with it."

A long pause. Then I say, "And we will find a way to deal with it when I see you."

"You had the gall to not tell me you'd be in Iowa."

"I didn't have the gall to tell you I was going to be in Iowa? It didn't matter. I'm going to be in Iowa – I could have told you I was going to be in southern California! The ability to leave from wherever I am and come back to Minneapolis is the same no matter where I am."

"I feel like I've wasted the last eight years of my life with you. It's not fair."

"The ride is temporary. That's the part that's fair to you."

"How is that fair to me?"

"It won't last very much longer. It'll be over soon."

While this conversation took you about ten minutes or less to read, these conversations took place at least twenty-five of the fifty days I was away from home. These were the conversations at bedtime, after riding until I was exhausted. The average call time was about thirty minutes. There were a lot of pauses in the conversations.

"Okay," she said, "I'll come on Monday to Phoenix."

"Great," I said, "I'd love it if you could ride with me a couple days."

"I have to come back Tuesday."

"Alright. I'll plan the ride for Monday and Tuesday to Lake Havasu City with you on the back."

Gettysburg, Pennsylvania

Wednesday morning was the first time in a long time that I didn't set an alarm to wake up. This was a day I was looking forward to for almost the entire two and a half years it took to plan this motorcycle ride. This day had gone into the schedule almost right away as the day I spend at Gettysburg.

I rolled into town without a clue. Didn't have any idea where to go, or what would be important to see. I had one thing in my mind: I wanted to see the bed where Lincoln slept when he visited this battle field of the Civil War. I remembered David Wills was the name of the primary architect of the national cemetery and the events surrounding its dedication. He is the lawyer who offered a room to the president on November 18, 1863. It was in this room that Lincoln reportedly put the finishing touches on the famous *Gettysburg Address*. There are five copies in existence today, and these copies are now residing in the Library of Congress, the Abraham Lincoln Presidential Library and Museum, the south wall of the Lincoln Memorial, and one privately owned copy which resides at the Kroch Library at Cornell University.

Lincoln has been a hero of mine since I returned from the Navy. In those days, I was less sure of my life than I am now (not that I have much of a clue about my own life now) and I would attend day-long seminars. In hindsight, these day-long seminars that I would attend were less informative and more sales pitches, but I always learned from them. It was during a sales pitch for a product designed to teach you to read very fast that Lincoln was brought up. The quote they had attributed to Lincoln was, "Everything I want to know is in books; therefore, my best friend is the one who gives me a book I have not yet read."

To this day I have not been able to verify that quote and attribute it to Lincoln. However, it is a good quote.

Within a short time, I found another list of things about

Lincoln. This one read:

> Age 23 – Lost election to state legislature
> Age 24 – Failed in business
> Age 26 – Sweetheart died
> Age 27 – Nervous breakdown
> Age 29 – Lost bid to be speaker of Illinois house
> Age 34 – Lost election to Congress
> Age 39 – Lost election to Congress
> Age 45 – Lost election to US Senate
> Age 47 – Lost bid to be vice-president
> Age 49 – Lost election to US Senate
> Age 51 – Elected president of the US

When I realized what a great man Lincoln is known to be and I saw this list of failures, Lincoln immediately became a source of comfort for me. His speeches became my recreational reading. His antidotes and jokes became the stories of legend for me. I studied everything I could get my hands on including learning about Mary Todd Lincoln, whose very brother was an officer for the Confederates during the war.

One of my favorite stories comes from a book of Linolnania that was published during the great depression by the granddaughter of William Herndon. William Herndon was Lincoln's law partner for twenty years, and upon Lincoln's death, took the responsibility of recording everything he could from every person he could find who ever came in contact with Abraham Lincoln. It's a good bet that every book ever written since 1885 on the subject of Lincoln uses information that was gathered by William Herndon.

Herndon himself drafted a book about Lincoln, but it turned out Herndon was not a very good writer and his booked flopped by all accounts. I cannot find a copy. However, the notes he accumulated by spending twenty years following Lincoln's footsteps and talking with everyone who ever came in contact with Lincoln, are an incredible collection. During the Great Depression, the granddaughter of the law partner of the great Abraham Lincoln earned herself a little money by publishing all of William Herndon's notes.

This book, now eighty years old, contains the exact words of every letter William Herndon wrote, every answer he received, and every un-edited note he wrote when speaking with those people who knew Lincoln, but couldn't read or write; therefore couldn't answer his letters. He traveled the country finding and talking to everyone who ever knew Lincoln.

In this collection of all stories Lincoln, comes the story of a traveler who came into Springfield, Illinois one summer day in the late 1840's. He sat in his saddle while his horse walked a leisurely pace into town. He had just passed a large two-story house, when he heard a door slam once, followed almost immediately by a second slamming. Looking toward the house, he saw the tallest man he'd ever seen running from the back of the house toward town. No sooner had the tall man reached what appeared to be the end of his property than a short, very round woman was seen chasing him, screaming at him, and swinging a meat clever!

Just about that moment, the tall man spotted the rider on the horse, stopped running, grabbed up the little round woman by the back of her house dress, and said, "That'll be all, Woman," and he escorted her back to the house, holding her collar with one hand, and her apron strings with the other. The man telling that story never saw Lincoln again.

I was born in a small farm village myself. I could relate to Lincoln. If Lincoln could do it, so could I, not that I'd ever been chased by a round woman with a meat clever (it's been close!), but I did know what it was like to be poor in a small town.

I was certainly familiar with failure.

Lincoln was invited to come to Gettysburg, Pennsylvania, by David Wills, in the fall of 1863, to say a "few appropriate remarks" to the crowd that would be assembled there for the dedication of the national cemetery.

Here I was in Gettysburg, Pennsylvania. I rolled around casually, until I found the battlefields. I saw on one side of the road the battlefields and those historical markers indicating this or that act of bravery, and on the other side of the road, the tower. While I knew nothing of this tower, I was able to assume that from its perch, the entire battle field could be seen. I wanted to go there.

There's an eerie feeling when you are all alone among thousands of people. At this point in the ride, I still wasn't sure what the ride itself meant. I didn't really understand my place in it. I only knew I had to do it. I was right in the middle of thousands of people who lived there, who traveled there, who were, like me, completely amazed by the place, and I was all alone.

I parked near the base of Longstreet's Tower (also known as Eisenhower's Tower, because it is built on the land that was owned and occupied by President Eisenhower), finding the perfect spot in the shade to leave the bike, I started up the steps with a camera in hand. The tower is called Longstreet's Tower because it is built on the location where General Longstreet's headquarters were set up during the battle. I recorded all that I could on the tiny GoPro camera that I held in my hand as I climbed the seventy-six foot structure.

Once at the top, enjoying and trying to memorize the out-of-this-world view I was absorbing, being sure to record it because even as I looked out on the battlefield, I knew I would forget. I realized I waited too long to eat, and I started to shake.

I turned off the camera and started down. I imagined as I descended what it might be like to pass out from the "hypos" as I had come to call this weird condition whereby I need food. I call it the hypos because that's what Lincoln called his condition. Arguably, Lincoln suffered from what we now call by-polar disorder. In his day, or at least in his writings, he referred to it as the hypos. For him it was depression; for me it was low blood sugar.

Of course, this has never been diagnosed by a doctor for either Lincoln or me, so we're going with this just because we can.

While I did imagine passing out and falling down the steps, most of the images in my mind were comedic. I made it to the bottom without passing out anyway, so it was all good.

Sort of. I was still shaking. The fact that the temperature was eighty-five degrees in the shade didn't help matters much. I opened the trunk of the bike and started digging for anything that had calories. I did find two bags of peanuts and I still had a bottle of water from this morning. I sat in the shade and chewed and drank for about twenty minutes.

Rolling into town, I found the Wills house, which is now a national museum, sitting in the very middle of the town of Gettysburg. I managed to park the motorcycle very near the front door, and decided to stop for ice cream first and then hit the museum. I was still feeling the low sugar weakness, and felt that ice cream would be perfect, given its nutritional value. The bike was directly outside the door of The Cannon Ball Old Tyme Malt Shop.

The stories I was able to share with Greg and Tina (the owners) were a lot of fun, and the feeling of connection to these two in Gettysburg seemed strong.

Greg told me that he searched all of history to find his own personal connection to Gettysburg, since Tina had family who fought there, and his search led him to a man who lived nearby. Turns out, there was a Union messenger traveling from Gettysburg to inform more union troops that reinforcements were needed. This messenger was traveling throughout the day and into the night, when he came upon a farm house. He knocked on the door wearing a soldier's uniform, and the house occupant fired a shot, killing the messenger.

The owner of the farm was charged, and later exonerated for the killing. It was considered self defense. That farm owner was Greg's distant relative.

Talk about shooting the messenger!

Greg and Tina bought me a burger, fries and a fantastic strawberry malt, so if you're ever anywhere nearby, please stop in and buy an ice cream from them. The place is wonderfully historic, and you should hear the history from them.

Yes, it's true, I didn't know anyone there, and having conversations with people was still having conversations with strangers, but walking through the streets left me with the feeling that I was supposed to be here.

I parked the bike near the actual cemetery – the original cemetery. I walked up to the Lincoln monument that has been built there. I walked along the gravesites of the original stones marking those who died in battle. Gettysburg National Cemetery has grown in massive amounts since its beginnings on November 19, 1863, but I managed to stay close to the original plots.

As I walked, all alone, passed those stones that are now one hundred, fifty-five years old, worn as they are, small as they are (those original stones stick out of the grass about three or four inches, and are about twelve inches across left to right and about eight inches across top to bottom), and in some cases, crooked as they are, I was still made to feel very small.

I recorded myself walking there. My actual words took a long time to formulate, but I said to the camera, "There's just something about walking around here that makes me feel like I'm rather insignificant."

When I stood in front of the bed where Lincoln slept, again, I was moved to just stop and be in awe of the circumstances of the man and the moment. I looked at the desk, and tried to imagine what was going through his head as he sat in the chair and did the math so he could tell the people how old our country was. What made him decide to use the language, "four score and seven" when he could have easily and more understandably said, "eighty-seven"? How did he concentrate on the incredible state of the union, with soldiers – US soldiers – dying every day by the thousands, all while his wife was behaving so erratically?

If Lincoln can do it, I can do it.

Out on the street again, I noticed a Harley Davidson dealership just a few feet from the bike. I walked in. Remember, at this point in the trip, I had not stopped in a single Harley Davidson dealership because I had, up to this point, less than good luck talking with them about what I was doing. This time, I decided to walk in. I started talking with the two sales women who were working there, who asked me if I was there for bike week.

"Don't know anything about bike week," I said, "I'm here for this," I said, handing them a brochure.

"I've heard of this," the older one said.

"Turn it over," I instructed, "to see the map. That's what I'm doing right now."

"That's amazing!" the younger one said. Let's be honest, the older one was in her early forties; the younger one was in her late thirties.

"A lot of places I go are really happy to make a small contribution to the cause," I said.

"Oh, you'll have to take that up with the management," the older woman said, "we're just a shirt store here."

"As a coincidence," I said, with all the charm I could muster, "I'm only interested in a shirt. By the way, how do you like mine?" I asked, pulling my vest open to reveal the letters on my shirt, which read;

MY DD214
CAN KICK YOUR
MBA'S ASS

"Well," the older one started to respond slowly, "I don't know what a double D two one four is, so I can't say."

"It's a brotherhood. I can't tell you."

"Oh, that's too bad," the younger one offered.

"I'll tell you what," I offered, again, keeping whatever I considered charm poured on thick, "I'll give you one of mine if you give me one of yours."

"On one condition," the older one leaned forward, putting her elbows on the counter, "tell me what yours means."

"A DD two fourteen is military discharge papers," I said quickly.

"Oh," the said together.

I went out to the bike and found a shirt for them, and traded for a "Battlefield Harley Davidson" T-shirt. Then, I saddled up and pointed the bike toward Philadelphia.

Philadelphia, Pennsylvania

Getting to Philadelphia included many small elements that had no method with which to plan. I started by using GPS on my phone to find a cheap hotel in the area of downtown Philly, because, since I'd never been there before, I wanted to experience the heart of the city. The hotel I found had an attractive price and a phone number. When I called the number, a nice (and defensive) woman answered the phone, and explained that yes, she had a room for rent on a daily basis, and yes, it was available for the night. I explained what I was doing with the Gold Star Ride Foundation and she said she would donate a room. She asked me to call if I was going to be later than sunset.

I set the GPS to guide me to the address, and studied the maps so I had a working knowledge of the area, or so I thought. I plugged in the ear buds and started to ride.

The ride to get there was fantastic. The GPS took me through winding roads and large hills engulfed in massive trees and the sun was going down providing the perfect light for the ride.

GPS was speaking into my ears, but I couldn't look at the maps. GPS told me to turn here, then turn there, then I found myself *leaving* the downtown area of Philadelphia and heading back toward Gettysburg and directly into a blazing sunset. I rode to the next exit from the highway, pulled off and studied the maps.

I was pretty sure I knew what I was doing, so I called the nice lady again, and told her what happened, and said I'd be there in about twenty minutes, even though I was rather certain that I was within a couple blocks the first time around. I started riding again, without the GPS.

Once parked in front of her door, I called again. She met me at the door of her three-story home, and invited me inside.

"This is nice," I said once we had seen the entire place. "I'm a little worried about leaving my motorcycle parked on the street though."

"There's a mini police station right around the corner," she told me. "Maybe they will watch it for you?"

I walked around the corner and found the mini police station. Everything about this downtown was a new experience for me. The buildings were so close together. Beautiful three story houses had no lawns at all. The buildings were so crammed together. The police station was no different.

The mini station, which is what it was actually called, was long and narrow. I walked in the door, and found myself standing on a ramp that led down to the desk area, where there were four desks neatly situated in the room. There was one officer inside, who greeted me as if I was reporting a crime of some minuscule importance.

"I'm with the Gold Star Ride Foundation," I said, handing him a brochure.

"Oh," he responded with some surprise, "How can we help you?"

"I'm in town visiting Gold Star Families," I said, "and I'm staying around the corner. I'm just a little worried about leaving my bike out on the street with so many people walking around."

"Oh, why don't you bring it here?" he asked.

"Inside here?"

"No, around back. I'll show you." He took me through the mini station to the back door, and showed me the place I could park. I liked it immediately and left to get the bike.

Back in my room, I found myself on the phone with MSL. There was some excitement because she was finally coming to visit me on the road.

"I'm booked on the flight to Baltimore tomorrow."

"OK, great," I said, "that's only a two hour ride from here. I'll be there to pick you up."

I performed the rest of my daily routine, which was important today because I had all the video footage of Gettysburg to download to the computer. I fell asleep around one AM.

To Baltimore and Back

I woke up without an alarm and packed the bike. I was in Philly, and I wanted to take advantage of this location, so I rode the three blocks to the downtown area. Some of those cobble streets made riding difficult, but it was worth it. I managed to park the bike on the street between two cars that had left about five feet between the bumpers.

When I returned after touring Independence Hall and visiting the Liberty Bell (something I suggest everyone do), I sat on the bike for a few moments, studying the maps to the Baltimore airport, when a young man in a delivery truck made a comment through an open window about taking my parking spot when I left.

"Sure," I said, "I was just saving it for you!" Of course, there was no way a forty foot truck was going to fit into that "half" parking place where I was.

He put on his flashers, leaving the truck in the driving lane, and walked over to say hi.

"What's with all these stickers on your bike?" he wanted to know. I explained. "I spent eight years in the man's Army," he told me.

"Eight years," I said, "you were almost halfway home."

"Just couldn't do it anymore," he shook his head.

"It's not for everybody. Thank you for your service."

He gave me a perspective on enlisted men in the military that I hadn't heard before, about the degrading way junior enlisted were treated in the Army. My Naval experience wasn't quite like that.

I let out the clutch and rolled toward the toll road that would lead me to Baltimore.

The Delaware Po Po

The road skirted through the Wilmington, Delaware, area and I needed gas, so I stopped. After pumping gas, I noticed the time and thought, "I need to call into the podcast today. I need to find a place to do that."

I rolled a few blocks toward the houses on that busy

street, looking for a quiet place to park. After a few blocks, I turned right, rolled a block, then turned right again. I wasn't far off the main road, but I was happily nestled into a residential neighborhood. It was quiet and the large mature trees offered the nicest shade.

The houses in this neighborhood were big. All of them either two or three stories, all of them with at least three car garages, and all with big trees and large lawns surrounding them. I stopped the bike in the shade, not quite in front of any house in particular.

I had just turned off the engine when my phone rang. "Tony here," I said.

"Hi this is Christy, the Gold Star Mom of Tony."

"Christy? Oh, Christy. I'm planning to see you tomorrow, right?" I asked.

"That's right. I'm just calling to make sure we're still on for that."

"I should be there to meet you at lunchtime," I said, "but I'll call you when I get close to confirm our location and time."

"I think what you're doing is so special. Thank you."

"I'm glad I can do it. I have to call into a radio program now, is there anything else I can share with you today?"

"No, thank you again, I'll see you tomorrow."

I hung up the phone with her – actually, I didn't hang up, I just touched a button that made the call disconnect. I suppose phrases like *hung up the phone* let you know how old I am. Nobody really hangs up any more.

I called into the Tom Barnard Show, podcast number 1421-2, for those of you who like to listen, at about twenty two minutes into the program. We talked about silly things for a while, like movies (like I've had a chance to see any movies) for about ten minutes, when I get disconnected. I call back thirty seconds later to hear a joke about me being wanted for murder, then I have to excuse myself because I see in my rear view mirror that I am now blocked into the street – and can't leave if I want to - by law enforcement. I hang up quickly from the broadcast, saying, "I have to talk with the local law enforcement now."

Two police officers, and I'd mention their race if I thought it mattered, walk toward me with one hand on their hip. A third police officer stands in the open doorway of his patrol car. Two more patrol cars are seen coming around the corner a block away, to make sure I can't go anywhere, I only imagine.

"Are you having some trouble?" the male officer asked as they approached. I disconnected the phone call.

"No, I just stopped here for the shade," I responded. I had been sitting on the bike for the phone call, but I got off the bike and leaned on the seat as they approached. Normally, I think this tiny piece of information is worthless, but when telling the story of interaction with police officers, it seems more important.

"So, everything's alright?" the female officer asked, because when you're talking with police, you have to repeat everything so everyone can be sure.

"I'm a little warmer than I like," I said, "but that'll go away on the highway."

"What are you doing *here*?" she wanted to know.

"I'm traveling the country for Gold Star Families," I started to say.

"I see the stickers on your bike," she says.

"Well, my job is to ride this bike all over the country and do whatever I can for Gold Star Families," I conclude with, "can I get you a flyer from the bag?" Because when you have two police officers, each with a hand on a gun, talking to you, you ask for permission to do anything.

This is a bit of a defining moment for me. As I turn to open the saddle bag, I realize what these houses look like. I realize that the longest amount of time possible for me to have been here is maybe twelve minutes; possibly thirteen. These police officers are not here because they were just in the neighborhood, they were called, and they responded very quickly.

I picked up three brochures from a saddle bag and turned around. The older officer, who had been waiting by his car was now approaching. "Here," I said, handing the brochures to them.

"Oh, I've heard of this," she said, "this is really cool!"

"So, no trouble with the bike?" the older officer asked.

"Bike is fine," I offered.

"So, you just ride around the country?" the young male officer added.

"Yes, I'm on my third week."

"This is really cool," she repeated, then added, "Can we get a picture with you?"

"Sure," I said, being more than a little surprised, "but I get one, too."

The two younger officers and I all reached for our phones at the same time. The young woman asked the older officer to take the pictures.

"Unless you want to be in one," I said, "I don't want you to feel left out."

"Oh, I won't feel left out," he said, lining up the camera.

When the pictures were done, everyone put their phones down, and I looked up at the police cars. There were four of them now, with five police officers. The young officers and the first older officer were standing near me. We had our arms around each other for the picture pose. "I just thought of something," I started, "someone in one of these houses called you."

"Yes, that's right," she said.

"And now they're looking out their window wondering what you're going to do about me," I added. "Now, they see us with our arms around each other."

The two younger officers and I broke into laughter. The older officer just smiled. The other two stayed far away and I don't think they heard me.

"I actually have to be at the Baltimore airport by four," I announced. "Will I make it?"

The two younger officers each looked at their watch. They started to talk to each other about the time, but I didn't really care about that any more. I knew what I was up against, so I put my helmet back on, and swung my leg over the seat.

Yours, Very Sincerely and Respectfully

"You should make it," the younger male officer told me.

"Maybe you could answer one other question," I said, "What's the helmet law here?" This was a question I was asking while strapping the helmet to my head.

"You don't have to wear it, but you have to have it on your bike," she informed me.

"I'm sorry," I started to reply, "I don't have to wear it but I have to have it?"

"That's right. And it needs to be visible on the bike."

"If you don't mind my saying so, that's the dumbest helmet law I've ever heard of," I said.

"We don't write 'em," the young male officer was shaking his head, too.

"Are we done here?" I asked, waving my arm to show them to move their vehicles.

"Oh, yeah, we'll get out of your way," the older officer said, walking back to his car.

I hit the starter and let out the clutch, rolling to the end of the street, where I turned around to see that the older officer was following me. I navigated around him and casually rode back to the highway, giving a big whole arm wave to them all as I rolled passed.

I hit the highway and did my best to make the other cars on the road seem slow, and it didn't take long for the traffic pattern to make everyone go slow. I wrote previously about the young woman who nearly ran me over while texting. That occurred on this part of the trip.

I stopped for all the toll booths, and paid fourteen dollars to get to Baltimore, and didn't feel a single raindrop until I was on the edge of Baltimore, Maryland. In the rain, I pulled into a nearby truck stop to check my maps and messages.

I didn't look at the maps, because MSL had sent me a message from the plane. The message said,

> They're diverting us to Philadelphia because of
> the rain.

I immediately sent her a text back.

I'm in Baltimore. I'll be back to Philly in two hours.

Good news. I didn't have to ride in the rain anymore. Well, not much anyway. The rain dried up by the time I was three miles from that truck stop. I was paying the tolls to ride back the one hundred or so miles to get to Philly.

The day was getting long by the time I pulled into the airport in Philadelphia, but I got there just about the same time MSL came walking out to greet me. She hadn't waited long at all. We strapped her down on the bike – metaphorically speaking – and started to ride west.

We didn't have a plan, or a place we had to be. We had about twenty four hours to do whatever we thought was important. To me, the most important thing was that she was sitting on the bike with me; not getting ready to call me while I was in a cheap motel so we could have one of our nightly conversations.

Even though we hadn't spoken much in the previous weeks, once we were rolling down the road, we didn't talk much there either. We spoke when we needed to, otherwise we just pointed in the direction of whatever we wanted the other to see. We headed west from the airport without much of a plan. It was a good choice. Once the road was moving under us at sixty miles an hour, the scenery was beautiful. It's not the destination; it's the journey.

We rolled along, enjoying the wind and watching the sun sink in the western sky before us. The miles drifted passed, and we didn't even notice that we'd been riding for almost two hours. The bottom of the sun was just starting to touch the horizon and we started realizing the need for a change in plans.

Maybe when I was twenty-five, I could have just kept riding until I ran out of gas, but that was more than half my life ago. "We better find a place to stay," I said, above the sound of the wind and the bike.

"I'm hungry, too," she added.

"I'll stop at the next motel I see," I said, thinking that was a good plan. The motel appeared a few minutes later, just after we passed the city limit sign identifying *Paradise, Pennsylvania*. You'd think it was an omen, and maybe it was; or maybe it was ironic.

The owner would have nothing to do with a donation, and it turned out to be a dive. The sort of dive I would stay in by myself, but I'd never want to ask MSL to stay there; but we did. To give you an idea of the sort of motel this was, we walked by a vending machine on our way to the room – and it was completely sold out. Not a single chip left in it. When I went looking for the ice machine, I learned that they didn't have one. The TV only played local channels, and it was a TV that featured a cathode ray tube. For those of you too young to remember, that was the really big TV technology; the kind of TV that has a screen three feet away from the wall. To their credit, the TV did have a working remote control.

The owner of the motel said we could find food just a little ways down the road, so we unpacked the bike, then got back on it to go find food. The sun must have gone down much later than we had anticipated, because restaurant after restaurant was closed.

Of course, as we looked for the restaurant, we drove by six more motels, all of which gave the impression that they were nicer than the one we chose.

After twenty minutes of looking, MSL pointed to a truck stop and said, "Go there." I obeyed.

I've been in many truck stops in my lifetime. This wasn't much of a truck stop. It was a glorified gas station with parking for about ten big trucks out back. There was no restaurant; however, they did have a food counter that pretended to have hot, fresh food in it. She chose a couple pieces of chicken and an ear of corn. I chose the chicken with a baked potato.

One other thing that showed up at this truck stop, while we were milling around, looking for nothing and finding most of it, was a bandana. Up to this point, I'd been wearing a black bandana, but I found a nice red, white, and blue number which featured stars and stripes. I folded it, wrapped it around my head and tied it.

"That completely changes your look," she told me. I was ready for the change.

We packed up our food and a few bottles of water and headed back to the motel. Unfortunately, a bad meal will have an effect on your mood. Our fresh, hot meal was neither fresh nor hot, and our mood changed to match our meal. Most of our conversation in the motel that night was just like the conversations we had on the phone.

In the morning, I turned on my laptop and suggested we go visit a place just up the road before we head to the airport. Sort of like a mini vacation for an hour or two that we were still together on the road. She thought that would be a good way to spend the day, so I wrote the directions on a small piece of paper that would sit on my gas tank, and we packed up the bike again.

The view of the mountains around Paradise, Pennsylvania was very enjoyable. We may struggle to find things in common, her and me, but this was one thing we liked. An hour later, we pulled in to the parking lot of our destination.

We were about to start a tour when an employee said, "You came on your motorcycle?"

"Yes," I said.

"Aren't you worried about the rain?" she asked.

"Well, I wasn't worried about it until just now," I said. I sat down and looked at my phone's weather radar app. Ouch. Everything around us was green, and there was a lot of darker green coming toward us. Green is the color of rain, and dark green is heavy rain. Yellow, orange and red are more severe storms. While it wasn't close to us, there was yellow on the radar map, too.

"Dear," I said, "we're going to have to make a move."

"What's going on?" she wanted to know.

"Rain. And lots of it. What airport do we need to get to tonight?"

"Baltimore," she said.

"What time?"

"I need to be there by four."

"And would you like to arrive wet?" I asked, already aware of the answer.

"No. Can we get around it?"

"Let me study for a minute or two," I said, but I could feel myself becoming agitated. I finally had a chance to spend some quality time with MSL and the weather was planning a rain dance.

Sometimes I get lucky and I'll be the first to admit it. I studied the route to the airport, and I studied the weather radar. In the Navy, I was a weather forecaster, and that particular skill was coming in handy as I studied.

After about ten minutes, while she was taking in the local sites, I said, "Let's go." She followed me to the bike.

"What did you find out?"

"I found out that the entire western half of Pennsylvania is getting wet, and it's going to get wetter. That rain is going to pound us and there really isn't much we can do about it."

"We're going to get wet?"

"We are," I said matter-of-factly. "But maybe we can get lucky. You see this spot where there isn't any rain?" I pointed to the weather radar on my phone. I tiny spot without green was right in the middle of that large area of green covering my phone.

"Yeah," she said.

"You know, it's not raining there, right?"

"Yeah."

"That's where we are now. I think that little circle of no rain will move this way, and I've found all the local and county roads we need to take to stay inside that little circle of no rain."

"I'll keep my fingers crossed," she offered.

"So, let's pack up to get wet," I said, removing all the cameras from the bike and packing anything not waterproof into the saddle bags. "Can you ask them for a garbage bag?" I asked.

"Do you have some garbage?" she asked me.

"No, I'll use it to waterproof your backpack."

With that done, we were on the bike, rolling out the driveway. A few raindrops hit the windshield. "Here it comes," I said. I could feel her sigh.

We rolled on to the gate of the place, and the rain stopped. The clouds were all around us; not even a little tiny piece of blue sky. I was ready for it to open up, but I was hoping it wouldn't.

I turned right. Then left. We were out in the farm country. No streetlights, no traffic lights, not much of anything but fields in every direction. We were on a two lane road with very little traffic. These roads were designed for farm trucks and tractors. We came across a few of each of those.

We came to a stop sign. I looked at my directions on the little note stuck inside my gas cap, and turned left.

An hour passed, and still we were dry. The airport was a three hour ride from our starting point. We were *still* dry.

Every twenty minutes or so, MSL would pat me on the shoulder and say, "Good job," like it was really me who was keeping us dry. We could actually see the rain falling about a mile away in every direction. The road was wet, but we were still dry.

We didn't want to go on the interstate highway, but there really wasn't any choice. We rolled down Interstate Eighty-Three into downtown Baltimore. I'm not sure why the GPS took us that way, but it did. Sprinkles started hitting us just as we pulled off the interstate into downtown. We rolled to a stop at the first traffic light, which was red, and the road was inclined; we were facing uphill.

Then, just as we came to a stop, the clouds opened up with all the fury of a summer thunderstorm.

Being wet is not that big a deal, as any biker will tell you; a road changing from dry bricks to slick rectangles of grease, however, is a slightly different experience. Even with the slippery roads, that wasn't the toughest challenge. Being overloaded on the bike wasn't the toughest challenge either. With the rain falling that hard, the biggest challenge was visibility. My glasses had water streaming off them, and so did the windshield on the bike. The windshield also found this opportunity to fog up on the inside. Add to that the good people of Baltimore are not the most courteous drivers, and things get a little hairy.

I was looking for any opportunity for conditions to improve, but now we were also right down to the wire for MSL to catch her plane.

The next intersection also had a red light. And the next one. And the next one. I was moving a block at a time, on slippery roads, with moods changing from a little anxious to extremely tense, and the rain was not in the mood to fall lightly.

Ten blocks, stopping at every intersection, getting wet – no, getting soaked – and doing a miraculous job of not getting hit by a car, were behind us as I came to a stop at yet another red light. "I'm stopping there," I said, pointing to a gas station on the right that had a shelter above the gas pumps. We didn't need the gas, but I needed to get out of the rain for a minute or two.

Once stopped, she said, "I should probably take a private taxi from here." She started looking at her phone.

"You check that, I'll check the radar."

We didn't talk much more than that, each of us trying to dry our glasses.

"Driver will be here in three blocks," she said.

"And the airport is fifteen minutes away," I offered.

"And my plane leaves in an hour and a half," she said. We have flown enough to know that two hours in a busy airport is often not enough to get through security in time to catch a plane.

Three weeks were nearly completed on this ride, and I hadn't spent any quality time with her for ten days. The last time she flew out to meet me was in Cleveland, and that day rained, too. Now, we'd managed to be together for less than twenty-four hours, and she was leaving again, and it was raining again, and I didn't know when I'd get to see her again.

The private driver pulled up, and I opened the back door for her, hugged her tight, told her I loved her, and let her get in the car. Then I opened the front door. The driver was a forty-something woman. "Make sure you take good care of her," I said.

"Oh, I will," she replied.

"She's the most important person in my world and I'd hate to have to come and find you." I knew the words would have a different meaning coming from a man with a three day beard, soaking wet, and covered in leather from chin to toe.

"OK," she said timidly.

Then I winked at her, and she smiled.

The car disappeared with me standing on the sidewalk in Baltimore, apparently not smart enough to get in out of the rain. I stood there watching the car disappear, then stood there staring in that direction for a minute or two after they were gone.

I was alone again.

I saw the casino across the street and went there. I parked in the garage and walked in all wet. I was hungry, too.

I tried to be pleasant to everyone I talked to, but quite frankly, you'd have to ask them if I was successful. I know I was thinking about an old quote as I walked into the casino on the third floor:

> *Take a man when he is wet and hungry; if he is amiable then, dry him and fill him up, and you've got an angel*

and I had hoped I was amiable, walking in so wet and hungry, and it wasn't the first time, but I know I felt lonely.

I was less wet and a little more nutritionally satisfied when I left, and I set my GPS to get me out of there. It was still rush hour, and I tried to pick a road that would keep me out of traffic and off the freeway.

The roads were bumpy. Probably the worst roads in the entire country were the roads I traveled leaving there. I wasn't sure I should do it, but Washington, DC, was in between where I was and where I was going, so I pointed that way. The rain was all cleared now, and the sky was blue and beautiful.

As wonderful as the weather had become, the opposite was true of the roads, which sucked! I don't think my wheels made a full rotation without hitting a bump for three hours!

GPS sucked! I stopped every fifteen to twenty minutes to ask that stupid thing where the heck I was. This was one of the most challenging days of riding. Started out great with MSL on the back, then dodging the rain for three hours, then getting wet, then bad GPS and bumpy roads, then DC, which, looking back, I should have gone around. I did go right to the Mall, though, then went right under it and popped out the other side.

Finally out of the city, which seemed like I had been in it for days, the road opened up and I rolled south.

I slept that night in a small town called Warrenton, Virginia. The name of the place was Rip Van Winkle, which I thought had a nice ring to it. The owner, although he thought what I was doing was awesome, didn't think donating a room was a good idea. It was already dark, so I didn't argue.

The room had a nasty smell. I spent the first hour downloading my video to the computer with the door open, trying to get fresh air inside. I had no phone service here either, unless I went outside and walked fifteen or so feet to the edge of the property, which came with the added inconvenience of standing next to traffic, which wasn't much being in a small town, but it was something. That's where I was when I called MSL.

We both had the same thoughts this night. We missed each other.

The fog rolled in overnight, so when I started about thirty minutes before daylight, I was wearing full leathers and riding in poor visibility, but Christy was expecting me for lunch, so ride I did.

Chapter Nine: Smaller, But Significant Stories

Singers Singing a Sad, Sad Song

Sometimes, life throws lemons at you. Of course, it is a metaphor, and of course, the cliché is to make lemonade.

I rolled down Fisher Road Northeast, and stopped at Capitol Inn and Suites, in Salem, Oregon. The owner there was kind enough to donate a room to the Foundation, but it came with its own complications. First, he said to meet him at his other hotel, because this one was full. At the other hotel, which wasn't far away, he said we should go back to the Capitol Inn.

The Capitol Inn and Suites is a little difficult to take when you first walk up to the doors. The parking lot is filled with pot holes, the front doors need repair, and the lobby is under RE-construction with lumber and broken furniture in all sorts of madness. The overall look of the place is one that would make you want to turn and run.

The room, itself, on the other hand, is where this new owner spent his time and effort. The room was very comfortable, with what seemed to be a relatively new bed and furniture. The TV and WiFi were above average hotel fodder. The room was incredibly quiet, even though when I looked out the window, I could see the heavy traffic on Interstate Five.

Still, I was thankful for the room, and a little concerned that I would wake up tomorrow and find that I no longer had a bike. I found myself walking outside the front door to sit on the bike three or four times throughout the evening, even though it was parked in the valet area of the front door. (No, there was not a valet.)

The three men trying to fix a car two parking spots away from the bike could not be ignored, but the two men in the adjacent parking spot to the bike were, shall we say, interesting?

Each time I went outside to check on the bike, I was greeted by those two men who would never be accused of

---

spending a lot of money on their clothes. The white man wore his hat backwards so I could see the adjustment strap and know just how big his head was. The Black man sat quietly smoking and sipping. The white man was in his late twenties. The Black man was in his sixties. Both were occupying the parking spot adjacent to my bike. The older man sitting in a folding lawn chair, the younger man was constantly pacing left and right.

"I'm Tony," I said, sticking my hand out toward the seated man. We talked for a little bit, and I asked if I could make a little movie. They agreed.

"Tell me your name," I said, first to the seated man.

"Greg," he said, "I'm born and raised in Mount Pleasant, Texas. I know every Cowboy who ever played the game!"

"Never you mind about those damn Cowboys," the other man offered.

"Tell me your name and where are you from," I instructed.

"I'm Jared and I'm from Gary, Indiana, Chicago, Atlanta, Houston, Texas, all over."

"Where are we now?" I asked to keep the recording going.

"We are in Salem, Oregon," Jared announced, as if it was his job to announce such things.

"Salem, Oregon," I repeated.

"Salem, Oregon," Greg repeated.

"It's pretty soft from where I come from," Jared said.

"But it's not where you at, it's who you are," Greg instructed.

"Home is what you make it, right?" Jared offered.

The spoke very quickly back and forth.

"Nuttin' better under the sun," Greg said, then, with his elbows propped up on the arm rests of the lawn chair in which he was planted, started to sway his hands back and forth. "Papa was a rollin' stone," he sang, "wherever he lay his hat was his home."

"I know that," I said, trying to be one of them, but it

was feeble.

"It's real though," Greg added, no longer singing.

Jared started a monologue, "We come from a different place, man. We got that southern hospitality and we try to bring that here to where we are."

"And where are we?" I wondered out loud.

"I don't give a sh... wait," Greg pronounced the S-H without pronouncing the I-T, "hold on and let me think."

"We at the Capitol Inn and Suites," Jared informed, unaware that he failed to use a verb.

"The Capitol Inn and Suites," Greg repeated. Then Greg offered, "and this boy," shaking a pointed finger at Jared, "has got it."

"Got what?" I asked.

CLANK! "Damn!" one of the guys fixing the car dropped a wrench on the ground and made sure to let us know about his disappointment.

"Listen," I said, "I'm gonna post this video on social media and both of my friends are gonna like it."

"It's going viral," Greg offered.

"We're going viral," Jared complimented

"It's going viral," Greg repeated. "Show him your stuff," he said to Jared.

Jared didn't wait or waste time. He started swaying back and forth just enough to show a rhythm. "Bmpt schtt bmpt schtt," he repeated a few times, then without stopping his swaying, he started rapping:

Will somebody please tell me my words mean somthin'
Speakin' all your words now, homie, tell me why they never
mean nothin'.
You coulda caught me in the streets bumpin',
But speakin' all your words now again,
Tell me why they never mean nothin'?
...
No discrimination; I'm hatin' on every faction
Every fraction of life that ain't with this pain I'm packin'
You got the passion a-Christ, you see my pain and you

laughin'

...

If you truly loved me you woulda worked to make somethin work
You wouldn't worry about nothin'; you woulda put me first.
But I'm back to the old me who thinks he's cursed.
Went back to the same dude who put your new boo under six feet of dirt
Tell anybody here and go ahead try me, watch shit get worst.
My voice is a little tired but I do anything aside to make sure the fam don't shine
This is for everybody who died from Day Day to Tye
I'm gonna do everything I can to keep your names alive.

Now, I've dabbled in the music business a bit going back to the eighties, so I've heard a tale or two about street musicians, and mostly how bad they are; never how good they are. With Jared, I was really impressed.

It's possible that what impressed me the most about Jared was that last line, *I'm gonna do everything I can to keep your names alive.* With this, I knew I had more in common with this homeless man in Salem, Oregon, than I did in contrast. Even if he didn't rap about people whose lives are lost in the military and the same is true about Greg.

"I'll watch over that bike;" Greg said, "make sure nothin' happens to it all night."

I slept soundly all night. Woke up when I wanted to, and went outside when I was ready to go, and I found Greg sitting in his lawn chair in the parking space next to my bike, just as he had been the night before. Nothing on the bike had been touched.

I just felt like it was going to be an awesome day.

Richard's Coffee Shop, Mooresville, NC

There were moments on the road that were so emotionally charged that I needed to insert them into this story; their own story. Richard's Coffee Shop in North Carolina was one of those.

I had finished with Gold Star Families for the day, and started south again, hoping to make it to Savannah, Georgia, then on to Jacksonville, Florida, where I was hoping to stop by the local television station for a little blurb on the news (I was invited). I stopped at a motel two hours south and east of Charlotte, North Carolina, in the small town of Laurinburg, North Carolina. The motel would not donate the room, but they did donate a few other things. For example, they printed some documents for me, and they did my laundry for me. I was waiting for clean clothes when someone reached out to me.

"I heard you were traveling the country honoring Gold Star Families," he started.

"I am," I replied.

"I'd like you to stop and see us at Richard's Coffee Shop," he said.

"We've been known to make stops like that," I said.

"We'll be waiting here for you tomorrow," he said.

"I'll be there as soon as I can tomorrow. My map program says you're a four hour drive. I should be there shortly after noon."

I didn't know what was in store for me. After making those plans, I looked over the itinerary for the rest of the week. Savannah, then Jacksonville, then a few days rolling around Florida, then heading west next week along the Gulf States. It looked like things were shaping into a rhythm, and I could handle a little rhythm. That's when the phone rang. MSL had different things to discuss, all of which were listed in a previous chapter, so I won't list them here. After about thirty minutes of that negative talk on the phone, I set my alarm and went to sleep.

I loaded up the bike at first light, and off I went back to the north side of Charlotte, North Carolina. This is where I woke up the day before. I felt a little, well, silly, when I thought about all that riding I did, seemingly for nothing.

There's always a rhyme and reason; often I just don't know it. Ask God.

I was late arriving at Richard's Coffee Shop, but when I found it, the person who had invited me was nowhere to be seen. The people that were there, well, they didn't know I was coming.

"We're about to lock up," he told me, "not many people come in for coffee this late in the day."

I glanced around for a clock on the wall. Found one. It was thirty minutes passed one.

"Okay," I said, "I get that. But would you mind horribly if I just take a couple pictures since I'm here? I'll be three hundred miles away by tomorrow at this time."

"Okay, come in," I followed instructions and entered. I was carrying my GoPole, which is the fancy name for the selfie stick that GoPro camera people provided for me.

"As you can see," he started a semi guided tour for one, "we have displays here in order, of every major military involvement the United States has been in since 1775. This is not the uniform George Washington wore, but it is exactly like it. Over here, we have uniforms from the War of 1812." He didn't slow his cadence as we moved through the coffee shop, which, at this point, did not have an odor of coffee.

"This is Chief Warrant Officer Richard Warren. He flew a Huey in Vietnam." We were stopped in front of a large portrait of a man with white hair, mustache, and wire rimmed glasses. "He originally named the place 'Pat's Gourmet Coffee House' after his wife, Pat. But after Richard passed away in 2009 from issues with Agent Orange, a bunch of us regulars got together to make sure his dream didn't die, too." My guide was on a roll now, there was no sign that he started this tour by telling me he was closing the coffee shop for the day.

"Richard made it a point to welcome anyone who came in for coffee with a traditional Veterans' Greeting. *The State*, which is a state wide magazine here in North Carolina, said Pat's Gourmet Coffee House was the most patriotic coffee shop in America. It is today the only non-profit coffee shop and living military museum in the entire country."

He paused for a moment while my head started spinning toward all the different niches in the shop. The place was larger than the average coffee shop, but only a little, and every square inch of the walls was covered with something from one war or another. Niche after niche surrounded the half dozen or so folding banquet tables that were centered in the coffee shop.

This place is amazing! I was shown the flags set into displays from local Gold Star Families to represent the local people who had volunteered and lost their lives in the Middle East. I saw collections of ribbons and medals from military men and women from the Korean War (which, incidentally, is still being fought as I mentioned in the chapter about Lockport). I saw flags, posters, and photographs from every possible era.

The Civil War was represented along an entire wall. Vietnam had its own place as well, complete with autographs of every Vietnam Vet who had ever stopped in for coffee.

There are framed newspapers announcing the most important military news. For example, and this seems a little odd, but the framed headline HITLER DEAD is only a few feet away from another newspaper headline: FDR DIES. Both of these headlines are mounted to a wall above which flies a six foot replica of a World War II fighter plane.

"You see this?" he asked me.

"I do," I answered.

"This is the bombardiers' scope from a B seventeen bomber."

I looked at the black device that resembled an old movie projector sitting on its side, displayed under a glass box.

"And now, this here," he said, guiding me about six inches left, "this is a special interest. This is Thomas Ferebee," he said.

"Is he, or was he famous?" I asked, looking at the framed picture which had an autographed eight by ten black and white picture in it.

"He was the bombardier in the Enola Gay," he said.

"The plane that dropped the bomb?" I asked, my voice going up a bit.

"The very same one. He grew up just down the road from here. This is Ferebee, who slept in the plane the night before the bombing, and the night after the bombing, and after the war, he stayed in the service. It was the Army Air Corp then. He retired a full Colonel after about twenty five years.

"Colonel Tibbets was the pilot, and he lived just a few miles down here," he said, pointing at the wall, but indicating a far off place. "This ninety-some year old woman knew him, and knew all the guys in the crew, because they come to visit; have reunions up here, and she knew all of 'em, or almost all of 'em."

"That's a pretty big piece of history," I mumbled after a moment or two of silence.

"It's considered local," he explained.

I took as many pictures as I could, made as much movie as I could, and purchased a shirt from the store. "U S Navy," I told him as we looked at the variety of shirts they had for sale.

"You served in the Navy?" he asked me.

"Yes. I've never had a Navy T-shirt," I said, "I figure I should have one now."

We finished choosing the shirt, "Come with me," he instructed.

We walked up to the coffee counter, because it is a coffee shop, remember? He went behind the counter, coming back out in seconds. He approached me squarely and we stood face to face.

"Now," he began, "I'm gonna welcome you home." He held a small key chain stretched between both hands so that I could easily see it. Two strands of beads, varying in red, white, and blue colors. First, he held out the red and white beads saying, "This represents the flag we sailed under," then he flipped it over to reveal the blue and white string of beads, "This represents your Navy service." He stretched his left hand toward mine, "Let me have your left hand and your right hand," he gripped my left hand with his, holding the key chain between our joined left hands, and grabbed my right hand with his right hand. With our arms crossed, he shook both hands once and said, "Welcome aboard," then shook both hands once again saying, "Thank you for your service." He shook both hands again, one time, saying, "We leave our rank and our politics outside," he shook hands one more time, "God's always welcome," and he shook hands again, "Because we don't have atheists in foxholes or firefights," and he shook them again one time, "Again, Thank you for your service," then got animated. The shaking of the hands was more pronounced; assertive, but still only once, and he spoke again, "Welcome Home," one shake, "Welcome Aboard," one shake, "You're now a member of this place," and then he shook my hands one last time and released.

As complicated as it was to read that paragraph, or as complicated as it was to write that paragraph, it does not come close to the complications I felt at that moment. It had been ten thousand, sixty-four days since I came home from the Navy. More than twenty eight years. No one had ever given me such a formal, sincere, heartfelt welcome. I was shaking, just a little bit.

The Sisters in Oregon

Some days, you just feel like the ride is perfect. There was a day in Oregon that felt like that. I started the day with mountains all around me, but I wasn't riding in or on the mountains. I was in a high plain, and I followed that route for three hours.

Three hours later, I found myself in a gas station which was not able to donate any gas, and I was in Oregon, where self-service gas stations don't exist.

I had phone service for the first time in a few days, so I spent a little time talking with MSL. The call was a little like a long awaited reuniting that both of us had been waiting patiently to have. For reasons I cannot explain, I felt very optimistic about the day before me, even with empty bank accounts.

I pulled away from the gas station and rolled down the road and without any thoughts one way or another, the bike pulled into a restaurant. I wasn't necessarily thinking about food, but here I was.

The place was called Rigoberto's Taco Shop. Hindsight being all things it is, I guess the name of the place was rather unusual, at least to me.

Once inside, I was greeted warmly by a nice woman, who appeared to be a Latina (surprise – it was a Mexican restaurant) and although it didn't seem likely when I heard the Spanish accent that she would understand me, I told her about the Gold Star Ride Foundation anyway. She smiled and donated my breakfast.

It was a good thing, too, because it was a hearty breakfast, and I ate every morsel of it. Getting back on the bike, I headed toward Oregon Route two-forty-two and followed the signs toward *Sisters*.

Sisters is the name given to the route, and it's because of the twin peaked mountains named *North Sister* and *South Sister*, which the highway circles around to the north. Normally, I wouldn't write about a specific mountain or two, but this warrants sharing.

Remember, I was in the high plains area between Burns and Bend, Oregon, and now I was headed down the mountainous area toward Salem. Oregon is such a magnificent place; I wish I had more time to spend there. Just outside of Bend, on the aforementioned route, the road started to descend. I like mountain roads as much as the next guy, but I wasn't prepared for this.

I downshifted, accelerated, leaned left, leaned left again, upshifted, leaned right, accelerated, downshifted, braked, upshifted, leaned left, leaned right, accelerated, upshifted, over and over and over again.

On a good ride, this activity may be repeated for fifteen minutes. In Minnesota, this ride couldn't happen without some significant travel involved. Here I was, upshifting, down-shifting, leaning left, leaning right, braking, and accelerating over and over again. The only part of riding that I did not do on this road was cruise straight with a steady speed.

After two hours of riding, I stopped at a wide spot on the road, and just looked around in awe of the place. I was looking at giant trees, huge mountains, and a bright red ball in the sky crossing from the east.

I started riding again and the same thing continued.

Four hours after I started riding down this hill, with all

the curves, shifting, braking, accelerating, and leaning again, (and passing through one of my favorite small town names, Nimrod) I found myself in Lebanon, Oregon, and pulled into a grocery store parking lot. It took four hours to go just under a hundred miles. That's an *average* speed of twenty-five miles an hour.

I'd been riding for almost six weeks when I stopped in this parking lot, but I still wasn't prepared for what I had just gone through. Four hours of aggressive riding on an eleven-hundred pound machine. I put the kickstand down on the edge of the parking lot, pulled myself off the bike, and laid myself down on the pavement.

I could feel my body shaking. I wondered if I could have made the trip at all without that wonderful breakfast.

While the sound of traffic around me piqued my curiosity, I forced myself to stay on the ground for at least two songs.

I did get up and go inside the store. I found a snack that looked nutritious and sat at a picnic table outside the front door and rested. I stayed there, resting, almost an hour.

The best part of this story is, I'd been riding six hours, and I had nearly completed all the riding I was going to do today. Salem was just down the road, and I was meeting Gold Star Families there.

Lindsey's Restaurant, Van Horn, Texas

"I'm a lucky man," David began, "and I know I'm a lucky man, and I'll tell you why I'm a lucky man."

David was an interesting fellow, who I had only known about three minutes before I heard that line come out of his mouth. I had just finished eating lunch that he made in his restaurant and I had shared with my waitress that I was with the Gold Star Ride Foundation, and I gave her a brochure.

"You'll want to talk to David," she explained, in a thick Spanish accent.

"Could I have another bottle of water, too?" I asked, as she quickly carried the brochure to David. It didn't take long

---

for him to stop what he was doing to come out to sit with me.

His first minute and a half was spent checking me out. You can never be too careful, right? "So," he spoke very softly and deliberately, "you've been riding your motorcycle across the country?"

"I have," I said, also speaking softly and slowly. Not as deliberately, though.

"And you stopped here? How is it that you stopped here?"

"I left San Antonio this morning," I said, "riding up US Highway Ninety. I didn't want to stop at the chain restaurants; I like local food wherever I go in the world. So, I came into Van Horn looking for some good food. And I found it."

"Thank you. I enjoy cooking. It's not what I've always done, but I like what I do now."

He paused a very pregnant pause, and I was about to say anything to break the silence when he broke the silence telling me how lucky he was.

"God has taken care of me," he spoke with a Spanish accent, but not much of one. Just enough to let me know that Spanish was his first language, but he had clearly been speaking English a very long time.

David was a short man, about five feet five inches tall, with a round, weather beaten face and a complexion that showed years of working outdoors. These things made me think he was older than I was, but I never did learn his age.

"I had a landscaping business in Grand Prairie, [Texas]," he explained, "and I was doing well. I had maybe twenty employees, and I was making a lot of money. And then, business started to slip, and I started drinking. It slipped some more, and I started drinking some more, and the more business would slip, the more I would drink. Pretty soon, I had no business, but I was still drinking."

I was thinking, "and you're lucky?" but he continued the story.

"I didn't know what I was going to do," he spoke with the attitude that suggested there was some sort of happy ending to this story. "I lost my house next."

I glanced around at where we were. This restaurant looked like every bar from every old time western movie I ever saw, except there was no swinging doors, and there was glass in the windows. The other side of those windows featured a small town where tumble weeds were the peak activity of the day, with a side order of dust and heat. Sure, my meal was good, but this town was a ghost town waiting to happen. There were not many inhabitants in this town. (Incidentally, the 2010 census puts the population at just over two thousand people, down by nearly five hundred from the 2000 census.)

"After a few months," David was still telling his story, "I was looking for a way to commit suicide. I wanted to end my own life."

That got my attention.

"I was writing the note," he said, leaning over and digging in his pockets. He produced a folded up piece of lined paper and shook it at me. "When the phone rang," he paused his story and put the paper back in his hind pocket. "It was a friend of mine. He told me he fired his manager of his restaurant and he wanted me to go run it.

"He called me, and asked me to run his restaurant when I had the note written and the gun on the desk."

I looked at him a started to raise just one eye brow when he continued, "I know, right? I've never run a restaurant before. I don't know what I'm doing."

"You must have learned quick!" I interrupted, "because I liked what I ate."

"I learned fast," he said, nodding. "And after a month, I called him and told him I would try it for three months. That was seven years ago."

"And did you buy it from your friend?" I asked.

"Yes, I did. I bought it after eleven months. And I know I was lucky," he brought me back to being lucky. "My wife and my daughter help here, and my daughter will leave in the fall because she has been accepted in college. She's the first one of my family to go to college."

"That's pretty awesome," I said.

"I told you I was lucky," he continued, "come over here.

This place is famous," we walked across the tiny restaurant together, passed all six tables.

"After I took over, Tommy Lee Jones came and asked to make a movie here. These are the pictures of Tommy Lee Jones and the rest of the cast. This is the newspaper story."

"So, you took a run-down restaurant and made it famous?" I asked; more to prove I was still listening than anything else.

"I did," he said. I took a picture with the two of us, with all the famous pictures in the background.

The movie is called *The Three Burials of Melquiades Estrada.*

"God took care of me," he continued as we walked back to the table where we started, "so I take care of other people. I'm buying your lunch today, just like a few years ago, when a couple of young people came in and they were broke. I fed them and they had little kids, so I gave them five hundred dollars to make sure they got down the road. When people come in here hard on their luck, I remember when I was hard on my luck, too, and I help them."

Conoco Gas, Wamsutter, Wyoming

I handed the woman behind the counter a brochure. She looked at me a little funny, not noticing the brochure much. "I'm traveling the country honoring our nation's fallen heroes by taking care of their families," I said.

"Oh!" she said, getting excited after listening to me.

"I like to tell people that before I pump my gas because once I didn't and they got mad at me because apparently they wanted to buy the gas for me. It is a charity after all."

"Are you thirsty, Sweetheart?" she asked, in a way that sounded like Georgia, but I knew we were in Wyoming. "Why don't you get yourself something to drink?"

"OK, thank you, I will," and I turned around to get a water from the refrigerated door and then came back to the counter. That's when I noticed her name tag: Bobby Jo. "Do you know about Gold Star Families?" I asked.

"Yes, I do. I'm very supportive of our military. My

whole family is. My sisters, Betty Jo and Billy Jo, we do a fund raiser every year to help veterans."

"Oh, that's so wonderful of you to do that!" I said with sincerity, "and your sisters are Betty and Billy? And you are Bobby Jo? I think your parents had a sense of humor."

"*Petticoat Junction*," she said, nodding and rolling her eyes. "But we have a lot of fun with that, too."

(If you who are not sure about this reference, there was a TV show created by Paul Henning, who also created such wonderful gems as *Green Acres, The Beverly Hillbillies,* and *the Andy Griffith Show.* He did many more as well. You could say he was the Chuck Lorre of the 1950's and 60's. *Petticoat Junction* was the story around a single mom operating the Shady Rest Hotel in the middle of nowhere with her three teenage daughters. It had a small town feel and it was on TV for seven years.)

I laughed a small laugh, and kept on smiling. It was still early in my day, having just started the day a few miles back – and by a few, I mean seventy-five.

"How much gas do you need Honey?" she asked, as I gulped down the water.

"No more than four gallons," I said, returning the cap to the bottle.

"OK, I've got it covered," she said.

"How much do I owe you for the water?"

"I got that, too," she said, "I just love what you're doing, and I wish I could do more."

"Tell some people," I offered. "You'd be surprised how on any given day, I might talk to twenty people, and nineteen of them don't have any idea what a Gold Star Family is."

"Oh, but around here, we've got a military base, and everyone loves our military, so they all know."

"Not always. I tell military people with some regularity about what we do and what Gold Star Families are. I even, one time, told a Gold Star Dad that he was a Gold Star Dad. He didn't know what it was."

"Oh, that's just too bad," she said.

"I'll pump my gas right there," I said, pointing out the

window to the bike.

"It's all ready, Honey," she said, nodding her head.

"I'll never forget you, Bobby Jo," I said and I meant it. I smiled as I walked out to the bike, remembering the beautiful white Samoyed my son and I had when he was little. The dog's name was Bobby Jo. I didn't tell Bobby Jo that I once had a dog named Bobby Jo. That's just not something you do.

I smiled about that for a long time. I rode after leaving there about five hours before stopping in Colorado. I thought about all the wonderful years I had with Bobby Jo (my dog) most of those hours. It's the smallest things that give you the greatest strength to do what has been put before you to do.

Sundowner Motel, Burns, Oregon

Six hundred, nineteen miles. That's what the map program said was the distance I had to ride that day. It was all at various places in the Rocky Mountains, so it was going to be a pretty ride. The destination today is Bend. There was some talk of a large group of Gold Star Families meeting me there, so that was the goal.

Eight hours into the ride, I filled my tank just on the north side of Boise, Idaho, and headed west.

The law changes when you cross certain state lines, and I did not have to, by law, put my helmet on for a long time this day. The last state to require a helmet was Tennessee. That was three weeks ago. Going into Oregon, I knew I'd have to stop and put it on, and sure enough, as soon as I crossed the state line, I found a law enforcement officer behind me and closing the gap. I turned off the road to the right when he was still a block and a half behind me, and I saw him turn right at the same time. I thought he was trying to "head me off at the pass" as they say. I stopped the bike in the parking lot of a hardware store in the little town of Nyssa, Oregon.

I walked into the Nyssa Coop Supply store, covered in leather, bandana on my head, sunglasses hiding my eyes, and said, "Where might I find a ball cap?" I'm not sure they weren't completely stunned.

"You mean like a baseball cap?" one young employee decided to respond.

"Yes. I'm riding west, and I could use a sun visor as I go."

"Oh, follow me," he offered, jumping down from his seated perch on the counter near the cash register and leading me around the corner.

I thanked him for the hat, and adjusted it for my larger than average head, and put it on. Then, I put on the helmet, which seemed to fit over the hat rather comfortably, all things considered. I saddled up and off I went, with helmet on, and sun visor in place. It was a really good idea.

Oh, that law enforcement person? Yeah, he saw me pull out with the helmet on and then he disappeared as well.

I started riding into the mountains, not realizing what was in front of me, but ride I did go. The views were spectacular, and the ride was smooth enough. I was slowing down for the corners, and having my breath stolen from me by the magnificent views. The road was not crowded, but I was always concerned when I saw a big truck in my mirrors. You never know when thirty-five tons will lose control going down a mountain road. Last thing I wanted was to be a bug on a big truck's windshield.

I had been enjoying this ride and watching the sun go down after having been on the road for about ten hours. I was getting tired, there's no way to deny that. I had about seventy miles between myself and that nice Nyssa Coop Supply Store when I rounded a corner, passed an off ramp, and looked straight at a sign that said,

NEXT GAS 68 MILES

I looked down at my gas gage and it said I had a half full tank. Well, I've done this before, I can go that many miles on that much gas, so, *verrrooooom!* off I went into the crazy Oregon Mountains.

Well, the curves were a little more than I planned, so I was riding slower than I'd planned, which of course, had already led me to believe that I was not going the entire six hundred, nineteen miles for the day. At this point in the ride, the only thing I knew for sure is that I had to stop for the day very soon. The curves kept my speed down, so when I had finally come to the part of the road that was sixty-eight miles after the sign that said no gas for sixty-eight miles, I was pretty happy to pull off the road. I glanced at my gas gage to see I was on empty. Not close to empty; empty. I planned it right, but I couldn't have planned it much farther.

The best laid plans always go to waste, right? I looked up to see the gas station was closed.

I looked around only to see more mountains, which after this extremely long day was the last thing I wanted to see. Of course, my phone didn't work, which meant my GPS didn't work. I couldn't call anyone, I couldn't see where I was in the world, the gas station was closed, and my tank was empty.

Yeah, sure, I planned it well.

I took a deep breath, walked around the bike a couple times, got back on and started down the road in the direction I was headed, because the only certainty I had was that I could not turn around and make it sixty-eight miles back from where I had come.

I did my best to keep my RPM's low, hoping to conserve gas. My Boy Scout trick to recognize the daylight left suggested that I had about thirty minutes at the most before sunset. I didn't know how far I had to go to the next town; nor, more important, to the next gas. The *low fuel* warning light came on as soon as I hit second gear.

I guess God had sent his gas angels to help me. I rolled about twenty-five miles with the warning light on when I found myself at a gas pump in a little town called Burns, Oregon.

The most expensive gas on the entire trip was there in Burns. If you're reading this to learn where the best gas prices in the country are, well, I can't tell you that, but I can tell you the worst prices are (were) in Burns, Oregon.

There was a little talk between me and the man working at the gas station. He pretended he wasn't the owner and that only the owner could say if he would donate some gas or not. I was empty and I had no idea how big the town was that I was standing in; since it wasn't my destination, I didn't even know it existed before arriving there, but I still think he was the owner.

He told me, and I believed him, that Bend, the town I was trying to get to, was a full two hour drive away, and as he told me that, I looked at the sun. The bottom of the sun was touching the horizon, so I wasn't going to make it there. I was only off by about a hundred miles on the day, and this was the town that would be my reluctant host for the night.

With a full tank of gas, I rolled back toward the way I came, and started pounding on doors, looking for a little room at the inn, so to speak. One motel after another had no vacancies, even after stopping at four motels. The surprise here is that there were still more hotels and motels to investigate. I was surprised to learn that I could be turned away four more times! Of all of these, only one had rooms, but the room price was twice as much as I had.

God has provided so far, right?

Burns, Oregon, it turns out, is the county seat of the ninth largest county in the entire United States. Since you're reading this book, if nothing else, you've learned that the United States is a very big place. Even with that large county claim to fame, Burns only has about twenty-eight hundred people.

Still, twenty-eight hundred is about twenty-seven hundred more than I imagined when I arrived with an empty gas tank. I passed three more gas stations before I found a motel willing to provide me with lodging. Incidentally, all of those gas stations had less expensive gas than where I stopped.

I found myself on the road to Bend, without knowing I was on the road to Bend, and on the very outskirts of Burns, on the opposite end of town from where I started.

This little lodging facility (to make sure I'm nice) could also be compared to that family's lodging that was looking for a place to have a baby on what would become Christmas more than two thousand years ago. This place was a great place to keep the animals! I've told the story before, on radio and in a few other places, about how I was awakened in the middle of the night by an insect crawling on my cheek. I swatted it away then opened my eyes to see what it was. I didn't recognize it. I'd never seen anything like it before. It was about an inch long, had six legs and clear wings, and it featured a bright green thorax. It looked like a giant, florescent green mosquito. Apparently, it couldn't fly – at least not after I brushed it off my face.

I brushed it off the bed and pulled the blankets up close to my eyes.

It's odd that I would start the description of the motel with a bug that crawled over my face in the night. There was much more to this place than that, and it really starts with the guy who greeted me when I arrived. While his tank-top T-shirt could have suggested I go a different way, I'd already been denied a room by what I thought was every other motel in town. I was actually starting to worry when I arrived, because the sun was gone.

He was actually an extremely nice human being, and it was easy to talk with him. He was quick to decide to take the tax deduction for the room that was still unoccupied for the night, after which he immediately scribbled, "NO" on a sign and hung it in the window next to the "VACANCY" sign, which was also hand-written.

He was very friendly, and informed me that the WiFi didn't work in the room he had assigned to me; which was the very last one in a line of fifteen rooms. If I wanted to use the WiFi, I'd have to come outside and walk toward the office, where it would work just fine.

I parked the bike right next to the room, number fifteen, and unpacked into the room. It was during this part of my day I realized I was sleeping in a room that had open cracks in the door which would allow anything smaller than a seven inch salamander to enter the room without a key. The key did unlock the door, but it wasn't really necessary, because the door didn't latch, which rendered the lock nothing more than a decorative object in the middle of the door.

Inside, the TV on the wall was working, but there were only two electrical outlets in the room. The TV needed one, and the satellite dish needed one. I could plug in my laptop, or the TV, or the satellite, but not all three.

The refrigerator, which is found in every hotel and motel room in the country any more, didn't close properly, so there was no way to use it to keep anything cold. The half full bottle of water that I found in the refrigerator must have belonged to the cock roaches, because I wasn't about to admit to owning it.

The bathroom was clean. In fact, the entire place was clean. Run down, broken, full of holes, yes, but clean. Ironically, the shower was broken. I turned on the water, which ran out trying to fill the bathtub, but the button to change it from a bath to a shower was gone. Not broken, gone. There was no way to move the water to the showerhead.

I know what you're thinking: take a bath. Well, I thought of that, too, even going so far as to imagine relaxing in a very hot bath. Well, there wasn't a drain plug in the place, so that couldn't happen either.

I did my best to make things work, and when I walked outside after doing my best to clean myself in that bathtub, and walked close to the office, my phone picked up the WiFi signal. (I didn't have any cell service there either.) Once on the WiFi, I found myself standing in a dark parking lot which was in desperate need of maintenance. I was barefoot, and thanks to WhatsApp, which allows for calling without a cell signal, I found myself having another conversation about why I'm on the road, and why don't I fly home from Portland, and a few more ideas that didn't match the goal of helping Gold Star Families.

The families in Bend had cancelled, but I had three families waiting for me in Salem, and I was determined to see them tomorrow.

Corner Coffee Shop, Bellevue, Idaho

It was about seven in the morning when I parked my

bike outside the Coffee Corner in Bellevue, Idaho, and walked inside. There were three young ladies working in the coffee shop that day.

"Hi. I came in to have coffee with Arnold Schwarzenegger," I said, starting off what I thought was a funny dialogue. "Have you seen him?"

"Not today," I heard the taller blonde say.

"Maybe tomorrow," the girl with darker blonde hair said.

"What time were you supposed to meet him?" came the question from the third girl working there. All of these women were young, I would guess early twenties, if even that old.

"Oh, you know, I probably should have told him I was going to meet him here, huh?" I said, bringing in the punch line to the joke.

Bellevue, Idaho is just a few miles – and this is a few by anyone's definition, not just mine – from the tiny little ski hamlet of Sun Valley, Idaho, which is where many celebrities have homes. I heard Bruce Willis had his house up for sale, and I thought I'd swing by and ask him to donate it to the Gold Star Ride Foundation. An *ask*, incidentally, that still has not occurred, even though I've reached out to his legal team to start the dialogue.

Sun Valley is also the location of Steve McQueen's last days. For a motorcyclist, who often thinks of Steve McQueen riding along that fence in the *Magnificent Seven*, that tidbit is important as well.

"Since you're the boss here, I wanted you to know about the Gold Star Ride Foundation and the work that we do," I said to the third young woman.

"Oh, what's that?" she wanted to know, taking the brochure from my hands that I was holding over the counter. I explained.

"Oh, can we donate to that?" the second young woman wanted to know.

"Sure, since I'm a volunteer and we are a charity, we live only by donations from others," I explained.

"That's so cool," the first young woman chimed in. "We

should put some of those brochures over there so people can see 'em."

"That's awesome," I said, "I'll get you some for that table. And you know I was only joking about Schwarzenegger, right?"

"Well, I do now," the third woman was rolling her eyes at me. I guess I just don't understand the younger generation.

While I did pay for my coffee, two of those women made donations to the Foundation through the website, and we appreciate that.

The Corner Coffee Shop is a really neat little place, and the coffee is pretty good as well. The people are charming, just like you'd expect from a local little coffee shop in a touristy part of town. Bellevue is more tourism than locals. One day, I'll be back there.

Bellevue, Idaho is about twenty miles north of the Oregon Trail, which you may remember from your history books. Within a few miles, or maybe I should say an hour or two, you can find some of the most unusual terrain in the country. I freaked out when I saw Lava Fields of *Craters of the Moon* National Park. I didn't have time to stop for it, but I rolled on by, thinking, *how in the world did covered wagons and women and children travel along this pass to get to Oregon, a place that it took me three days of hard riding*?

Craters of the Moon is a place with giant black rocks, six to twenty feet across, scattered as far as the eye can see, or in my case, for twenty or thirty miles along the road. It looked like jagged coal and lava mixed.

When I looked out at these huge rocks, scattered as they were, I couldn't imagine walking through that field today. Not even on foot. My mind could not find a way for a wagon drawn by a horse to navigate that terrain. Yet, it was the Oregon Trail.

River Wind Ranch, Estes Park, Colorado

One day, way back in the beginning of going out to see Gold Star Families, I found myself on the phone with a senior enlisted Air Force man. He'd been in the Air Force for almost two decades and was being processed out because his knee was injured beyond repair. He was receiving a medical discharge, but he didn't want to stop taking care of veterans, which, as other enlisted folks know, is what senior enlisted people do.

He found a camp, and while I might be a little out of school telling the story, I'll tell it anyway.

He called me in January and told me his story. He's the only person I've ever met who actually received benefits from one of those other veterans' organizations. I've always been someone who keeps his mouth shut when he can't say something nice, so I'm keeping my mouth shut about this other organization. That being said, that organization made arrangements for him to receive his medical discharge papers from none other than the Commander in Chief, President Donald Trump. I thought then, and I still think, that was pretty awesome.

He told me about a camp for veterans. He told me how this camp provides a place for healing for veterans coming home from the fight, and how entire families are involved. The whole family comes to the camp, and they all find ways to learn how to be back in society. I thought it was something that needed my support, as well as everyone else's support. I wanted to know more about this place.

"It's situated in Colorado," He told me.

"But I thought you were in South Dakota?" I asked.

"Yeah," he responded, "I'm known to go back and forth a lot. Home for me is actually Texas. This River Wind Ranch," he changed the subject back to the important stuff, "brings in families of those who saw action, and helps them and their entire families come back to civilian life. Sometimes that's really hard to do."

"I'm not sure I ever came back," I said, "and I've been home almost thirty years." I wasn't lying; while I've done okay as a civilian, there are those who would argue that there is something wrong with me.

"Do you think you can bring your ride to the camp?"

"I'll do everything I can to get there."

"Don will take care of you when you get there," he said.

Here I was, in the heat of August, riding through the Rocky Mountains, headed east on US Highway Forty, headed to the River Wind Ranch. I glanced at the GPS and it told me the quickest way to get there was US Highway Forty, then turning off this highway onto US Highway Thirty-four.

It was Colorado, and the weather was perfect. The views were spectacular. By this point in the story, you've probably read so many times that the views were spectacular that it doesn't mean anything anymore. Well, when I started in Colorado, it was pretty flat. It was still great, but mostly flat. When I turned west on Highway Forty, things got a little more exciting. Mountains grew from the flat farm country into giant trail signs that touched the sky. Hay became the most common commodity being transported on the highway, and fence-lined properties were the only thing visible on the landscape that wasn't a towering rock formation trying to touch the stars.

Well, that's the metaphor, even if it was daytime. I would have said clouds, but the few clouds that were in the sky that day were closer to me than the tops of the mountains.

I rode east on and on, and after an hour, I rounded a corner and saw the clouds, but they weren't the natural formation of water molecules in the sky. These were clouds of smoke, streaming across the sky in massive bands of dark gray.

The Rockies were on fire here, too. The wind out of the south made sure of two things; first, that the fire had plenty of oxygen to continue burning, and second, that I had plenty of struggles to hold the bike upright in that powerful crosswind.

While I was trying to keep the bike on the road, the road was twisting and turning, doing its very best to keep me alert. This was a mountain pass; Rabbit Ear Pass, to be specific. Mountain passes always add an element or two that you don't find crossing the wheat fields of Nebraska. Mountains dictate the direction and elevation of the road, and while those engineers who designed and built the highway did their best to make the road easy to navigate, sometimes nature has a better idea of what to do with those designs.

The highway builders often would remove the top of the mountain and make a small valley. I will refer to these topless mountains with the term "cutaway" because that seems to be the best word. The top may be twenty or so feet above the roadway, but the road is cut through it, making walls of mountain rock crop up on both sides of the road for short distances; usually about thirty to fifty feet. These cutaways would have rock walls on either side of the highway, which was only one lane going in each direction.

This sounds easy and peaceful enough, I know, but let's add Mother Nature to the equation. The air is full of smoke. Visibility because of smoke has been reduced to a mile or less. Nature is trying to spread this fire with a thirty or forty mile per hour breeze. This breeze (being a little facetious here) was making it impossible to hold the motorcycle straight up and down on the highway. I was constantly leaning to the right.

Then I'd hit one of these cutaways. Well, the wind is blowing a little breeze between these tiny mountain walls, too. The result, somehow, is that the forty mile per hour breeze would immediately shift from the right to the left. The result would be that while I was leaning to the right to correct for the wind, then hit one of these cutaways at roughly sixty miles an hour, and faster than you could blink, the forty mile an hour crosswind would shift by one hundred eighty degrees. The wind would now be *pushing* me to the right, which is the direction I was leaning.

After seconds of trying to correct for this, I would find myself leaning to the left, fighting the wind that was pushing me to the right, only to pop out the other side of the cutaway and find the wind pushing me left again. I crossed the centerline of the roadway at least once during these treacherous conditions.

Every once in a while, Nature would mix with Man in order to provide an even more exciting experience, and put a semi-truck and trailer in the oncoming lane, traveling about sixty miles per hour, and pushing the wind in two new directions. At least once on this part of the ride, I met an oncoming big truck inside a cutaway.

That will make your knuckles turn white.

Then the hills tapered off a bit, and the ride became,

once again, easier and more enjoyable. Except of course, that now I was extremely tired, and I'd been riding for nine hours. I could feel my blood pressure drifting downward as I rolled passed Muddy Creek in what seemed to me to be a downhill direction.

I stopped the bike in Kremmling, Colorado, in the first parking lot I could see. As a tiny coincidence, it was a liquor store, and I thought it might just be a nice night to have a Scotch nightcap.

This is worth mentioning, because while I was still shaking when I stepped into the liquor store, the nice lady working there wanted to know more about me, the bike, the Foundation, and the ride. I shared with her the usual information, and handed her a brochure. She – on a personal level as opposed to a store level – donated to the Foundation.

I could feel myself trying to stay, but I knew I was expected farther down the road, even though my phone had no service at this stop. I forced myself to go back outside, and saddle up. I pulled the bike out to get back on the road, and as I did, I looked back toward the mountains I had just crossed over, and saw them still on fire, smoke still rolling toward me, but now with something a little unexpected. I saw one of those programmable DOT signs on the side of the road for the westbound traffic. The sign read:

ROAD CLOSED DUE TO FIRE

I sighed with a long exhale and accelerated in the other direction. That was the second time in as many weeks that the road closed due to fire immediately after I passed.

I stopped to fill the gas tank before leaving that little hamlet stuck somewhere in the Rocky Mountains, then continued my journey.

I have to talk about the things we all need to know about GPS and electronic maps. I looked at the maps and found the shortest highway, and figured that the shortest highway would get me to my destination is the shortest amount of time. Until I try that other highway, I guess I'm not sure if it was faster or not. What I did *not* see on the electronic map, nor had I any experience to this point of the ride, was the *elevation* of the highway.

Down the road I went, trying to find the River Wind Ranch on US Highway Thirty-four. The road curved this way and that. In fact, it curved so much that there was never a spot on the road that remained straight for more than about two hundred yards ("meters" if you are reading using the metric system).

The speeds on this road were never above thirty-five, and usually around twenty-five, with curves that slowed to fifteen. This isn't a good way to make good time on the highway.

It was on this road that I slowed down for a herd of elk that were crossing the road.

After the elk crossing, I noticed it was starting to get cold, and the clouds that were smoke an hour ago were now water molecules and the elevation of the highway had me riding in fog. Cold and wet, higher and higher I went.

Remember, I started riding in Colorado many hours ago, and it was a hot August day. I was wearing a T-shirt and a leather vest. It was getting cold. I spotted a wide spot in the road and decided to stop and put on my jacket.

At this stop, I realized I was dizzy. Not a lot, just enough to notice it. I walked around the bike a few times, but it didn't get any warmer. I took a few pictures, and read the plaque that described what I was looking at, and it said:

Never Summer Mountains

I started to understand why I was high. Colorado Rocky Mountain High. Not like, well, you know. Just like the John Denver song.

I pulled my leather jacket out of the trunk and put it on; took a deep breath; and got back on the bike.

It was about seven o'clock at night now, and I had nearly eleven hours into the days ride. I was late. Just like every other day.

I kept riding, around hair pin turns with speed limit signs of fifteen miles per hour. Every once in a while, there would be a straight stretch of road and I could hit the gas and get up to thirty or even thirty-five miles an hour. With each passing hairpin curve, the temperature went down.

As I went higher and higher, still not understanding why a US highway would wrap itself around a mountain like this, the road seemed to get more and more narrow. One side of the road was up against the rocks that make up the mountain, the other side of the road was an incredible drop off, so far down I can't even speculate how far it was. It looked like many thousands of feet down.

The scary part of this is, well, I'm used to riding on roads with guard rails along the side of the road when there is a dangerous drop off of even as little as five feet. These drop offs were many thousands of feet down, and there were no guard rails. There was no room to build guard rails. There were no shoulders on the road either.

The relief I felt when I reached the parking lot at the top was palpable. I could feel my grip relax on my handle bars, and my breathing started getting deep. I put my kickstand down and slowly got off the bike.

Dizziness was unmistakable now. Where I thought maybe I was dizzy before, I was definitely having difficulty holding myself upright and walking in a straight line. Walk I did, thinking that would help me feel better. It made me feel colder.

I dug the chaps out of my saddle bags and zipped my legs into them. I was already cold, so I knew I should walk around a bit to warm up before I started riding again. I walked to the viewing wall and took some pictures. I saw the sign that identified the elevation level at that spot. I was Eleven thousand, eight hundred feet above sea level. I made a "selfie" movie with my phone, saying, "If I was on an airplane right now, I could use my electronic devices."

I looked at the snow capping the distant mountains from my current location and thought, "Isn't it August? Since when do we see snow in August?"

Then snow pellets started falling on *me*!

"What, God, are you trying to tell me?" I thought. "This mountain has the ability to kill me on a clear day. Now, I have to ride down in the snow?!"

There were some other guys up there on bikes, but they were riding BMW's. They didn't have a big heavy bagger like I had.

"You look warm," one of them said to me.

"Don't be fooled by my looks," I responded, still shaking a little under my skin from the cold, and still dizzy.

They got on their bikes and took off. I thought they were going way too fast for the conditions, but off they went. I followed them from about a quarter mile behind. They stopped a half mile away at a wide spot on the road, and I rolled passed them.

I could feel my knuckles turning white with my grip, I could feel my knees shaking from the cold even as I tried to squeeze the gas tank with my knees, and I was breathing shallow again, partly from fear, partly because I could feel the tiny snow pellets hitting my cheeks.

I wondered, rolling along about ten miles an hour, how this story would be told in the newspapers. I imagined headlines like

National Motorcyclist Falls Off Mountain

Or

Frozen Motorcyclist Found Thawed After Six Months

About thirty minutes after starting down the mountain, I could see breaks in the clouds, and I could feel the temperature increasing. Along with this new found comfort, I found a car crowding my ass on those dangerous curves. The curves going down on the east side of the mountain were just as precarious as those going up on the west side of the mountain, and here I had a young man – appeared to be in his twenties – who was just inches away from the back of my bike.

I wanted to pull off and let him pass, but the road was too narrow and the right side of the road was a massive drop into oblivion. After what seemed like hours, although I'm sure it was only a few minutes, a wide spot in the road showed itself, and I pulled in. The car sped around me and disappeared around the next corner. I came to a stop and put my kickstand down, taking advantage of a safe place, but before I could turn off the bike, flashing red and blue lights whizzed passed me down the mountain.

My break in the wide spot of the road didn't last long, but I did stop there long enough to be completely amazed at the beautiful sunset to the west. It was nearly thirteen hours now since I began my day, and I was still stuck on the side of a very large mountain. I took a picture of the sunset, hoping that just a little of the amazing glow of reds and oranges from around the mountain peak might show up in a picture. It was a beautiful explosion of color.

I started the bike and again, a little dryer now, and headed down the mountain. Two curves into this part of the ride and I found the police officer, stopped behind that car that was pushing me down the road. The driver of the car was on the receiving end of a ticket. While I don't know what the ticket was actually for, I like to think it was for tailgating a motorcycle on a dangerous mountain road.

The ride got easy after that, and within minutes I found myself at the gate of the Wind River Ranch just outside Estes Park, Colorado. I was supposed to be there for dinner, four hours earlier.

The Wind River Ranch is a special place. They immediately met me and started sharing stories with me. They thanked me for doing the work that I do, and shared just one story with me.

There was a man who served his country faithfully in Afghanistan and after a four year hitch, took off his uniform and tried his hand at being a civilian. The struggles were more than he thought he could handle, and he found the Wind River Ranch and brought his family for a week here.

The very first night of his stay, the regular activities kicked in, and there were things for him to do immediately. There were meals to eat, people to socialize with, horses to ride, campfires to light, and things to do.

The next morning, more things had to be done. More family activities, more horses, more barn dances, and more stuff had to be done. Then the next day. Then the next.

On the sixth day, the veteran pulled one of the camp's many counselors aside and shared with him that he was a new man now. He loved his wife and kids, and he felt like his life had more purpose than ever.

Then he went on to explain that he had a plan. The plan is gone now, but the plan was to get his wife and kids situated into their rooms for the night, then he was going to end his own life. He'd had enough. He had his note written and his method ready.

The activities of the first night changed all that. He was going home happy. His wife was happy. His kids were happy. That particular veteran found what he was looking for.

In the first few minutes that I was there, I learned about the life of a veteran that was saved at Wind River Ranch.

The good people at the camp took care of me, found me a warm bed at nearly seven thousand feet elevation, and fed me a hot meal; although I can't say where they found it so late at night.

It took a while for me to figure out how to call MSL from that hotel in the mountains, and eventually, I was connected to WiFi and called the same way I had called from Burns, Oregon, only I didn't walk outside barefoot. Even knowing that there were only a few days left on this ride, MSL wasn't happy because I was still away from home.

The next morning before I saddled up – pardon the pun; it was a horse ranch – and had a little breakfast. Then a tour of the facility, and a chance to meet a few people. Most of those I met were volunteer staff members. I said hi to a few campers, too.

Nestled in the majestic mountains of Colorado, Wind River Ranch offers a peaceful and beautiful setting for you and your family to enjoy a restful getaway from the norm which includes a ton of hard work.

Don is the manager of the place. We posed for a picture, Don and I, and as we did, he said, "Check out those mountains in the background! They almost look real, don't they?"

We both laughed.

"All I've ever wanted to do," Don explained to me, "was manage a Christian Dude Ranch. That's what I do."

The Wind River Ranch is one of those places that you never hear about. It sits quietly amid the mountains of Colorado at about sixty-five hundred feet, and no one really notices it's there. It's just quietly there, changing lives for the better on a scale that the average human can't understand. Can't understand, that is, until you get there.

The truth is, I do not possess the words to adequately describe it. Put a visit on the top of your bucket list. If you can describe it, please share your description with me.

David Butler

Dr. Thomas Wilston was a surgeon during the Civil War. On April 15, 1865, Dr. Wilston was in Washington, DC, across the street from Ford's Theatre. You may remember that's when and where Abraham Lincoln breathed his last. I can't add anything to that story. I was told that he was there; however, my own research suggests that when I was told this piece of information, it may not have been accurate. I can't find proof that he was, and I can't find proof that he wasn't. I like the idea that Dr. Wilston was there.

Dr. Wilston was assigned to the 92nd Illinois Infantry and traveled and camped with them. This part has been proven many times over, so we can talk about that.

Also in the 92nd Illinois Infantry was a young man named David Butler. David was born in 1832, so in 1864 he was thirty-two years old. That's young by my standards.

David was on "picket" on April 24th of that year, when he, as well as the entire 92nd Illinois Infantry, was overrun by

Confederate forces which, from most records, only say the Confederates had an "overwhelming" number of troops. During the firefight that ensued, many of the 92nd ran deep into the woods to escape, many were killed outright, and the remaining twenty or so, many of whom had been injured, surrendered. David was among those injured who had surrendered.

The Confederates that day decided not to take any prisoners, as the story goes, and they opened fire on the wounded and disarmed 92nd. After the guns stopped, they marched onward, sparing no effort to disrespect the deceased; many were kicked, or hit about the head and face with the butts of the muskets. Their bodies were strewn about and left. This occurred at a place called Nickajack, in the Appalachian foothills of southeastern Tennessee.

It was a day or so after the attack, which didn't last very long (because of the overwhelming force), when reinforcements of Union troops arrived, bringing with them Dr. Wilston. The troops quickly prepared the earth for the sort of burial that was common during the Civil War. As the troops were throwing dirt on the bodies, Dr. Wilston was examining them as best that could be done for that sort of medicine at that time in human history, when, suddenly, he shouted, "Stop, there's still life in this one!"

The troops pulled David out of the dirt covering the mass grave that was dug to bury as many as twenty-four of the soldiers from the 92nd Illinois. He was taken to a Union hospital and nursed back to health. It was weeks before he regained consciousness, and nearly two years before he recovered enough to be discharged from the hospital.

The rest of the 92nd Illinois, and there wasn't much, was converted to mounted infantry on July 22, 1863, and assigned to Brigadier General John T. Wilder's Lightning Brigade. For David, that was two months too late. Dr. Wilston then followed General Sherman on his famous March to Savannah.

The Civil War ended, and David Butler was sent back to the area of Rockford, Illinois, where he began his Civil War adventure, but the journey took him several months. Since the war had ended so long before he was discharged, and the walk back to Rockford with one leg shorter than the other, a nose so crooked it looked like it was mounted on his cheek, and most of his teeth missing (from the butts of the muskets), when he arrived at his own doorstep his wife was challenged to recognize him. His two sons, who had grown nearly four years in his absence, were now nearly teenagers.

Within days of his return, his wife died of pneumonia.

It was nearly ten years later, with his sons grown, that David decided to marry again, to Charlotte. Charlotte was a widow of the Civil War, and the two had three more children, the youngest was a daughter they named Mabel.

David breathed his last in 1890, when his young daughter was seventeen years old. Charlotte chose to allow Mabel to marry a nearby farmer named George, who was nine years her senior. George wanted a better opportunity for his new family, so they moved west from the area in north-central Illinois, to a place in north central Iowa.

Their family grew, and by most accounts, they were good farmers. They had nine children, and their third son, Emery, was born in 1905. Emery was twelve when Mabel "took sick" from the great flu epidemic in 1917. Another casualty of World War I, Mabel died that year. She was only thirty-six years old.

Emery married Gladys, and their third son is the father of the author of this book.

David Butler is my great, great grandfather.

I hope Dr. Wilston was with Lincoln on April 15, 1865, because I like the connection to Lincoln. I just can't be sure.

Joey Nova's, Excelsior, Minnesota

Meals are mentioned elsewhere in this story. Talking about food is always difficult, because we (people who talk about food) have to come up with words that create a memory of a taste for you. This is easy with common foods like strawberry flavored ice cream or inexpensive fast food cheeseburgers. What if you've never tasted the food before?

What if the desired result is to get you to create a sensation in your mouth or on your tongue that you've never had before?

Los Roberto's in Blackfoot, Idaho, comes to mind. Rigoberto's in Bend, Oregon is another. Lindsay's in Van Horn, Texas, is a great spot. Of course, the Amery Family Restaurant in Amery, Wisconsin, and Grumpy's in Roseville, Minnesota, are all great examples of great places to eat. All of them can be described with some rather common flavors, and most have already been discussed.

When you add just the right amount of oregano, or your use of garlic is perfected, it becomes a little more difficult to describe the flavors that are exploding in your mouth. That's the task of talking about food at Joey Nova's in Excelsior, Minnesota. Joey Nova's takes the simple act of adding ingredients to an artistic level.

At its core, the restaurant features Italian flare and flavoring. To be sure, its pizza alone is widely praised. The other Italian offerings are just incredible.

That would likely be enough for me to want to write about it. It's certainly enough for me to be motivated to make the car ride out to the Tonka Bay area, where no road travels straight more than a hundred feet or so before curving around a lake, an inlet or a bayou. Tonka Bay is known for many things throughout the summer months, like boating, fishing, water skiing, and motorcycle rides along the naturally perfect scenery. Joey Nova's may not be the thing it's remembered for now, but it is soon to be.

The exterior and parking lot are quite unassuming as you approach; simple strip mall on a curve. Once seated inside, Gary, (the manager) and all of the staff will work to obtain nothing less than praise from you.

This was not different when we called in late August.

"Gary?" I asked.

"Yes, this is he," he replied over the phone.

"Are you busy this afternoon?" I asked.

"Well, we're open. I'm working, but I have a table for you, if you like."

"You remember me telling you about the Gold Star

Ride?" I asked.

"Yes, I do."

"I'll be back in Minnesota today at three and I'll pull into your parking lot."

"Oh! My! Gosh!" Gary was excited to hear this. "Oh, my gosh! I'll be ready for you! I can't wait to see you. You'll have to tell me all about the ride!"

"See ya at three," I ended that call. The Gold Star Ride Foundation would finish the ride at three at Joey Nova's in Tonka Bay.

I pulled in just a few minutes late, and now that you've read this much of the story, you might think a few minutes is about an hour and a half. No, this time, a few minutes meant three. I pulled in to the parking lot at three minutes passed three in the afternoon, on the nineteenth day of August. Fox Nine (a local FOX Network affiliate) had a camera man recording me as I pulled into the parking lot.

I parked and, when approached by the camera man to be interviewed, excused myself to give MSL a long hug hello.

My brother-in-law, Wayne, was there waiting as well.

Then the news producer asked me, "Why did you do this?"

"Because," I said on camera, "that person died so the rest of us can do whatever the rest of us do, and I firmly believe that if you're not volunteering or donating, it's just lip service."

He asked a couple more questions, but they all landed on the cutting room floor.

Gary came running out to greet me, and we sat talking for a few minutes, then his staff brought out the first meal I had in Minnesota in seven weeks.

MSL and I enjoyed the perfect weather and the table on the patio (so to speak – it may have been more like a table on the side walk) for about an hour. As usual, there was more food than I could eat, and we were treated like royalty.

Then again, that's why we go to Joey Nova's.

The Midwest

One day, in the middle of the afternoon, I stopped for gas in Iowa or Missouri or Kansas or Nebraska (I forget which), went inside to tell the manager about my work.

The woman standing behind me in the line interrupted, "you do what for Gold Star Families?" There was a sadness in her eyes.

"Are you a Gold Star Mother?" I asked, hoping that she wasn't.

"No," she said. "Where are you going next?"

I explained and excused myself to pump my gas. She came out a moment after me.

"It's really a great thing you do," she said, a little shyly.

"Thank you."

"Nobody did that sort of thing when I was in," she offered.

"Thanks for your service to our country. When were you in?" She had my full attention now.

"I was in in seventy-eight. My daughter was in for two and a half years and my son is still serving over in the Middle East."

"Forgive me for asking, but your daughter was in for two and a half years?" The number seemed strange to me.

"Yeah," she said slowly, her eyes moistening, "she's one of the twenty-two."

I immediately understood. Twenty-two is the official number of veterans who take their own life every day. "Oh, my God, I'm so sorry to hear that. That makes you a Gold Star Mom in our book. I'm so sorry." My eyes were getting moist, too.

"The Army didn't see it that way."

"We are not the Army," I said, using the words to enforce some stoicism, which in hindsight seems completely unnecessary.

"Thank you," she said, pausing and looking away a little. I could see she was looking for words.

"I've got something I'd like to share with you," I said, putting the hose back into the gas pump. I walked around the bike and opened a saddle bag, retrieving a plaque. "You don't know me," I offered, "but when I meet a Gold Star Family, I leave them with this plaque. If you'll accept it, I'd like you to have this."

"Okay," she said, a little shocked.

...but I cannot refrain from tendering to you...

She wiped a tear from her eye, then reached out to accept the plaque I offered to her.

"You know," she said, not taking her eyes from the plaque, "so many people need just a little help. Sometimes the bravest thing you can do is ask for help."

"I think that is totally correct," I said, fumbling for words.

"I wasn't sure what I would do; I was on my last ounce of strength," she paused. "Then, when I couldn't deal with it anymore, I went to the VA."

"Are you service connected?" I wondered out loud.

"No, but I missed my daughter, and I served in the Navy, so I went to the VA."

"And they were able to help you?" I asked.

"They," she stumbled over the words, "Well, they helped a little," she spoke like someone who was still hurting. "But the bravest thing I ever did was find the strength to call them and ask for help."

"It's not something we like to do."

"No, it's not, but when it was done, after I went to see them, they were able to help me cope a little; it wasn't so bad. I don't know why it was so hard to do," she explained the feelings of depression and sadness that so many veterans and Gold Star Families know about.

"I'm glad you found the courage to do it."

"I wouldn't be here if I didn't," she said.

"It saddens me. I hate hearing about the twenty-two a day. It's really a lot more than that, but one is too many. I understand how horrible it is to lose a child, and I'm so sorry for your loss."

"I'm so glad I stopped to talk to you," she said, "but I have an appointment. Can I hug you?"

"Of course," I said. We gently embraced. Then she turned and opened her car door. I waved as she drove away, then turned to get back on the bike.

I never did learn her name, but she knows mine and she's welcome to call anytime.

I'm not sure about this story but here goes. I was riding something like thirty-two days in the peak of summer when I arrived at a restaurant to meet not one, not two, but three different Gold Star Families. I was surprised to see local news cameras waiting for me in the parking lot. Just to make it official, I circled the lot once or twice to make sure they could film something with me on the bike.

Kickstand down, I pulled myself off the bike, and in a good mood, well rested (which was highly unusual), I walked toward the camera and a small group of people who looked like they were waiting for me. I stole a line from Bill Murray in the comedy classic *Stripes*, saying as I walked, "What? A surprise party! Whose idea is this?" I don't think anybody understood the joke.

We greeted each other warmly, everyone anxious to know everyone else. The Gold Star Brother had not met the Gold Star Mother and neither of them had met the Gold Star Son. After the introductions we went inside to a table that had been waiting for us.

We sat around a large table and the camera operator did his best to make sure we could all be captured and heard, and the dialogue rolled along casually.

"What do you think you'll have?"

"How was the ride over here?"

"What's your favorite part of the country?"

You get the idea. That sort of talk continued for a while. The waiter delivered our lunches and everyone was chewing and wiping the crumbs of food from the corners of their mouths, when the Gold Star Mom looked at me directly. "I just don't know," she said as her eyes glistened with the formation of a new tears, "why my son would take his own life."

The people at the table, the camera operator, and the people at the surrounding tables, all fell dead silent.

I'd like to share with you how I thought about what to say, but I didn't. I didn't know what to say, and to this day, I have no idea from where this came, but I acted and spoke without hesitation, and without a crackle to show my nervousness. I placed my right hand on top of her left hand and just let it lay there. As I looked at her eyes, I could see the blank sadness that comes from wishing you knew why something very sad had to take place, but you just can't figure it out. I moved my lips and allowed words to fall out of my mouth. It was unscripted, unplanned, but altogether quite natural. "He didn't take his own life," I said, quite matter-of-factly, "it was a sniper's bullet from seven thousand miles away."

It was as if I had reached across a sink and turned the water on. I can't recall ever seeing a pair of eyes moisten and drop tears so quickly and easily. I felt the tears trickle down my own cheeks as well. After a moment or two, when I thought it seemed okay, but before anyone spoke, I glanced around the table and realized there wasn't a dry eye in the place. Out of respect, we all stayed quiet for another moment.

Then, someone said, "These mashed potatoes are so much better than I thought they would be."

As quickly as it had changed, the conversation changed back. We were all happy to be there. We finished our meal, made jokes about the waiter mixing up the drinks, asked the camera operator when it might be on the news, paid the bill, and walked out to the parking lot.

"I didn't know what to expect," the Gold Star Mom shared. She seemed like she was still a little shy about talking with me.

"I didn't either," I quipped. It was true. I never know what to expect when I meet a Gold Star Family.

We thanked each other, and we parted ways. I climbed back onto my motorcycle and started it up. The first few minutes of riding after meeting a family are always the most surreal. Nothing seems like it should. Going sixty miles an hour feels like fifteen miles an hour. Ten miles of highway feels like two.

I rode south to the next state, turned west to the next Gold Star Family – another Mom, then I rode west some more and some more. After a few days, I turned north to ride to other states, cover more miles, meet other Gold Star Family members.

After about a week of riding, nursing sunburn, trying to live through heat exhaustion, I showered in the cheap motel and found this in my email from the best friend of that Gold Star Mom:

*I wanted to share with you that your visit
to us was very special. After you left, she
tore up her own suicide note.*

I couldn't see the computer screen through the
moisture that formed on the surface of my eyes
involuntarily, so I buried my face in my hands and
allowed myself to weep for a short time.

Tyrolean Lodge, Sun Valley, Idaho

Ski lifts and motorcycles have little in common. Yet,
here I was, riding through a town made famous by movie stars
who purchase houses in this community so they can ski. Bruce
Willis, Demi Moore, Arnold Schwarzenegger and Steve
McQueen have all purchased homes in this community, which
is really not very large at all, and it's not very easy to get to,
unless of course, you have a private plane. Donald Trump's
plane, however, is probably too large to land in the small air
field on the south edge of town.

I'd never been there before, which is true of almost
everywhere I've been on this trip, and I was more than a little
surprised by the appearance of the place. I arrived after visiting
the Oregon Trail, and riding through forest fires on the west
side of the state of Idaho. The sun was going down, and finding
a hole-in-the-wall, small motel with cracks in the door and TV's
that doesn't work was not in the cards. The entire community
was first class, and the most modestly priced hotel was a
couple hundred dollars for the most modest room.

I stopped on the edge of town for gas, and went inside
to introduce myself and The Gold Star Ride Foundation to the
clerk and asked for a donation of a tank of gas. During the
entire trip around the country, I don't remember anyone with
as profound a look of bewilderment as this clerk.

"You need gas?" came a voice from behind me.

"Well, I'm working for a charity honoring our nation's

fallen heroes," I said, spinning around.

"I heard you," he said, "I'll be happy to buy you a tank of gas."

"Are you a Gold Star Family member?" I asked, a little surprised since I had never had the guy in line offer to buy my gas anywhere in the country.

"No, thank God, I'm not," he said, "but I think I understand what you're trying to do, and I'll be happy to pay for your gas."

I rode away from those gas pumps with a smile and a feeling of hope and optimism.

I went to the first hotel as the sun encroached the horizon. The desk clerk was kind enough to call the manager, who decided there would be no donations today. Sadly and disappointedly, I got back on the bike.

The next hotel had the same reaction. The third hotel, although I held onto my optimism, said the same thing. So did the fourth and the fifth.

It was dark now, and my optimism was changing to pessimism and fear. I was only days from arriving back home, but the bank accounts could not buy me a room in this area. If I didn't find a hotel, I'd be looking for a park with a picnic table to sleep under, but at this elevation, it promised to be a cold night.

I found myself on the west edge of town asking God what I should do in this dilemma. I didn't hear his reply, but I'm pretty sure He said, "Keep trying."

I followed a dog leg to the left and the right, and a sign popped up above the trees indicating a hidden hotel behind the trees. I pulled into the Best Western parking lot.

I must have been quite a sight walking slowly up to the front desk of this hotel with wonderful amenities in the lobby. The couches were pristine white leather and the water cooler featured slices of fresh lemon floating in the dispenser. I felt both out of place and extremely comfortable simultaneously.

"I'm with the Gold Star Ride Foundation," I introduced myself at the front desk. "I'm riding around the country in support of Gold Star Families. Do you know what a Gold Star

Family is?"

"I do!" he responded with a pleasant excitement that wasn't too overbearing.

"That's why I'm in town, and I wonder if you have a room available?"

"We do have a room," he smiled and started moving the mouse and looking down at his computer.

"Would you like to donate a room to our cause?" I have to admit, optimism did not feel like it was in my voice.

"I have to make a call, but I'm going to do all I can to get you a room," he said. "My father was military and I will absolutely get you a room." He picked up a phone and dialed a number.

"Yeah, this is Jerry at the front desk. I've got a guy here with the Gold Star Ride Foundation and he needs a room. Can I comp it?" he looked at me and smiled. "Yeah, he's riding all over the country for Gold Star Families, you know, when someone gets killed in the military? Yeah, he's just here for the night." Then he dropped the phone from his chin and asked me, "It's just the one night right?"

"Yeah."

He picked the phone back up, "Yeah, it's just the one night. Just one person, yeah. Okay, thank you very much," and he hung up the phone.

I could feel a sigh of relief leaving my body. I tried to hide it.

"This is the sixth place I stopped," I said.

"You should've started here!" he said with excitement. He was actually filled with joy and I could feel it.

"I'm trying to get some video to make a documentary about my travels," I said as he handed me a key card. "I'd like to interview you on camera since you were kind enough to get me a room."

"That'd be great!" he said.

"Just let me dump this stuff in the room, and I'll be back in a few minutes to talk.

The room was spacious, and I felt like I could get some rest there. Not since I slept in Lake Havasu City had I been in a hotel room this large. There was a quaintness I felt walking through the hallways to get to the room, which were narrower than most hotels.

True to my word, I walked back down to the front desk about fifteen minutes later, camera in hand. "Ready?" I asked.

"Yeah, let's do this," he said, coming out from behind the front desk.

"Before we begin, I just want to say thank you once again, for helping me and the Foundation tonight with this room."

"We love to donate to charities and whatnot; especially anything to do with the military," he started right in. "We love the military around here so if we can help out somebody who's helping military families, we're absolutely for it." He spoke as if he'd done this before.

"What do you think I should know about this hotel?" I asked like a true reporter.

"Oh, wow," he sounded a little shocked by the question. "This is Best Western Tyrolean Lodge in Ketchum, Idaho, which is an Austrian based and styled hotel. It's been here since the early forties or fifties if I'm not mistaken. It's one of the originals that was here when the place was founded in the 1930's. It's one of the first ones. It's also across from the first, uh, ..." He pointed to his left across the street.

He stuttered just a bit so I offered to help with, "Ski lifts?"

"Yeah, first ski lifts in the entire country and from what I understand the entire world."

"Wow," I said, "and it's right across the street?"

"Right across the street," he went on, "wonderful skiing area, people literally walk across the street to the lifts all the time. It's just a beautiful area – small town, wonderful people."

"And it's not really easy to get to," I offered.

"No, it's not. It's up in the mountains; it's like a little valley way up in the mountains. In wintertime it's really hard to get up here."

"How far are we from a recognizable city?" I asked.

"Three hours from Boise [Idaho]. About an hour and a

half from Twin Falls [Idaho]."

"In a beautiful valley currently not on fire," I tried to joke about the nearby fires.

"No, not here; just about fifteen miles up the road, but we're not on fire here."

"Thank you very much, Jerry," I concluded.

"Absolutely. Thank *you*. My father was military and I love doing this stuff," he said again.

I wanted to talk to him more in the morning, but he was gone, and so was I shortly after the sun came up.

Fifteen minutes down the road, almost as if it were planned, I found a couple fire fighters on the side of the mountain road. It was a wide spot where I could safely pull off, so I stopped.

They explained the fires in that area were likely to be contained soon.

I continued to ride in smoke for the rest of the day until I stopped for the night in Wyoming.

The Last Gold Star Mom of the Year

It's difficult to describe what it's like to meet Gold Star Moms and Dads and Brothers and Sisters and Sons and Daughters. It really is.

It's difficult to describe in a way that makes you understand why I feel so compelled to do anything I can for these Gold Star Recipients. If you ask MSL, she won't be able to explain it to you. She can tell you what it is, but not even she can explain why.

In the previous pages, examples of extreme misery, joy, contentment, and peace; extremes of weather, road, and other riding conditions; and mechanical failures have all been detailed. Perhaps from what you've read already, you've come to understand.

After more than fifty days of grueling riding; heat, rain, wind, and extremely long hours every single day, I found myself rolling down the east side of a mountain in Colorado. A song kept running through my head:

Somewhere along a high road
The air began to turn cold
She said she missed her home
I headed on alone

Stood alone on a mountain top,
Starin' out at the great divide
I could go east, I could go west,
It was all up to me to decide
Just then I saw a young hawk flyin'
And my soul began to rise
And pretty soon
My heart was singin'

If you've ever been there, it's one of the most remarkable scenes around the Rocky Mountains. You come down the hill, and the mountains just disappear. Nothing but flat fields of grain as you roll east.

I knew the song was pretty cool that was running through my head – music has that sort of power. I also knew it was wrong. I didn't have a choice, really, about going east or west. I was going east. Well, northeast. It may have been up to me to decide, but that decision was made a long time ago.

As I got close to sea level for the first time in two weeks, I turned north and enjoyed the summer ride. It was wonderful here, but very lonely. I managed to ride north into Montana and east into South Dakota. Part of me was thinking how close I was to home, and how I was excited to get there. Part of me was thinking it was a wonderful day to ride in some remote locations. After riding north into Montana, I turned east and rolled passed a sign that said:

NEXT GAS 72 MILES

I knew I was in a desolate place. I double checked the gas gage, which said I had plenty, and rolled that throttle on.

Somewhere about thirty miles toward the next gas, I

found the Meridian Rest Stop and pulled in. I had pretty close to three hundred miles on my butt for the day already, and just wanted to get off the road. I had a thermos full of espresso from the morning, so I just sat with that at a table. I wasn't really hungry at this point, although I hadn't eaten much yet for the day and it was about three in the afternoon.

After sitting for a moment or two, I laid myself down on the bench and closed my eyes.

A semi-truck pulled into the rest stop with the engine brake making a very loud noise which woke me up. I looked at my phone and realized I'd been there over an hour. I also noticed that I had no phone service. The surprise would have been that I *did* have phone service.

Down the road I went. It was a two lane road, deep in southwestern South Dakota. It was a long ride, but I just kept rolling. I stopped for gas at the seventy-second mile, and grabbed a granola bar while I was there, then down the road I went some more.

As I left that small town, feet up on the highway pegs, a young man in an old Firebird pulled into the lane to my left and pretended to race. It was about a 1975 year model, so I was a little impressed with that; I like old cars. I smiled at him, gave it a little more throttle, and he disappeared in my rear view mirror, and that little experience made me smile for quite a few miles.

When the gas gage was pointed toward E again, the sun was threatening in the west. My Boy Scout trick helped me guess that I had two hours left, maybe two and a half as I pulled into the gas station.

I filled my tank and did my usual routine at all stops, then walked back out to the bike. A car had pulled into the gas pump on the opposite side of the gas island from the bike, so it was easy for them to hear me when I spoke.

"Gonna be a nice evening," I said to the woman working the gas pump, who was probably twenty years my senior.

"But it's been hot all day," she replied.

"We gotta take the good with the bad."

"Nice day to ride," she offered.

"It is," I said, "and I've been riding about four hundred miles so far today."

"Oooo, that's a lot," she said, "where you been?"

"I started in Colorado," I said, "and I'm on my way to Aberdeen. I have to go see a Gold Star Mom."

"Oh," she said, and then became silent.

After a pause, I said, "You know what that is?"

"Yes," she said without making eye contact as she hung the hose back on the pump. I could see her face was showing sadness suddenly.

"You're not a Gold Star Mom, are you?" I asked with as much sympathy as I could muster in my tired body and mind.

"No," she replied slowly, "but my best friend lost her daughter a few years ago. I lost my husband last year after forty five years."

"Did he serve?" I asked, not sure where it would lead.

"No, he didn't. But I miss him." The sadness in her voice was measurable.

"I'm very sorry for your loss," I offered, not sure if I sounded sincere or like a platitude. I paused and offered, "I know it hurts when you lose someone close."

She sniffled once, but showed no tears, and her voice didn't crack, but the sadness was there. "Yes, it does." She stood there as if suddenly she didn't have any place to go.

"I wish we could have a pill that makes those painful things just go away; well, some would argue that we do and it's called booze," I tried to sound funny.

She smiled and looked at me. "Yes, that might be nice sometimes."

"But then again," I continued, "if we didn't have the sad times, we wouldn't know it when we had the good times. We have to have something to compare it to."

"How far do you ride that motorcycle for families?" she asked, coming back to the current world and leaving the sadness again.

"About fourteen thousand miles in the last two months," I admitted. "Here," I said, offering her a business card, "this is who we are."

She accepted the card, glanced at it, and slipped it into a pocket. "It's a good thing you do."

"How far is Rapid City?" I asked.

"Oh, not far," she said, "about two hours."

"I better go," I said, "I'm hoping to go a lot farther than that tonight, and I don't like to ride after dark."

"You should make that by dark," she said, opening her car door. "Take care." Then she was gone.

I rolled north, enjoying the changing scenery as I put pavement behind me. After two weeks in the Rocky Mountains, the Black Hills were an incredible change. The road curved, climbed, and fell. It curved, climbed and fell the way it does in the Black Hills; a little more gentle, a little less extreme, and a few more trees.

As I pulled into Rapid City, South Dakota, the highway changed to something that resembled a city street. That is, I found myself downshifting and stopping for traffic lights. As I pulled up to the second traffic light, noticing that the big round ball was starting to touch the horizon off to my left. I pulled in the clutch and pushed down the shift lever with my left foot and found nothing there. I couldn't shift.

I held the clutch tight and steered into a gas station on the right side of the road, remembering I was still in fourth gear, and coasting to a safe parking spot. My shift linkage was broken, and I couldn't shift the bike.

I dug through the saddle bags and got lucky. All the parts were still there, they had just disassembled. I found some tools in the saddle bag and put it back together. The top of the big red ball was almost completely covered by the horizon when I started riding again.

I slept in Wall, South Dakota that night, and that has been discussed in earlier chapters.

The next day, I rode hard toward Aberdeen. I started riding at nine in the morning, stopped for gas in Pierre, South Dakota around noon and kept riding. I should have made it to my next gas stop in two and a half hours, but there was some road construction, so it took more like four hours. At one point, in the middle of nowhere, a two mile line of cars was just parked for fifteen minutes while we waited for oncoming traffic to clear on a one-lane road. Well, it was one lane during construction.

I stopped outside of Aberdeen to fill the tank at a place called Mellette Travel Plaza, which is located on the intersection of US Highway Two Eight One and South Dakota State Route Twenty, about ten miles south of Aberdeen.

As I pulled in, I knew I was in the right place, even if I was two hours later than expected, because I saw motorcycles lined up in front of the truck stop like an honor guard making sure only the best people would walk into the place.

They were part of the Old Cronies.

I stopped for introductions, small talk, and pictures, then went inside to tell the people working there what was going on. It was those nice people who shared with me that the bikes had been waiting for two hours. It was also very kind of those employees to donate my gas.

We rode together down the road, the Old Cronies and me, and they let me ride in the back of the pack through town and up to Viola's house. The meeting of all the different faces started slowly and I shook everyone's hand. I quickly set up the cameras to record everything on and around the table in the back yard.

"OK, everyone, I'm gonna record this." With a sweeping arm I added, "Everybody" then pointing to the camera, "whole world," then with a gesture toward the camera, I added, "Whole world," and another sweeping arm motion toward everyone, I said, "everyone." It was my way to start things off light, with a comedic homage to Bill Murray from the movie *Scrooged*. Most of the people chuckled a little.

"I keep a bottle of Cuban rum on the bike, just in case I meet someone who served in Vietnam," I said.

"Cuban rum?" Darrell asked.

"Well, I figure you had to go through some stuff when you came home, and it's my little way to say, 'welcome home,' to you. I figure it's about time someone did," I explained.

"Well, let's bring it!" he said, with a giant smile on his

face.

"I've got cigars, too," I added.

"Bring them, too!" he said, with a gentle chuckle. All the others chuckled at that, too.

"You know, in Cam Ranh, were I was stationed, if you were a short-timer," Darrell was telling a story about Vietnam, "a short timer was someone with less than thirty days, but if you were a short timer, you had to buy a bottle of VO – a quart – and on the bottle was a ribbon. Now, the rule is, you crack that bottle, and the bottle had to be gone that night..."

"Seems like a fair rule to me," I added.

"Yeah," he said.

"Cause you have to carry stuff," I said.

"You had to take the first drink and then give it away. Whoever you gave it to had to take a drink, but every time you gave a drink, you had to take a drink."

"And I spent my night in the 'out mode' but I still have my short timers' ribbon."

"So you get the ribbon right from the label?" I asked.

"Yeah, if you go to a liquor store and look at VO..."

"U-huh," I added.

"There's a black and white or black and oh, what the heck color is it? I'm colorblind, maybe red with white stripes on it. So, next time you go to a liquor store, just look at a bottle of VO."

He paused then added, "Then you tie it to a buttonhole and then everyone would leave you alone."

By now, everyone who wanted one had a cigar lit, and I poured a shot of rum in a small glass for Darrell. "Is there anyone else here who served in Vietnam?" I asked.

"Yeah, Chuck," he said.

I turned to the group, most of which was behind me or to my left, "Chuck?"

"Yeah," Chuck replied.

"You served in Nam, you want a shot of Cuban rum?" I asked.

"No, thanks," he said.

"You want me to have it for you?" I asked.

"Yeah," he said, "and I usually have a double, so you pour a double."

"Well, I'll save one and a half of those till I get done riding today, but thanks," I said, pouring the drink.

We shared many stories about riding motorcycles, the work of the Old Cronies, who like to raise money for veterans and all things related to veterans throughout the Aberdeen area, and just about any other subject that would come up.

"You like my shirt?" Revi asked me. I glanced at his T-shirt, which he proudly opened his vest to display. It featured a United States flag along with these words:

AMERICA
BACK TO BACK
WORLD WAR
CHAMPIONS

"I do!" I said with some enthusiasm. It was true. I did like it.

There was more small talk about cigars, fundraisers, the strange story of the guy trying to stop at every Harley Davidson dealership in the country, who, for some weeks, seemed like he was right in front of me out on the road. Several stops that I made, including the Burns, Oregon motel, told me he had been there just a day or two before me.

There also was a universal agreement that certain brown liquors are better when served chilled.

We talked about some of the breakdowns I had on the road, and I mentioned how my gremlin bell must be faulty, because the gremlins definitely jumped into my bike during the ride.

"Do you want a cigar, too?" I asked Viola, the guest of honor, "did I ask you that yet?"

"You did," she said, "but I don't know what I'd do with it."

"She's never smokes or drinks," Darrell offered, "because she likes the taste so much, she's afraid she'll become addicted."

"That's exactly why I try to only indulge at night," I said.

After a bit of a pause, I looked at Viola. "Tell me about Ron," I asked, cigar smoke wafting into the summer air.

"He died in 1967," she said, in that slow speech that is only delivered by someone with a lot of experience.

"He loved baseball," Darrell offered, "he was a good catcher, and he loved airplanes. He was in the Civil Air Patrol before joining the Air Force."

"Wait, he volunteered rather than, oh what's that fancy word? Conscripted?" I asked.

"He graduated in May and left in June," Viola contributed.

"You know," I said directly to Viola, "this is the first time I get to do this with a cigar." I reached for the small plaque I had brought with me. "In my travels to Gold Star Families, we do a lot of this sit and visit and it's a lot of fun," I said, waving an arm in the air. "We do this reminiscing and we tell stories and we enjoy the time.

"But at the end of the day," I continued speaking to only Viola, but letting everyone else hear my words, "the reason that I came here is because you lost your son." I paused.

"So," I continued my monologue, "to remember that I came here, I brought you this plaque. So, you get to keep this, and I'm gonna read to you what it says, okay?"

Viola nodded. I remember now, writing this, how her dark glasses did such a fine job of hiding her less obvious emotions.

Slowly, I started to speak the words;

> *I feel how weak and fruitless must be any words of mine which should attempt to beguile you from the grief of a loss so overwhelming. But I cannot refrain from tendering to you the consolation that may be found in the thanks of the Republic they died to save.*
>
> *I pray that our Heavenly Father may*

Yours, Very Sincerely and Respectfully   245

> *assuage the anguish of your bereavement, and*
> *leave you only the cherished memory of the*
> *loved and lost,*

I paused. There was a noticeable lump in my throat, and I was trying to maintain my delivery before I continued;

> *and the solemn pride that must be yours to*
> *have laid so costly a sacrifice upon the altar of*
> *Freedom.*

I paused again then ended with:

> *Yours, very sincerely and respectfully,*
> *Abraham Lincoln.*

The group applauded rather loudly.

Darrell was the first to speak as the clapping became quiet, "That was super nice, Tony," he said. "Thank you."

I noticed that Viola was more pensive than she had been at any other time in my visit. I leaned close to her as she looked at the plaque, "We'll send you his name so you can put it right here," I said, pointing to the spot left empty to add a name later.

"Will you send us that video, too?" Darrell asked.

"If I got a video," I said sharply, which made everyone laugh once again, "I don't know if it's recording."

"That's very nice," he repeated, "Thank you very much, and thank you for coming."

"You say that like I have to leave," I said, sparking some more laughter, "I'm not done with my cigar yet." Then, gesturing toward the video camera, "Look, I've got nine more minutes on the camera."

Even Viola smiled big at that joke.

"I can't believe," Darrell broke the silence again, "all the miles you've come and you end up in the little town of Aberdeen, South Dakota, to visit a my Gold Star Mother. That's cool. I thank you so much for doing that; for taking your time to come here."

"It's the only reason I left home in the first place," I said, "and you're welcome. I'm glad to do it." I was moved by his comments to me, but it was just a taste of what I was coming.

I learned later that Darrell, or Angie, or Chuck, or Revi, or someone else from the Old Cronies, made a call to the local newspaper, which came to interview Viola about the visit. At the end of that interview, which appeared in the *Aberdeen News*, Viola was asked what she thought of the visit. She responded simply, "We need more people like him."

I was noticing that others were leaving the party, and realizing that it was my twelfth hour since I started riding early in the day, and I hoped to go another two hundred miles before sleeping. It was time to go, so I made that announcement and stood to gather my things. I reached with my right hand to grab the rum and the cameras off the table, the latter having long since beeped that they were done, when I felt the gentle touch of a caring finger on the back of my left hand.

I turned to see what or who was touching me and found myself looking into the eyes of Viola, whose lips moved, but no sound came out.

"Thank you." I'm sure she said. I gently held her hand with both of mine. "Thank you," she repeated; still with no sound.

"I'm so glad I could do it, it was my honor," I whispered.

No one else there heard that exchange; at least, not that I am aware.

Twenty minutes later, no longer in Aberdeen, South Dakota, but watching the sun stretch for the horizon in my rear view mirrors;

I thought about all the heat.
I thought about the elevation sickness.
I thought about riding in snow.
I thought about the mountains
I thought about nearly running out of gas.
I thought about lying in the grocery store parking lot.
I thought about all those days in the rain.

I thought about all those miles in road construction.

I thought about all those miles in the dark.

I thought about all those miles in road construction in the dark.

I thought about all the times GPS took me the wrong way.

I thought about the breakdowns.

I thought about all the nights I laid awake wondering why I should do this.

Then I thought about Viola touching my hand, and I didn't wonder why any more.

I looked at the open highway in front of me, and rolled that power on.

I wasn't alone anymore.

Yours, Very Sincerely and Respectfully,

Anthony Price – Citizen

Post Script:

Viola was the last Gold Star Mom on the lengthy cross country ride described in these pages. She is not, unfortunately, the last Gold Star Family for us or for you. I rode on a month later to Arkansas, Missouri, and Iowa.

In 2019, even as this book was being created, we found and visited and helped more Gold Star Families. We found homeless and nearly homeless Gold Star Families who need didn't need tuition help, they needed rent money.

Also in 2019, we rode again in six separate rides, covering another fifteen thousand miles, more than twenty states and thirty families.

That's what we wanted to do when we started. That's what we still do. That's what we will do. You help us, we help them.

Thank you for taking the time to learn this story. And please reach out to us and share your thoughts now that you have.

info@goldstarride.org

www.goldstarride.org
651.417.3317

Name	Location	Contact	Notes	Level
Tom Barnard Podcast	online		tombarnardpodc ast.com/	Platinum
TCNT Twin Cities News Talk	FM 103.5 AM 1130		twincitiesnewsta lk.iheart.com/fe atured/justice-drew/	Platinum
Savannah Harley Davidson	1 Fort Argyle Rd, Savannah, GA	912 925-0005	savannahd.com major repair	Platinum
Art, Bill and Joe	Louisville, KY		Raised over $3K at work!	Platinum
Richard's Coffee Shop	165 N Main St. Mooresville, NC	704 663-0488	Living Military Museum	Platinum
Steve's Custom Cycle	6095 Robinson Rd Lockport, NY	716 625-4372	Harley - David's son	Platinum
Cowboy's Alamo City HD	11005 North, I-35, San Antonio, TX	210 646-0499	cowboysalamoci tyharley.com	Platinum
Barnett's Harley-Davidson	Las Cruces, NM 88005	575 541-1440	barnettslascruce shd.com	Platinum
Twin Cities Harley-Davidson Blaine	1355 98th Ave NE Blaine, MN	763 786-9079	TWO back tires	Platinum
Back Street Cycle	220 E McLeod Ave Ironwood, MI	906 932-9080	repairs	Platinum
WDAM 7 TV	Hattiesburg, MS		news story WDAM.COM	Gold
Margy Trade Winds Bed and Breakfast	943 Lombard St Philadelphia, PA	215 592-8644	lodging	Gold

Harley Davidson Louisville	1700 Arthur St Louisville, KY 40208	502 634- 1340	oil change	Gold
Brandl Motors	14873 113th St Little Falls, MN 56345	320- 412- 3940	www.brandlmot orscdjr.com	Gold
CBS47/FOX30 TV	Jacksonville, FL		Actionnewsjax .com	Gold
FOX 29	San Antonio, TX		Foxsanantonio .com	Gold
River Wind Ranch	5770 CO-7 Estes Park, CO 80517	970 586- 4212	food / lodging cool place helps vets	Gold
Amery Family Restaurant	418 Keller Ave S Amery, WI 54001	715 268- 2100	food and donation	Gold
Deerwood Inn	155 SW Old St Augustine Rd Madison, FL	850 973- 2504	Deerwoodinn .com	Gold
Lindsay's Café	802 W Broadway Van Horn, TX	432 207- 8248	lunch	Gold
Cannonball Olde Tyme Malt Shop	11 York St, Gettysburg, PA 17325	717 334- 9695	lunch and ice cream	Gold
Mission BBQ	5045 Jonestown Rd, Harrisburg, PA	717 901- 4317	dinner	Gold
London Bridge Resort	1477 Queens Bay Lake Havasu City, AZ 86403	928 855- 0888	provided luxury suite for MSL and me	Gold
Battlefield Harley Davidson	35 York St Gettysburg, PA	717.39 8.2747	battlefieldharley -davidson.com	Silver
Balance Rock Eatery and Pub	148 S Main St Helper, UT 84526	435 472- 0403	waitress paid for my lunch	Silver

Rattlesnake Mountain HD	3305 W 19th Ave Kennewick, WA 99338	509 735-1117	T-shirt	Bronze
Harley Davidson of Scottsdale	15656 North Hayden Road Scottsdale, AZ	480 905-1903	T-shirt	Bronze
Stripes Gas	521 US-281 Johnson City, TX 78636	830-868-2800	Employee cash donation	Silver
Charin Inn	116 N Main St Clearfield, UT	801 825-2221	Room for the night	Silver
Silver Sage Motel	840 S Main St, Moab, UT	435 259-4420	Silversageinn .com	Silver
Sundowner Motel	416 Hwy 20Hines, OR	541 573-5000	Room for the night	Silver
Steak House and Lodge	15860 T Bone Lane Hayward, WI	715 934-4411	Ready to feed 80, and only 3 came	Silver
Hillcrest Motel	412 4th Ave Wall, SD	605 279-2415	Room for the night	Silver
Country West Motel	5956 Dewar Dr Rock Springs, WY	307 362-6673	Room for the night	Silver
Sunrise Espresso	West End of Main Street Grangeville, ID		next to Zip Trip helped without being asked	Silver
Friend's Corner	773 Kohler Rd Burbank, WA	509 380-0558	Mgr bought gas and water	Silver
BP	1121 Mebane Oaks Rd, Mebane, NC	919 563-1945	Manager made cash donation	Silver

Yours, Very Sincerely and Respectfully

Speedway	15852 TN-13 Hurricane Mills, TN	931 296-9008	mgr made donation	Silver
Blue Coffee Pot Restaurant	US-160, Kayenta AZ 86033	928 697-3396	manager bought lunch at checkout	Silver
Mountain View RV Park & beef jerky	1120 E Business Loop Bowie, AZ	520 847-2510	owner bought gas	Silver
Subway restaurant	2829 Lancaster Dr NE Salem, OR	503 587-8712	lunch purchased by Alysa	Silver
Los Roberto's	990 Market St Blackfoot, ID	208 785-2777	lunch	Silver
La Cabana	994 Yampa Ave Craig, CO	970 824-5051	lunch	Silver
Jeannie's Dream Motel	1354 Hwy 20, West Winfield, NY	315 822-3468	Room for the night	Silver
Best Western Tyrolean Lodge	260 Cottonwood St Ketchum, ID	(208) 726-5336	Jerry - room for the night	Silver
Mirabito Convenience Store	1 E Main St, West Winfield, NY	315 822-5785	manager paid for gas	Silver
St Croix Valley Riders	Motorcycle riding group		https://stcroixval leyriders.org	Silver
Manny's Steak House	825 S Marquette Ave Minneapolis, MN	612-339-9900	https://mannysst eakhouse.com	Silver
NYSSA CO OP SUPPLY	18 N 2nd St Nyssa, OR 97913	541 372-2254	hat	Bronze
BJ's - New Underwood	16098 Hwy 1416 New Underwood, SD	605 754-6778	gas donation	Silver

Mellette Travel Plaza	38620 SD-20 Mellette, SD 57461	605 887- 3364	gas donation	Silver
Maverick	891 E Main St Price, UT	435 637- 7457	employees pooled money for	Silver
Subway restaurant	1050 E Main St Worthington, PA	724 297- 3132	employee paid for lunch	Silver
Conoco Travel Center	7180 US-89 Flagstaff, AZ 86004	928 855- 0888	Employee paid for gas	Silver
Marathon Gas	1041 M-32 Gaylord, MI	989 732- 9063	employee paid for gas	Silver
Jake's Gas & Go	4108 James Madison Hwy Fork Union, VA	434 842- 1000	Employee donated gas and $20	Silver
Exxon gas	21535 Frontage Rd Deming, NM	575 546- 3698	employee bought gas	Silver
Downtowner Inn	113 E North St Grangeville, ID	208 983- 1110	discount room and breakfast	Silver
Texaco Dayton	533 W Main S Dayton, WA	509 382- 9952	Dalton bought my gas	Silver
Coffee Corner	120 N Main St Bellevue, ID	208 788- 0003	cash donation	Silver
Kremmling West End Liquor	200 Park Ave Kremmling, CO	970 724- 3564	cash donations	Silver
Butcher & the Boar	Minneapolis, MN	612 238- 8888	Butcherandtheboar.com	Silver

Rigoberto's Taco Shop	1913 NE 3rd St Bend, OR	541 388-6783	breakfast	Silver
Justin 7-Eleven	220 N Main St Moab, UT	435 259-3557	bought gas	Silver
Conoco	350 McCormick Wamsutter, WY	307 324-7807	Bobby Jo bought my gas	Silver
Super America	849 WI-46 Amery, WI	715 268-7654	gas donation	Silver
Capitol Inn and Suites	1875 Fisher Rd NE Salem, OR 97305	503 588-5423	room for the night	Silver
Fairfield Inn & Suites by Marriott	2525 South Univ. Mt Pleasant, MI	989 775-5000	two rooms, but we didn't make it	Bronze
Speedway	1500 S Market St Elizabethtown, PA	717 361-7887	Employee paid for gas	Silver
The Trophy Chick		612 715-7240	Printed all the plaques	Gold
You Have a Friend in Real Estate	Buffalo, NY	716 983-0448	laurafriendrealtor@gmail.com	Gold
Vets Campground on Big Marine Lake	Marine on St Croix, MN	651-433-2699	www.vetscampmn.org	Bronze
Print Media Minnesota	Minneapolis, MN	952-835-5155	http://printmediamn.com	Silver
GoPro Cameras			https://gopro.com/	Gold
Viking Bags	Extreme Fairings		vikingbags.com	Silver
International Cigars			itscigarrolling.com	Gold

Amery Free Press			Theameryfree press.com	Bronze
Cenex gas	Hurley, Wisconsin	715 561-3444	www.cenex.com	Silver
Hogs and Heroes Foundation	Lockport, NY		hogsheroesfoun dation.com	Gold
Jersey Lilly's	Hico, TX	254 796-0999		Bronze

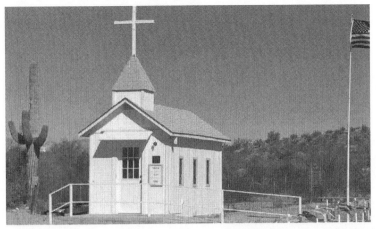

In western Arizona, the Little Road Side Chapel

Gordy and the DART truck

The Gold Star Family from Aberdeen, South Dakota

Gravesite of a fallen hero in Pennsylvania

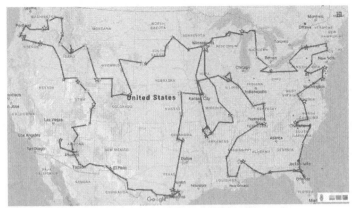

This map depicts the actual route of the 2018 motorcycle ride. 44 States, 17,487 miles, 64 families, and 58 days averaging over 300 miles each day

This sign in New Mexico lets you know how far you are: Denver, 748 miles; Bowie, AZ zero; Jacksonville, 1793; Las Cruces, 170; Houston, 966; Tombstone, 83; El Paso, 218; Geronimo Cochise, 0 (must also be in Bowie, AZ); Orlando, 1889.

Above: My first
encounter with
the law.

Right: Just
hanging with
another Gold
Star Family

Some meetings with Gold Star Families were incredibly serendipitous. This is Joe at the NY/PA state line.

Welcome Home!

This wild horse was captured grazing by the motorcycle camera somewhere near the AZ/UT state line. This was one of five in the herd.

Somewhere in the Rocky Mountains of Colorado.

Danger at every turn, this picture was captured in Utah and features a firefighting helicopter picking up a giant bucket of water to fight fire.

The challenges of riding a motorcycle across the country. This New Mexico state warning sign says; DUST STORMS MAY EXIST NEXT 10 MILES.

Sitting with Tom, whose son is memorialized on the
military memorial directly behind us. His son's name is
circled in red.

A quiet morning with MSL in front of the London
Bridge; at the Lake Havasu London Bridge Resort.
Can you tell from the picture that it's 110
degrees in the shade?

Bobby Jo, sister of
Betty Jo
and Billy Jo.

Sign outside SA in Amery, Wisconsin.

Sunset; just south of Moab, Utah.

Gold Star Son poses for pictures on the bike.

After dark, Lockport, NY, broke down at a gas station, trying to find a reason why it won't tart.

Below: South of Grangerville, Idaho.

TWO Gold Star Dads near Salem, Oregon.

"Those mountains look real, don't they?" That's what he said when we posed for this picture at the Wind River Ranch, Estes Park, Colorado. Elevation: 7522 feet above sea level

Gold Star Mom in Arizona

Arriving at a cemetery to meet a Gold Star Family.

Meeting Jerry in Ketchum, Idaho was a wonderful gift.

If I was on an airplane, I'd be high enough to use my electronic devices. Can you see how dizzy I am in this picture?

Posing for a selfie with one of the firemen working to put out forest fires in Idaho. This pose is near the Little Salmon River, about four hours from Boise **inciweb.nwcg.gov** is the website they recommend to learn more about current forest fires.

GSM in Pennsylvania

Tim and his mom came out to meet me on my way down the mountain in Colorado.

Zach at the Silver Sage Inn, Moab, Utah.

Made in the USA
Columbia, SC
19 May 2021